Connecticut
Driving Through History

Suzanne Staubach

Covered Bridge Press
North Attleborough, Massachusetts

For my mother, who gave me an appreciation of old houses.
For my father, who gave me his love of history.
For my children, Gretchen, Daniel, and Aaron.
And for Joe.

Cover photograph by Michael Tougias:
Bush Hill Road, northeastern Connecticut

Covered Bridge Press
7 Adamsdale Road
North Attleborough, MA 02760
(508) 761-7721

ISBN 0-58066-004-5

10 9 8 7 6 5 4 3 2

Contents

Introduction

Fiery volcanoes, towering mountains, mastodons, dinosaurs, a blanket of glacial ice, forests, no forests, and forests again, Connecticut is a state which has witnessed many changes. Today, two ranges of hills run north to south the length of the state, flanking the fertile Connecticut River Valley to the east and west. Hardwood trees—oak, hickory, ash and maple—cover much of the land. Rural villages, heavily populated suburbs, and cities make up a total of 169 towns. The state, the third smallest in the United States, covers 5,009 square miles, including 6,000 ponds and lakes, 8,400 miles of rivers and streams, and 253 miles of shoreline. Except for a sliver along the northern boundary, Connecticut lies entirely between the 42nd and 41st latitude.

Geologists tell us that 500 million years ago, the cluster of small continents known today as Avalonia, located in the ancient ocean Iapetos, began drifting towards each other. They drifted closer and closer for tens of millions of years until finally they smashed together in the Great Collision. During the Collision, the ocean floor of Iapetos was jammed under Proto North America, a huge drifting continent. The small Avalonian continents were crunched and disappeared, and other, larger, continents became welded together and formed a super continent, Pangaea. The landmass that became Connecticut was at the heart of this Great Collision, and was reduced from perhaps 2,000 miles across to less than a few hundred miles across. Intense heat from the Collision caused volcanoes to form from present-day Newfoundland to Georgia, and these volcanoes, which soared as high as the present-day Rockies, spewed molten lava over parts of Connecticut.

Two hundred million years ago, the super continent Pangaea cracked and broke apart, forming a new ocean. Connecticut cracked too, and the soaring mountain ranges formed by the volcanoes split into two roughly parallel ridges. A flat valley, named the Newark Terrane by geologists, spread out between these ridges. Later, the Connecticut River cut through the Terrane. During this Jurassic era, dinosaurs roamed the Valley.

Twenty to twenty-five thousand years ago, the entire region was covered with a layer of ice 6,000 to 7,000 feet deep.

Connecticut was a cold, barren and lifeless place. The glaciation lasted until 16,000 years ago, and then the earth warmed. The ice melted and retreated. The glaciers left in their wake the stone and gravel debris and the scoured and polished bedrock that make up the familiar New England landscape we see every day.

Life returned. Lichens grew on the sides of rocks and tender green shoots of grass sprouted in the newly exposed soil. Oak, birch, spruce and fir trees appeared. Mastodons, mammoths, beavers, squirrels, and deer came to feast upon the tender new growth.

Today, when we look at the western and eastern highlands of Connecticut, those picturesque rolling hills, we are looking at long dormant, worn-down volcanoes. Beneath them lies the ocean floor of Iapetos. When we see smoothly exposed and polished bedrock we are seeing the effects of the glaciers. The red sandstone of the valley was once part of Africa. The southeastern shores and the far eastern border of the state were once part of Avalonia. The northwestern corner of Connecticut was part of Proto North America.

Yet, when traveling through the state, visiting a particular town, commuting to work, it is the stories of the people who lived here only a few hundred years before us that capture our imaginations. It is these stories that this book focuses on.

Archaeologists are at work today, trying to discover details of the lives of the earliest hunting peoples who arrived in Southern New England 11,000 to 14,000 years ago. We know these Paleo Indians imported or brought with them flint spear points, knives and scrapers. They pursued the mighty mastodon and the mammoth as the glacier retreated and the land warmed. Paleo Indian sites have been discovered in several Connecticut towns, including Bolton, Glastonbury and Voluntown.

Around 5,000 years ago, migrants arrived from the west. They made bowls, pots, spoons and ornaments of soapstone, and from the evidence, appear to have been only semi-nomadic, compared with their predecessors. These Early Archaic tribes produced projectile points and perfected the spear for hunting swift-running caribou. They also fished and kept domesticated wolf-dogs.

The Woodland tribes, who flourished 700 to 300 years ago, hunted, fished, and raised crops of corn and beans. They produced pottery, baskets, hoes, mortars and pestles, canoes, warm winter clothing, and many other goods for daily use. They moved with the seasons, enjoying waterfront villages in the summer, and inland wooded villages in the winter. Their houses, or wigwams, were weathertight and comfortable.

Linguistically related, the Native Americans of New England were Algonkians. They were divided into tribes and subtribes, headed by sachems. Women cared for the children, raised the crops, and tended to most of the domestic needs of the family. The men were hunters and warriors. We know the names of the tribes by the names of their villages when the English arrived in Connecticut, or the names of the larger confederations.

Estimates of the indigenous population vary. By the time of European settlement in Connecticut, the Algonkians had already suffered from disease spread by earlier contact. The devastating plague of 1617 wiped out whole villages. Benjamin Trumbull, writing in the late eighteenth century, put the remaining number at 16,000 to 20,000. The nineteenth-century historian of Connecticut Indians, John W. DeForest, thought that estimate too high. The modern historian Francis Jennings estimates the post-plague population at 60,600 by the 1670s, and estimates the pre-contact population at as high as 150,000.

At the time of contact, the western parts of the state were thinly populated if at all. The lands were used for hunting grounds. However, as pressure from the waves of English settlers increased, some native peoples formed new alliances and tribes, and moved to the thickly wooded, hilly terrain of the northwest corner. Soon, however, pressure from settlement followed there too.

Tribal boundaries are inexact. Mathias Speiss, a Manchester historian, mapped out the major paths and tribal lands for the year 1625. In most cases, I have used his work as the basis for listing Native Americans for each town. In some instances, however, when it is known, I list the smaller tribe or village.

Currently, there are five Native American reservations. The census stands at around 300 on these reservations, and slightly more than 4,000 if those who live off of the reservations are included. Nevertheless, when driving around the state, the history and influence of the native tribes of Connecticut—the Pequots, Mohegans, Mahicans, Nipmucs, Podunks, Paugussetts, Tunxis, Siwanogs, Nehantics, Hamonassets, Massacoes, Sicaogs and Poquonocks—can still be seen and appreciated. Their language and place names survive in the names of ponds and rivers. Many of the first colonial roads followed the worn paths of the Native Americans. These paths became roads, which later became highways, such as parts of Route 44 and Route 1.

Curiously, the Native American place in the European imagination has been passed down in many towns via stories and legends, some of which repeat themselves in colorful variations. There are several lovers' leaps in Connecticut, associated with tales of doomed romances between Native American women and European men. There are caves where, according to local legends, solitary Native American women, usually the last of their people, lived alone. And there are a number of Toby's Hills or Toby's Mountains which are said to be named for the solitary Indian or African-American who lived there.

The history of Europeans is easier to trace, because they left behind diaries, town records, books and many descendants. Their towns are our towns. Some of their houses and public buildings remain.

The Dutchman Adrian Block sailed up the Connecticut River as far as the impassable Enfield Rapids in 1614. His exploration formed the basis for Dutch claims to Connecticut.

John Winthrop, the son of the Governor of Massachusetts, was instrumental in beginning settlement at the mouth of the Connecticut River.

Actual settlement did not begin, however, for almost twenty years. In 1633, the Dutch erected a trading post, the House of Good Hope, at present-day Hartford. Plymouth Colony erected a trading post at present-day Windsor the same year. Several Podunks, worried about the alliance of the Dutch with their old enemies the Pequots, trekked to Boston and invited the English to come and settle in their midst.

Shortly after, a settlement began in Wethersfield, and a group of Dorchester colonists joined the Windsor settlement. At this time a group of English colonists erected a fort at Saybrook. The following year, Thomas Hooker led his congregation on their famous overland journey to Hartford.

Relations between the English newcomers and the Native Americans were strained and fraught with misunderstanding, fear and deception. By 1637, Sowheag, the sachem of the Wangunks, who had sold the land around Wethersfield, felt that he had been betrayed by the English, who he complained now wanted all the land. He relayed his anger to the Pequots, and, as a result, in April of that year, several Wethersfield colonists were attacked and killed by Pequots. In retaliation, the colonists, intent on exterminating the Pequots, declared war. This war, the Pequot War, was an especially bloody conflict, beginning with the Mystic Massacre and ending in the Great Swamp fight of Fairfield. The colonists decimated the Pequots.

Thirty-eight years later, Metacom, or King Philip, attempted to save southern New England from being completely lost to the colonists. He formed a confederation of Native American tribes, many from Connecticut, and waged what came to be known as King Philip's War. Some modern historians believe that had the Indians made this attempt earlier, they might have won, and today Connecticut, Massachusetts and Rhode Island might be very different places.

An early settler. The first houses were often crude log affairs.

Settlement was not easy for the colonists. Winters were harsh, food was scarce, and the work of creating homesteads was rigorous. Despite the later conflicts, settlers frequently relied upon the local Native Americans for help and instruction in their first years in the New World. Early housing often consisted of dugouts, rude log cabins, and sometimes wigwams. These gave way to small one-room

houses with a chimney at one end. As circumstances improved, housing was improved, and a room would be added to the other side of the chimney, thus creating the familiar center-chimney farmhouse. Further expansion was carried out by adding a lean-to across the back, thus the also familiar salt-box. By around 1750, the central chimney design gave way to the central hall, with a chimney on each end of the house. An ell, placed at a right angle to the back of the house, replaced the lean-to. To protect themselves from the harsh winters, farmers often connected their barns to their houses, creating the rambling style seen throughout New England.

The first settlers, Puritans, formed their governments around their religion. Their meeting houses were the center of worship and government. In fact, it was not until after the Revolution that church and state were separated. New parishes or ecclesiasti-

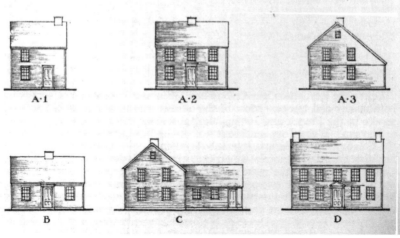

The development of the typical Connecticut house.

cal societies were formed to make travel to worship, particularly in winter, easier. These societies began within the bounds of the mother town, but in time usually petitioned the General Assembly to become towns in their own right. Thus, many of the earliest towns were subdivided into new towns. Later, particularly when the iron industry prospered in northwestern Connecticut, and when mills flourished along the rivers of eastern Connecticut, villages formed around industries. Towns sectioned off from other towns, and within these towns, villages formed.

Because of this, and because so many Connecticut towns were named for towns in England, the Connecticut traveler encounters such idiosyncrasies as the fact that the town of Hampton is nowhere near East Hampton, and is indeed northeast of East Hampton. Some of Connecticut's cities are within town borders, such as Willimantic in the town of Windham, Rockville within Vernon, and Winsted within the town of Winchester. Other towns are best known by one of the villages within. Storrs is a village in Mansfield, Mystic is in the towns of both Stonington and Groton, Falls Village is in Canaan, and Canaan is in North Canaan.

The first industries in a new settlement were the sawmill and gristmill, and virtually every town had at least one of each. The gristmill freed the settlers from grinding their corn by hand in a mortar, the way the Native Americans ground theirs. The sawmill made construction of houses easier. Only a few of these mills remain intact, but the stone foundations of many can be seen along rivers and streams throughout the state.

Connecticut was an active participant in the Revolutionary War, and responded to the Lexington Alarm with astonishing speed. The shoreline towns, especially in Fairfield County, saw battle. British Major General William Tryon attacked several of these towns, burning houses, warehouses and barns. Inland settlements sent men to fight and, often at great sacrifice, provided supplies. Several important players in the Revolution were Connecticut residents: Jonathan Trumbull, Thomas Knowlton, Nathan Hale, Ethan Allen, Israel Putnam and, alas, Benedict Arnold. George Washington, Rochambeau, and Lafayette were all in Connecticut during the Revolutionary War, and Washington visited several times.

Connecticut citizens have been industrious from the start. In addition to sawmills and gristmills, blacksmith shops, fulling mills, iron mines and foundries, shipbuilding and sea trade were important in the economic development of the state. Yankee peddlers carried Connecticut-made goods throughout the state, and up and down the coast. Textile mills took advantage of the abundant water power in eastern Connecticut. Tobacco farms flourished in the Connecticut River Valley.

Ironically, many of the prettiest towns in Connecticut, in the rural eastern and western highlands, were founded as manufacturing centers. The forests that covered the state disappeared, to make room for farms and grazing, and to provide wood for fuel, for ship's masts, for building materials and for charcoal. In the eighteenth century, Connecticut looked far different from the town greens, church spires, and white clapboard houses that we now cherish. Today, the trees have grown back, and the early industries no longer exist. Alas, some entire towns or villages have also vanished.

Farms disappeared, as the younger generations were tempted to work in the mills and factories, or to go west where the land was reputed to be easier to till. Grazing lands reverted to woodland. Left as evidence are miles of stone walls, an occasional crumbling chimney, and overgrown cellar holes in the forests where farmers once eked out a living.

Transportation has had a profound effect on the fate of individual towns. Towns with good harbors, either along one of the major rivers, or along the sound, quickly developed into prosperous centers of trade.

When the English arrived, Connecticut was already crisscrossed with a network of well-worn Native American paths. In the beginning, the English used these paths to lay out their own roads, but as settlement increased and the need arose, they blazed new roads. Towns along major thoroughfares, such as the Boston Post Road, enjoyed the opportunity to open taverns and derive income from the weary travelers who passed through. In the late eighteenth century, the turnpike system, which allowed fees, or tolls, to be charged and used for upkeep and maintenance, offered improved roads. Stage coaches made regular trips along these highways.

Then, in 1837, the railroad opened in Connecticut. By 1881 the railroad dominated transportation. By 1900, there were 1,024 miles of track in the state. Businessmen, subscribers and towns raised funds to lure a railroad to their locations, a practice which led to often circuitous routes for the lines. Towns which were bypassed were eclipsed by those with depots. Typically, Ashford, the town where I live, which was a stop on the Boston Post Road, with taverns and hotels, saw its hostelries fall into ruin. Conversely, neighboring towns, such as Mansfield and Willington, which were served by the rail, developed industries that took advantage of the opportunity to ship and receive goods.

Roads themselves changed from dusty in the summer aned muddy in the spring to smooth pavement. In the 1950s, under President Eisenhower, the interstate highway system was developed. These limited-access, multi-lane highways opened up previously remote areas, connected states, and were a factor in the rise of suburbs. Connecticut is crossed by several of these interstates—Routes 84, 91, 395, and 95.

Another, invisible network operated in Connecticut—the Underground Railroad. Some slavery was practiced in Connecticut, until it was outlawed in 1784. Native Americans, and more predominantly African-Americans, were enslaved by early wealthy colonists, and there is evidence that the extensive West Indies trade, which brought prosperity to the harbor towns, included trade in human cargo. Nevertheless, Connecticut was home to many active and outspoken abolitionists, including Harriet Beecher Stowe, John Brown and Prudence Crandall. Escaped slaves from the south were surreptitiously spirited through the state, usually under cover of night. Because of the secrecy of this operation, much of the specific history has been lost.

Early travelers included George Washington, as mentioned above, and yes, he "slept here." Madam Sarah Kemble Knight traveled from Boston to New York through southern Connecticut and wrote a small book about her travels. Such a trip was unheard of for a woman alone at her time, but she undertook it anyway, having business to conduct. In her narrative she comments on the roads, stages, and accommodations along her route, often with less than flattering descriptions.

Another interesting traveler was the Old Leather Man, a speechless recluse, who followed a regular circuit on foot through parts of southern and western Connecticut and New York State. I have included anecdotes of these travelers in the various towns they passed through.

It was not, however, until the popularity of the automobile that people traveled in Connecticut just for fun. The twentieth century brought both tourism and the Sunday drive. Today, tourism continues, but we have become a nation of commuters, so the notion of a drive on one's day off is no longer appealing. Still, there are many historically interesting places to visit and things to know about in Connecticut. A people on wheels— going to the grocery store, chauffeuring the kids, on the way to work— we pass through many towns daily, yet we often know little about the pasts of these towns. This book is intended to give you a peek at this rich and varied history. It is also intended to help you plan where you might want to go when you have some leisure or a few minutes to stop at a site while on your way elsewhere.

The book is divided into counties. This seemed appropriate, since counties are an historical remnant in Connecticut with no political or governmental meaning today. Towns are organized alphabetically within each county. This is to facilitate looking up the town you want to visit, or learning about the town you find yourself in.

I have made no attempt to include comprehensive histories of each town. Instead, I have included information

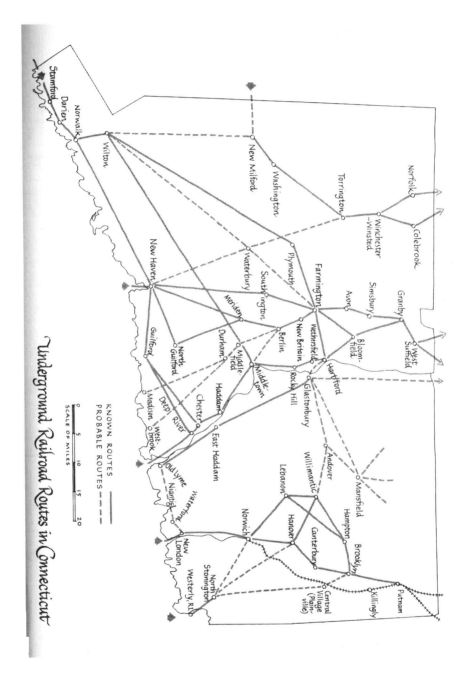

This map of the Underground Railroad in Connecticut was painstakingly researched by Horatio Strothers.

on the Native Americans, early settlement, inventions, business enterprises, anecdotes, stories, and other items that seem particularly interesting. I have also included historical sites, museums, official historic districts and houses of note. Where a phone number is not listed, the house is private and can be viewed only from the street. Historic districts vary from the well-marked (houses dated) and restored, to those areas designated to prevent further deterioration, but not yet restored. Some of these latter are the least immediately obvious, but worth a look if you are in the area.

I, of course, take full responsibility for what is said in this book. If you have comments, or pieces of history you would like to suggest for a subsequent edition, you can email me at sstaubach@snet.net

Enjoy your trip through Connecticut history!

Suzanne Staubach
Ashford, CT

Fairfield County

The county is 632 square miles, and has 23 towns: Bethel, Bridgeport, Brookfield, Danbury, Darien, Easton, Fairfield, Greenwich, Monroe, New Canaan, New Fairfield, Newtown, Norwalk, Redding, Ridgefield, Shelton, Sherman, Stamford, Stratford, Trumbull, Weston, Westport and Wilton.

Located in the southwestern corner of Connecticut, Fairfield County is tucked between the Long Island shore and New York State. It includes the wealthy suburbs of New York City, where artists, writers, actors and actresses as well as business executives live. It also has two of the state's largest cities, Bridgeport and Stamford, the 5,420-acre Candlewood Lake, and, inland, hill country.

There are many interesting architectural sites, including carefully restored houses. Fairfield County saw fierce fighting during the Revolutionary War, and suffered at the hands of the British Major General William Tryon, who torched the homes of many patriots.

Interstate Routes 84 and 95 go across Fairfield County. To really enjoy the county, however, you want to drive on the secondary highways, such as Route 37 in the northern towns, and of course Route 1 along the shore. The historic Merritt Parkway (Route 15) makes for a pleasant excursion.

Bethel

Routes 6, 53, 58, 302
Incorporated 1855

Native Americans
Paugussetts

Historical notes
Bethel was settled as part of Danbury in 1685 and organized as the East Parish of Danbury in 1759. It was nearly a century before the hamlet was granted town status. The inhabitants chose the name of Eastbury, but the General Assembly chose instead Bethel, after the Hebrew. Like its mother town, Bethel was a thriving hat-making center. Home to the Barnum family since before the Revolutionary War, P. T. Barnum was born here on July 5, 1810.

Notable buildings
Seth Seyle House, 189 Greenwood Avenue, now the Bethel Public Library. Three college presidents were born in this Greek Revival house. It was later donated to the town.

Bridgeport

Route 1. Incorporated 1821, chartered as a city 1836.

Native Americans

Pequonnock (or Gold Hill Band) of the Paugusssetts. The territory known as Pequonnock (means cleared field) included 200–300 acres east of the Uncoway River (Ash Creek). There were three villages, one on the western bank of the Uncoway River (Ash Creek), one at the base of Golden Hill, and a third, quite large, at the north end of the cove in Black Rock Harbor. Here there were planting fields, a fort, and a village of 150 wigwams.

Historical notes

The Parish of Stratfield, organized in 1690, was the first independent parish to form within the bounds of an existing town in the Connecticut Colony. Halfway between Stratford and Fairfield, it became the town of Bridgeport. Blessed with two fine harbors, Bridgeport Harbor at the mouth of the Pequonnock River, and Black Rock Harbor, Bridgeport became a bustling city. The turnpike, built in 1801, bypassed the then thriving Derby, and brought new goods and business to Bridgeport. In 1836, the Housatonic Railroad was chartered, and brought still more business. Bridgeport experienced rapid industrial growth and is today the largest city in Connecticut.

P. T. Barnum housed his circus in Bridgeport during the winter, and it is said that his elephants could be seen from the windows of passing trains. Barnum became deeply involved in the life of the city, serving as mayor and state representative. He was beloved for his many philanthropic acts, in-

Eastern view of Bridgeport Harbor, 1849.

cluding the development of Seaside Park. Tom Thumb, the stage name of the dwarf Charles S. Stratton, who toured with P. T. Barnum's Greatest Show on Earth, was born in Bridgeport. Twenty-eight inches tall, he gained international fame as the star of the circus.

Inventions, inventors and firsts

The Reverend Olympia Brown was the first woman in America to be formally ordained. She was called by the Universalist Church and served as pastor from 1870 to 1876. A century later, again in Bridgeport, the Rector Sandra A. Wilson became the first black woman to be ordained in the Episcopal Church.

Notable buildings

Barnum Museum (c. 1893), 820 Main Street, I-95 Exit 27 (203-331-9881). Changing exhibits related to the career of P. T. Barnum. This was erected by Barnum as the Barnum Institute of Science and History.

Captain John Brooks House (c. 1788), 90 Acre Park (moved from original site). Frame half-house with interior paneling, corner cupboards and Dutch stoop.

Penfield Reef Lighthouse, Long Island Sound off Shoal Point, and Tongue Point Lighthouse, west side of Bridgeport Harbor at Tongue Point. Both lighthouses are presently in operation.

Historic canal boats

Priscilla Daily and Elmer S. Daily, Bridgeport Harbor.

Historic districts

Barnum-Palliser Historic District, roughly bounded by Myrtle and Park Avenues and Atlantic and Austin Streets (both sides).

Bassickville Historic District, 20–122 Bassick, 667–777 Howard Avenue, 1521–1523 Fairfield Avenue and 1350–1380 State Street. This was once the manufacturing village of Bassickville, centered on the Bassick Company, which manufactured automobile hardware.

William D. Bishop Cottage Development Historic District (Cottage Park Historic District), Cottage Place and Atlantic, Broad, Main and Whiting Streets.

A Bridgeport furnace advertisement.

Black Rock Gardens Historic District (wartime emergency housing), bounded by Fairfield and Brewster Streets and Nash Lane, including Rowsley and Haddon Streets.

Black Rock Historic District, roughly bounded by Black Rock Harbor, Grovers Avenue, and Beacon and Prescott Streets. A Revolutionary War fort was located at Black Rock. Whaleboats were used as war boats in the effort for independence.

Bridgeport Downtown North Historic District, roughly bounded by Congress and Water Streets, Fairfield Avenue, and Elm, Golden Hill and Chapel Streets.

Bridgeport Downtown South Historic District, roughly bounded by Elm, Cannon, Main, Gilbert, and Broad Streets.

Deacon's Point Historic District, roughly bounded by Seaview Avenue and Williston, Bunnell and West Avenues.

Division Street Historic District, roughly bounded by State Street, and Iranistan, Black Rock and West Avenues.

East Bridgeport Historic District, roughly bounded by railroad tracks, and Beach, Arctic and Knowlton Streets.

East Main Street Historic District, bounded by Walters and Nichols Streets from 371–377 to 741–747 and 388–394 to 744 East Main Street.

Gateway Village Historic District (wartime emergency housing), roughly bounded by Waterman Street, Con-necticut Avenue and Alanson Road.

Golden Hill Historic District, roughly bounded by Congress Street, Lyon Terrace, and Elm and Harris Streets.

Lakeview Village Historic District (wartime emergency housing), roughly bounded by Boston Avenue, and Essex, Colony, Plymouth and Asylum Streets.

Railroad Avenue Industrial District, roughly bounded by State and Cherry Streets, and Fairfield and Wordin Avenues.

Remington City Historic District (wartime emergency housing), roughly bounded by Willow Street and East Avenue between Boston and Barnum Avenues.

Seaside Village Historic District (wartime emergency housing), east side of Iranistan Avenue between South Avenue and Burnham Street.

Sterling Hill Historic District, roughly bounded by Pequonnock Street, Harral Avenue, James Street and Washington Avenue.

Stratfield Historic District, Routes 59 and 1.

Wilmot Apartments Historic District (wartime emergency housing), junction of Connecticut and Wilmot Avenues.

Brookfield
Routes 25, 133, 202/7
Incorporated 1788

Native Americans
Pootatucks. Chief Pokono ruled for many years before the arrival of Europeans in 1636.

Historical notes

Parts of Danbury, Newtown and New Milford were brought together as the Parish of Newbury, which was later renamed in honor of the popular pastor, the Rev. Thomas Brooks, and incorporated as the town of Brookfield. Brookfield Center was also called the Iron Works, after its major industry. East of Brookfield Center was a lead mine.

During the nineteenth century, Brookfield was a busy little town, with stage coach stops, taverns and hotels. Sawmills, lime kilns, a gristmill, shear shop, comb and button factories, harness shops and hat factories, in addition to farms, occupied the citizens and brought prosperity. By the end of the century, there were two railroad stations in town.

Notable buildings

Brookfield Craft Center, Route 25 (203-7775-4526). This part of town is known as the Brookfield Iron Works. The center is located in a 1780 gristmill which overlooks Still River at Half-Way Falls. The grounds and gallery are open to the public.

Historic districts

Brookfield Center Historic District, Long Meadow Hill Road, Brookfield Center (Route 25). Included in the district is the former Town Hall, completed in 1875 at a cost of $4,000. The Town Hall is used by the Historical Society as a center for preservation.

Danbury

Routes 53, 39, 37, 6, 7, 202. Route 6 is at times Route 7 and at times Route 202. Parts of Route 7 are multi-lane.

Incorporated 1687, chartered as a city in 1889.

Native Americans

Paugussetts. Called area Pahquioque.

Historical notes

Eight families left Norwalk in 1684 to settle in Danbury. Though they wished to call their new town Swampfield, the General Assembly chose instead Danbury, after the English hamlet. No matter. In the early days, the settlement was commonly called Beantown because of the superior quality of the beans grown here. These beans were soon a crucial source of commerce for the settlement, making Danbury a key inland trading center. The town grew, the population swelling to 2,000 by 1750. During the Revolutionary War, supplies for the war were stockpiled in town, and hospital services were provided for soldiers. Major General William Tryon marched on Danbury in April 1777 and set several fires. Nineteen houses plus twenty-two stores and barns were burned. Three townsmen, including an African American, lost their lives defending the town.

Inventions, inventors and firsts

Zadok Benedict established the first hat manufactory in the country in 1780. He employed three men and turned out three beaver hats a day. Prior to Benedict's efforts, furs were sent to New York, where they were cut and sewn into hats. Benedict was followed into the business by other enterprising Danbury citizens, such as the ambitious farmer, Ezra Mallory. Though Mallory began in a little shop on his farm, he became so successful that the industry occupied several generations of his descendants. Hat-making flourished, becoming the principal industry in Danbury. As many as fifty factories operated at one time, and at the peak in the early twentieth century, millions dozens of men's hats were produced yearly. Danbury earned the nickname Hat City, and her hatters dominated the industry until the end of the 1950s, when fashion no longer dictated head coverings.

Notable buildings

Scott-Fanton Museum, 43 Main Street, I-84 Exit 5 (203-743-5200). Includes the John and Mary Rider House (c. 1785) and John Dodd Shop (c. 1790).

Charles Ives House (c. 1829), 7 Mountainville Avenue, the birthplace of the Pulitzer Prize-winning composer.

Danbury Railway Museum, Union Station (c. 1903), 120 Water Street, I-84 Exit 5 (203-778-8337). Restored station, vintage railroad cars, rides from an hour to a day long.

Military Museum of Southern New England, 125 Park Avenue (203-790-9277). World War II exhibits.

Historic districts

Main Street Historic District, Boughton, Elm, Ives, Keeler, Main, West and White Streets.

Darien

Routes 1, 106, 124
Incorporated 1820

Native Americans

Siwanogs

Historical notes

Once the first roads were cut through the woods, around 1700, the Darien area was settled as part of Stamford. In 1737 the area became known as the Middlesex Parish. Middlesex Parish was a frequent target of Tory raids. One July day in 1781, the British stormed the meeting house as the Reverend Moses Mather preached. It is said that some of the men hid beneath the voluminous skirts of the women and escaped undetected, but the British managed to round up the Reverend and forty-eight men and boys. They were shipped to prison in New York City, where they languished for five months. Some of the men died, but the survivors were exchanged and sent home.

In 1820, the parish was incorporated as a separate town, and, at the whim of a romantic sailor, named for the Isthmus of Darien.

Darien remained a quiet farming and fishing town until the arrival of the railroad in 1848. With rail service came an influx of Irish immigrants, followed by Italians. The population swelled, and gradually the town became a bedroom town for New York City.

Inventions, inventors and firsts

The nation's first home for disabled veterans and veterans' orphans, Fitch's Home for the Soldiers and Their Orphans, was built in the Noroton Heights section during the Civil War. It encompassed several acres on the present-day northeast corner of West Avenue and Noroton Avenue. The Allen O'Neill housing development for veterans is now on the site of the veterans' home.

Notable buildings

The Bates-Scofield House Museum (c. 1736), 45 Old Kings Highway North (203-655-9233). A classic saltbox maintained as a museum by the Darien Historical Society. Regional eighteenth and early nineteenth-century furniture is exhibited.

Bates-Scofield House, Darien.

Historic districts

Boston Post Road Historic District, 567–728 Boston Post Road, 1–25 Brookside Road and 45–70 Old Kings Highway North.

Easton

Routes 58, 136, 59
Incorporated 1845

Native Americans

Paugussetts. A rock known as Samp Mortar Rock, scoured by glaciers, was used for grinding corn (off Route 58). The pestle is now in the Peabody Museum at Yale. Below the rock was a cave, also used by the Indians.

Historical notes

Purchased from the Aspetuck in 1670 for thirty pounds and some trucking cloth. Part of Fairfield, known as North Fairfield and recognized as a parish in 1762, combined with Norfield to make the town of Weston in 1787. The North Fairfield section was then separated from Weston by the Connecticut General Assembly in 1845 to make the town of Easton.

Inventions, inventors and firsts

Samuel Staples left his entire estate to establish the first free academy and one of the earliest secondary schools in the nation. The first Methodist Society was established in Easton, in 1790.

Historic districts

Aspetuck Historic District (also in Weston), roughly Redding Road from the junction with Old Redding Road to Welled Hill road and Old Redding Road North past Aspetuck Road.

Fairfield

Routes 1, 58, 59, 135 and Merritt Parkway. Incorporated 1639.

Native Americans

Paugussetts. Site of the Great Swamp Fight. After the colonists, aided by Uncas and his Mohegans, burned the Pequot fort in Mystic, and massacred between six and seven hundred inhabitants, the chieftain Sassacus reluctantly led surviving Pequots (who had been in a different fort) away from their homelands towards the Hudson River. They were pursued by the Connecticut militia, led by Roger Ludlow, and by troops from Massachusetts. The colonists were intent upon exterminating the Pequots. On a hot July day in 1637 Ludlow and his men located the fleeing Pequots in a swamp in the land known as Unquowa.

Ludlow and his troops surrounded the Pequot encampment. Thomas Stanton, who knew the Pequot language, went alone into the swamp and convinced the Indians to let him bring the women and children out with him. The Great Swamp Fight ensued. Perhaps sixty or seventy Pequots escaped. The rest were killed or captured and sold into slavery. This ended the Pequot War.

Historical notes

Roger Ludlow returned with five companions from Windsor to Unquowa two years after the Great Swamp Fight. He purchased land from the Pequonnock on May 11, 1639. Fairfield originally also included what later became the towns of Weston, Redding, Easton, the western portion of Bridgeport and the Greens Farms section of Westport.

The battle of Fairfield Swamp, which ended the Pequot War.

Fairfield was an important player in the Revolutionary War and was visited by George Washington, Benjamin Franklin and the Marquis de Lafayette. The British looted and burned much of the town during the war, but it quickly recovered. Prior to the war, the young law student, Aaron Burr, secretly rode down from Litchfield to court Fairfield resident Dorothy Quincy. We will never know the particulars of the romance, but in 1775 Dorothy Quincy married John Hancock.

Until 1879, women in Connecticut had no rights to property, personal income or even the custody of their children. However, occasionally a circumstance necessitated a special act of the legislature. Such was the case of Sarah A. Sherwood, who had a substantial inheritance when she married Jessup Sherwood. Exercising his legal rights, Jessup demanded control of Sarah's property, and when she balked, he took the matter to the courts. Sarah was put in jail. Jessup remained comfortably ensconced in Sarah's commodious house and enjoyed her wealth. The women of Fairfield were outraged, and rallied to Sarah's support. In 1865, the legislature passed a special law in her favor.

Notable buildings

The site of the Great Swamp Fight has long since been filled in and built over. However, nearby, a monument was erected in the Southport section of town, just off and to the south of the Boston Post Road. The marker reads: "The Great Swamp Fight. Here ended the Pequot War July 13, 1637."

Ogden House Museum and Gardens, 1520 Bronson Road (203-259-1598). This building escaped the burning of Fairfield. It is a typical mid-eighteenth-century farmhouse, and has been appropriately furnished. The original tract of land was divided and dispersed, but enough remains for beautiful display gardens featuring herbs and vegetables that would typically have been grown during colonial times. The house is maintained by the Fairfield Historical Society.

Ogden House, Fairfield.

Historic districts

Greenfield Hill Historic District, roughly bounded by Meeting House Lane, Hillside Road, Verna Hill Road and Bronson Road. This district has the largest concentration of pre-Revolutionary houses in town (thirteen).

Fairfield Historic District (Uncowaye), Old Post Road from Post to Turney Roads. Includes the town green, and mainly eighteenth and nineteenth-century houses. The Beach Road section contains the oldest houses, and is a relatively intact example of an eighteenth-century cityscape. The Historical Society maintains its headquarters at 636 Old Post Road (203-259-1598) and manages four historic structures: the Sun Tavern, the Burr Homestead, and the Victorian Cottage and Barn.

Southport Historical District (Mill River), roughly bounded by Southport Harbor, the railroad, Old South Road and Rose Hill Road. Mainly nineteenth-century buildings, representative of most styles of that time period.

Greenwich

Route 1, Merritt Parkway
Incorporated 1665

Native Americans

Siwanogs

Historical notes

The adventurer and Dutchman Adrian Block sailed past what became Greenwich during his exploratory trip of 1614. A quarter century later, in 1640, Daniel Patrick and Robert Feake of New Haven colony paid the Siwanogs twenty-five English coats for the land between the Asamuck and Patomuck Rivers (present-day Old Greenwich). However, over the next decades, ownership was contested.

Greenwich was under British dominion for the first two years of incorporation. The Dutch of New Amsterdam asserted that, indeed, the settlement came under their jurisdiction as the Dutch had been there first, and for the next fourteen years, until 1656, it was governed under the Dutch manor system. In 1656, it reverted to British rule, under the New Haven colony.

Finally, in 1665, the colonies of Connecticut and New Haven granted Greenwich town status.

Seventeen years later, twenty-seven families purchased what became Horseneck Plantation (central Greenwich), from the few surviving Native Americans. A public pasture for horses was located at Horseneck Plantation, as well as a saltworks to supply the Revolutionary army.

Ghost stories and legends

General Israel Putnam had just begun his morning shave when suddenly he saw not only himself in the mirror, but approaching redcoats. Outnumbered, and fearing defeat, he ordered his men to retreat. To avoid capture, Putnam threw down his razor, fetched his horse, and raced down the stone steps of the tavern. He and his horse plunged from the summit of Put's Hill and disappeared entirely from view. Witnesses were astonished at the feat. Putnam and his stead survived and successfully escaped. The hill, along Route 1, has been pretty much graded away, but an enclosure and tablet mark the site.

Notable buildings

Putnam Cottage (c. 1692), 243 East Putnam Avenue (203-869-9697). The cottage began as a one-room farmhouse. Over the years it was expanded, and in 1734, became the Knapp Tavern. The Tavern was General Israel Putnam's headquarters, and is reputedly where he saw the redcoats in the mirror. Of heavy, hand-hewn post-and-beam construction, the house has seven fireplaces, two of which are massive fieldstone constructions.

Bush-Holley House Museum (c. 1732), 39 Strickland Road (203-869-6899). Connecticut's first art colony was founded in the Cos Cob section of town in what is now the Bush-Holley House Museum. The house was built as a home for the Bush family, wealthy merchants, farmers and millers. In 1882, the Holleys, who lived in the house, turned innkeepers and played host to such noted artists as John Twachtman, Childe Hassam, Theodore Robinson, J. Alden Weir, and Elmer MacRae. The guests were attracted to the Holleys' gracious hospitality, the proximity to New York City, and the picturesque grounds and waterfront.

Historic districts

Greenwich Avenue Historic District, roughly bounded by Bruce Park, Putnam, Greenwich, and Railroad Avenues, East Elm and Mason Streets, Field Point Road and Havemeyer Place.

Greenwich Municipal Center Historic District, 101 Field Point Road, 290, 29, 310 Greenwich Avenue.

Putnam Hill Historic District, Route 1.

Round Hill Historic District, roughly bounded by the junction of John Street and Round Hill Road.

Strickland Road Historic District, Strickland Road and Laughlin Avenue.

Monroe
Routes 25, 34, 111
Incorporated 1823

Native Americans
Paugussetts

Historical notes
Named for President Monroe. Originally settled as the North Division of Stratford about 1720, and organized as the parishes of Ripton in 1717 and North Stratford in 1744. The two parishes joined together in 1789 to break from Stratford and become the town of Huntington. In 1823, the old North Stratford area broke from Huntington and became the town of Monroe.

Geology
Monroe is rich in minerals, including tungsten, tellurium, native bismuth, copper pyrites, galena blende, and tourmaline, beryllium, rose quartz, and pegmatite, feldspar, albite, garnet, uranophane and flurospar. In years past, various mines have operated. The old Booth Bismuth Mine, a source for manganapatite, scheelite, and bismuth, is located on Barn Hill Road, about a tenth of a mile in from Route 110.

Other old mines in this vicinity include the East Village Pegmatite Quarry and Lane's Quarry. Most of these old quarries are behind houses on private land, but driving through town, it is interesting to note that this suburban town was once a rich source of minerals. A mile outside Monroe village, heading west on Route 110, is an old feldspar quarry. An abandoned lime quarry, called Devil's Den, can be found along the blue blazed Pomperaug Trail.

East Village Meeting House, Monroe.

Ghost stories and legends

When Ephraim Lane was tending his cows, he dug a shaft into the ground for a post hole so he could build a fence. To his surprise, he discovered a wealth of minerals: arsenopyrite, bismuth, marcasite, pyrite, rutile, scheelite, sphalerite, tungstite and a rich vein of flurospar. The phosphorescence of the flurospar was the talk of the town, and it was said that a pure green light shown from the mineral when it was taken into a dark room and placed on a hot shovel, and that the rocks remained wondrously luminous until they completely cooled.

Notable buildings

The Barn Hill/East Village one-room schoolhouse (c. 1790), junction of Wheeler and Old Tannery Roads (203-261-1383).

East Village Meetinghouse (c. 1811),

Barn Hill and East Village Roads (203-261-1388). Oldest Methodist church building in Connecticut.

Eliot Beardsley Homestead (c. 1760), Great Ring Road (203-261-1388). Excellent example of an eighteenth-century saltbox.

Historic districts

Monroe Center Historic District, Routes 110 and 111.

New Canaan

Routes 123, 124, Merritt Parkway
Incorporated 1801

Native Americans

Siwanogs. Chief Ponus, the leading sachem of the Siwanogs, lived here. The Siwanogs were members of the Wappinger confederacy. Their path to New York and the Hudson River crossed through Monroe. A boulder monument to Ponus, on Ponus Ridge Road, marks a place this now-vanished path once crossed.

Historical notes

Once a thriving shoe-making center, New Canaan is now primarily a residential town. Settled about 1700, the Parish of Canaan was organized in 1731 to serve families from the northern reaches of Norwalk and Stamford. When the town was incorporated in 1801, more lands were annexed on the southern and western boundaries.

Notable buildings

The Hanford-Silliman House (c. 1764), 13 Oenoke Ridge Road (203-966-1776). Built as a center-chimney saltbox by Stephen Hanford, a weaver and tavern-keeper, the Hanford-Silliman house was later altered by the Silliman family, who added a dining room to the rear of the house and a Greek Revival front.

Included on the Hanford-Silliman grounds are the John Rogers Studio and Museum, built in 1878, which now houses a collection of Rogers statuary; the Rock School, a one-room schoolhouse built in 1799; the Tool Museum; the New Canaan Hand Press, a recreation of a nineteenth-century printing office; the Town House and Library, built in 1825; and the Cody Drug Store, where furnishings from the original store are exhibited.

New Fairfield

Routes 39, 37
Incorporated 1740

Native Americans

Paugussetts. Chief Squantz of the Schaghticoke lived near the shores of what was later called Squantz Pond. West of this pond, on the top of Pond Mountain, is Pootaluck Council Cave, reputed to be the location of Schaghticoke meetings.

Historical notes

The early colonists negotiated unsuccessfully for the purchase of land, first with Chief Squantz, and after his death with his sons. In April of 1729, they bypassed Chief Squantz's family, and paid sixty-five pounds sterling to other Native Americans for the land. This, together with a tract known as

Mitchell's Purchase, became New Fairfield and eventually also Sherman.

Despite the rugged terrain, the stalwart settlers farmed and produced goods. However, by 1900, farming diminished, the manufacturers had closed up shop or left, and the population dwindled.

The Big Basin, a valley thick with white oak, deep in the shadows of Green Pond Mountain, Candlewood Mountain, Turner Mountain, and over the New York State Line, Mizzentop and Quaker Hill, stretched through the heart of New Fairfield and Sherman. Here the remaining rural residents shot clay pigeons, danced to the music of fiddles and banjos, and feasted at the famous clambakes hosted by the Talcott twins. They harbored a profound distrust of "Yorkers" or "insects," visitors from across the state line.

In 1927, the few remaining valley farms vanished when the Connecticut Light and Power Company dammed the Rocky River and flooded the Big Basin to create Candlewood Lake, the largest lake in the state.

Ghost stories and legends

Deep in the Big Basin, with Green Pond Mountain looming in the front yard, was The World's Smallest Store. Here Perry Boney sold cheese and crackers, bells, trinkets, foodstuffs and "specials," long blue shotgun shells that caused such smoke and noise no one bought them twice. The World's Smallest Store was so tiny it could only accommodate two very small children or one adult at a time. Still, it was something to behold. It boasted a "work of art," an oil painting of Custer's Last Stand with a whiskey advertisement beneath, and a front gate planted with petunias and candytuft, and hung with bells that tinkled when a customer arrived.

No one in the Big Basin could understand the mystery of Boney's shopkeeping. When his inventory was low, he would hike over Greenwood Hill to Sherman, an arduous five miles, carrying a covered market basket. At the general store in Sherman, he would replenish his stock, and then return with his basketful of goods to his own store, where he would sell them for the exact same price as he'd paid. It seemed he'd never heard of margins or profit.

There were other things about Boney no one understood. When he approached Sherman on his shopping excursions, a raccoon, the town mascot, would come out of the woods and Boney would talk to it in a strange tongue and whistle to it, and the raccoon would follow him to the general store, and wait outside for him. When Boney was ready to return home, the raccoon would walk him back.

The great sadness in Perry Boney's life was the loss of his true love. During their courtship, Boney's sweetheart planted portulaca seeds in an old iron kettle brought from the Salisbury hills. The kettle sat by the door of Boney's store. But before summer came, before the flowers bloomed, his fiancé died. Bereft, Boney tended his love's blossoms, year after year, covering them at each season's end with a net so he could collect the seeds.

One day, folks noticed that Perry Boney was not in his little shop, the door ajar. He had disappeared without a trace—gone, they say, to the fairies on Green Pond Mountain.

Newtown
Routes 302, 25, 6, 34
Incorporated 1711

Native Americans
Paugussetts. Site of a Pootaluck burial ground. The Mitchell family, the first white inhabitants of this tract, promised the Pootalucks that their burial ground would remain inviolate. However, despite the protests of local settlers, the grounds were excavated in the dark of night. Many artifacts now reside at the Peabody Museum in New Haven.

Historical notes
Known as Quanneapague and purchased from the Pohtatucks in 1705. During the Revolutionary War, Newtown was a hotbed of Tory sentiments. An important crossroads in its early history, and a bustling railroad town, Newtown was a center for mica and feldspar mining. In its commercial heyday, buttons, hats and fire hose were produced in the village of Hawleyville.

Inventions, inventors and firsts
James Brunot invented the game of SCRABBLE in Newtown. In the Sandy Hook section of town, Nelson Goodyear, the brother of Charles, operated a rubber factory in an old cot-

ton mill. He invented a process for making hard rubber.

Notable buildings
Liberty Pole (c. 1876).

Historic districts
Hattertown Historic District, roughly at the junction of Aunt Park Lane, and Castle Meadow, Hattertown and Hi Barlow Roads.

Newtown Borough Historic District, roughly at Main Street from Hawley Road to Academy Lane.

Norwalk
Routes 123, 1, 53, 57, Merritt Parkway
Incorporated 1651, chartered as a city in 1893

Native Americans
Siawogs, perhaps some Mohawks. In 1625 this was the site of the village Norwaake.

Historical notes
Adrian Block called the Norwalk Islands the Archipelago. The town name, however, derived from the Native American name Norwaake or Naramake, making Norwalk one of only two Connecticut towns to retain its native American name, albeit in altered form. (The other was Naugatuck, though there is some question whether the Indians themselves called it that.)

Part of the land was purchased by Daniel Patrick of New Haven colony in 1640, and the rest by Roger Ludlow of the Connecticut Colony in 1741, but neither man chose to live here. Ten years later, thirteen families from the Hartford area came and settled along the path that became the present-day East Avenue.

Like many shore towns, Norwalk was torched by Major General William Tryon during the Revolutionary War. Two churches, eighty-seven barns, twenty-two storehouses, seventeen shops, four mills and five vessels, plus the town's entire stock of wheat, grain and hay were lost in the devastating fire.

In 1820, a group of families who had suffered severe losses in the fire decided to head west to Ohio. They gathered their covered wagons at the Norwalk Green, and amidst the shouts, cheers and well-wishes of their neighbors, set off on the long journey. They founded Norwalk, Ohio.

Even before the Revolutionary War, Norwalk was an industrial center producing clocks, watches, nails and paper. The town became famous for its stoneware pottery. The first kiln was built in 1780 at Old Well, and was followed by several others. Domestic kitchenware was produced, most of it simple and utilitarian. The Norwalk potters were influenced by the increasing popularity of wares decorated in Chinese blue, and decorated some of their own pots with cobalt.

Goose Island was used by the Carnegie Institute as an experimental station in developing a serum for yellow fever. The serum was tested on rats.

The author/illustrator Johnny Gruelle was living in Norwalk when he created Raggedy Ann in 1917 and Raggedy Andy in 1920.

Ghost stories and legends

Three times Captain Joseph Merrill dreamed of finding pirate gold. In each of these dreams the location of the hiding place was revealed to him, on Pilot Island at the entrance to the western channel. After the third dream, he decided to pay attention, and went to the secret spot that had been so vividly revealed in his sleep. There—exactly as shown him in his dreams—he found a magnificent cache of Spanish gold! At least, that's the explanation he gave for the source of the Spanish coins he so lavishly spent.

When Elizabeth Fitch went out into the yard to tell her brother Colonel Thomas Fitch goodbye and good luck before he led his cavalry off to the French and Indian War, she was dismayed at the rag-tag appearance of both her brother and his men. Telling them to wait just one minute, she dashed to the chicken yard and quickly gathered a handful of feathers. "Soldiers should wear plumes," she told the men and handed them each a feather, which they stuck into their hats.

When Colonel Fitch and his troops arrived at Fort Calo, in Rensselaer, New York, Dr. Shuckburg, the British army surgeon laughed at the bedraggled men with feathers in their hats. "Now stab my vitals," he exclaimed derisively, "they're macaronis!" Macaroni was the slang for a dandy. Dr. Shuckburgh then wrote the song, "Yankee Doodle Dandy." The house where Colonel Fitch gathered his men is long gone, but it was located on Hendricks Avenue.

Notable buildings

Lockwood-Mathews Mansion Museum (c. 1868), 295 West Avenue, I-95 Exit 14N/15S (203-838-1434). This 52-room stone house was built at a cost of $2 million by LeGrand Lockwood, a railroad magnate and investment banker.

To put the price tag into perspective, consider that the carpenters brought from Italy to work on the mansion earned fifty cents a day. Stonecutters earned a dollar a day. One worker died during the construction.

The house was superior in the craftsmanship of its construction, its technological innovations and design, and was the inspiration for several mansions built in Newport, Rhode Island. Today it is considered one of the finest surviving examples of the Second Empire-style country house.

Lockwood's rise to extraordinary wealth, and subsequent financial ruin, resulted in the sale of the house in 1876 to Charles Mathews, a Staten Island importer, for $90,000. This is a story typical of the late nineteenth century.

The Lockwood-Mathews Mansion Museum is chartered by the State of Connecticut and owned by the City of Norwalk.

Norwalk Museum (old City Hall, c. 1912), 41 North Main Street. Colonial Revival style brick building. Exhibits and collections reflecting Norwalk's rich past.

Historic districts

Hanford Place Historic District, Haviland and Elizabeth Streets, roughly bounded by Haviland and Day Streets, Hanford Place and South Main Street.

Norwalk Green Historic District, roughly bounded by Smith and Park Streets, Boston Post Road, and East and Morgan Avenues.

South Main and Washington Streets, bounded by 68–139 Washington Street, 2–24, 11–15, and 54–60 South Main Street (east side only).

Redding

Routes 7, 53, 58, 107
Incorporated 1767

Native Americans

Paugussetts

Historical notes

Named for the eighteenth-century land speculator and lawyer, John Read. In 1714, Read purchased this tract of land from the sagamore Chicken Warrops (Sam Mohawk). Facetiously, Read called the area Manor of Chicken, or sometimes Lonetown Manor, and drew up formal papers installing Chicken as lord of the manor and himself as tenant. He built himself a house at Lonetown. The Connecticut General Assembly was not amused, and proceeded to auction the land off for settlement.

In 1729, Redding was made part of the Parish of Fairfield. It became an independent town in 1767.

During the winter of 1778–79, General Israel Putnam camped in Redding with three brigades. This was the "Valley Forge" of Connecticut. The men were scantily clothed, poorly fed, and after a fierce winter storm, freezing cold. Miserable and desperate, one of the brigades lined up to march to Hartford to demand redress, but Putnam convinced them to stick it out. Putnam's Brigades, the right wing of the Continental Army, were placed in Redding to be in a strategic position to fend off British attacks to either the west or the east. The encampment has been memorialized in a state park, The Putnam Memorial Camp Ground, on Route 58. Stones mark where the chimneys of the old twelve-man huts stood. The huts were burned before the army moved on. Also on the campgrounds is the Colonial Museum.

Mark Twain (Samuel Clemens) lived in Redding from 1908 until his death in 1910. Stormfield, the picturesque villa he designed himself, was on the ridge along Route 53, a half mile north of the junction with Route 107. It commanded an especially fine vista. Clemens founded the Mark Twain Library, a half mile from his house. It was endowed by Andrew Carnegie. Sadly, Stormfield was destroyed by fire in the summer of 1923.

Another writer graced the early days of Redding, the poet and statesman Joel Barlow, who was a member of the Hartford Wits. Though little read today, Barlow's poems were much admired by his contemporaries.

Geology

Redding is rich with minerals and has been extensively quarried. About seventy-five different minerals have been found in the Branchville Quarry, most frequently curved mica, beryl, calcite, dendrites, columbite, garnet, montmorillonite, pyrite, quartz, spodumene, staurolite and tourmaline. Specimens from this mine are exhibited in many of the larger museums in the country. Redding Garnet Mine, along the western banks of the Saugatuck River (between Routes 57 and 53), provided many garnets for sandpaper and the like.

Historic districts

Georgetown Historic District (also in Wilton), roughly bounded by Route 7, Portland Avenue, Route 107 and the Norwalk River.

Redding Center Historic District, roughly 4–25B Cross Highway, including Read Cemetery, 61–100 Hill Road, 0–15 Lonetown Road and 118 Sanfordtown Road.

Ridgefield

Routes 7, 33, 35, 102, 116
Incorporated 1708

Native Americans

Siawogs

Historical notes

Families from Norwalk purchased Caudatowa (meaning high land), encompassing 20,000 acres, from Catoonah, chief sachem of the Ramapoo Indians. They paid one hundred pounds sterling.

After burning Danbury in 1777, British General William Tryon evacuated his troops, leading them through Ridgebury, in the northern part of Ridgefield, and then on through Ridgefield itself. The fierce Battle of Ridgefield ensued, with colonial militia aided by local farmers. Tryon was forced back to Compo Beach on Long Island Sound.

Ridgefield remained an agricultural town until after the Civil War, when wealthy New Yorkers began to summer in the picturesque hills. Bypassed by the railroad, it retained its rural roots until 1870, at which time a spur line was constructed from Branchville in Redding, making access from New York City convenient. By the 1950s, the suburban spread outward from New York City had reached Ridgefield.

Keeler Tavern.

Notable buildings

The Keeler Tavern Museum, 132 Main Street, Route 35 (203-438-5485). The Timothy Keeler Tavern, a magnificent two-and-a-half story, gambrel-roof house, was built in 1713 by Benjamin Hoyt, and converted into a tavern and stagecoach stop by his grandson, Timothy Keeler. A cannonball fired during the Revolutionary War is still embedded in the cornerpost. The architect Cass Gilbert bought the property in 1907 and added a garden house for entertaining.

Another tavern, the Samuel Keeler Tavern, no longer extant, was near the cemetery in the Ridgebury section of town. It was, according to local tradition, a stopping place for George Washington on his secret 1780 trip from New Jersey to Hartford for his historic meeting with Rochambeau. Rochambeau had his headquarters at the Tavern in 1781, and celebrated his 56th birthday with his officers here.

Shelton

Routes 108, 110

Incorporated 1789 as Huntington. The borough of Shelton was incorporated as a city in 1915.

Native Americans

Paugussetts. The Pootatucks had a palisade fort above Riverview Park. Their burial ground was in the park.

Historical notes

In 1639, present-day Shelton was settled as part of Stratford. Later, the area organized as the Parish of Ripton. In 1789, Ripton and the Parish of North Stratford were incorporated as the town of Huntington. In 1823, the old North Stratford area broke away from Huntington to become the town of Monroe. Then, in 1919, in response to the growing strength of Shelton, and its charter as a city, the town's name was changed from Huntington to Shelton.

The harnessing of water power has had a profound effect upon the development of Shelton. In 1870, the Derby-Shelton dam was built, amidst controversy. As far upstream as New Milford, those engaged in shad fishing protested the building of the dam, contending that their livelihoods would be ruined. Experts were brought in by the Ousatonic Water Company to show that the dam would not hinder the shad, and as special appeasement, a special fish wheel was constructed. The dam fostered industrial development along the Housatonic River. However, the shad fishers were right, the fish wheel was useless, and the fish were impeded from swimming upstream to spawn.

The Stevenson Dam was constructed to produce power for electricity. Behind this dam is the eight-mile stretch of the Housatonic known as Lake Zoar. The lake is named for one of the many bridges which spanned the Housatonic during the tollbridge wars, a period when competing interests vied for the revenues generated by the collection of tolls.

By 1900, Shelton was very much an industrial town, producing pins, pianos and velvet. Tacks made by the Shelton Tack Company were literally worth their weight in gold. A pound of tacks in 1849 sold for $192 on the Pacific Coast, the exact value of a pound of gold.

Ship building was also an important part of Shelton's economy. Captain Edmund Leavonworth and his sons built twenty-one vessels in their shipyard a mile north of where the Stevenson Dam was later constructed.

By 1790, the census for Shelton listed 2,742 adults and 120 slaves.

Geology

At Indian Well State Park, located where Route 110 leaves the river, a stream cascades over cliffs to a pothole below. It is said that the Indians believed the pothole to be 100 feet deep.

Notable buildings

Shelton History Center, 70 Ripton Road (203-925-1803).

Sherman

Routes 37, 39, 55
Incorporated 1802

Native Americans

Paugussetts. A little brook which drains the upper valley of Sherman is still called by its Indian name NAROMIYOCKNOWHUDSDNKATANKSHUNK or Naromi for short. It means "water flowing from the hills."

Historical notes

Purchased in 1729 for sixty-five pounds from Mauwehu, the Indian sachem who lived in Potatuck (Newtown), by Captain Nathan Gold and others of Fairfield. The purchase included present-day Sherman as well as land that eventually was ceded by Connecticut to New York in settlement of a long-standing boundary dispute. Originally part of New Fairfield, and known as the Upper Seven Miles, the town was split off and incorporated in 1802. It was named for an early resident and cobbler, Roger Sherman, who was a signer of the Declaration of Independence.

In 1926, the Big Basin was flooded to make Candlewood Lake, fifteen miles long and 6,000 acres. One hundred houses were destroyed or moved. Housatonic water is pumped into the Lake to make it a power resevoir.

Ghost stories and legends

The Light family, who lived on top of Turner Mountain, often held "kitchen" dances. They would roll up the rugs and invite the neighbors, especially the young folks. An itinerant spice salesman would play guitar, accompanied by other musicians, and a jolly time was had by all. Kitchen dances were a popular entertainment in other Sherman households at the time, but those at the Light House in Sherman have lived on in memory.

Notable buildings

Northrop House Museum (c. 1829), 10 Route 37 Center (860-354-3083). Federal-style farmhouse. The cow barn in back was once used to dry tobacco. The parlor is furnished with items from the Tudor Haviland home, an 1870 Victorian lost when the Leach Hollow area was flooded to make Candlewood Lake.

Historic districts

Sherman Historic District, roughly the junction of Old Greenswood Road and Route 37 Center Northeast, past the junction of Route 37 East and Route 39 North and Sawmill Road.

Stamford

Routes 1, 104, 137, Merritt Parkway
Incorporated 1641

Native Americans

Siwanogs. East of the harbor, at Shippan Point, was the old Indian village of Shippan.

Historical notes

In 1640, Nathaniel Turner, an agent of New Haven Colony, purchased Rippowam from Ponus, sagamore of Toquams, and Wascussue, sagamore of Shippan. A year later, twenty-eight families came down from Wethersfield and settled in Rippowam. At first calling their new home by its Indian name, they quickly renamed the town Stamford after the town in England. Some of the families left, and went to Long Island to found Hempstead. In 1662, Stamford became part of Connecticut Colony.

George Washington passed through Stamford several times. In his diary for 1789, he writes that he breakfasted on Friday, October 16, and Thursday, November 12, at "Webb's, a tolerable home." Martha Washington is reputed to have stayed at the Webb Tavern, when she was on her way to meet her husband in Cambridge. The Webb Tavern stood on the corner of present-day Main and Bank Streets. It was taken down in 1868. During the Revolutionary War, Stamford Fort, located on present Westover Road, was built as protection against the British.

Madam Knight also passed through Stamford on her famous journey. She wrote in her account of the trip, "… we come to Stamford, a well compact Town, but miserable meeting house, which we passed, and thro' many and great difficulties, as Bridges which were exceeding high and very tottering and of vast Length, steep and Rocky Hills and precipices."

Madam Knight was Sarah Kemble Knight (1677–1727), a Bostonian, who recorded her impressions of a trip she made from Boston to New York via Rhode Island and Connecticut in 1704. This was then an almost unthinkable trip for a woman to make alone (although she did hire a series of guides). Her account of the trip was published in 1825 by Timothy Dwight as *The Journal of Madam Knight,* and makes fascinating reading to this day.

Two years after Madam Knight's visit, a new and spacious meeting house was built. Soon transportation to and through Stamford became far less arduous. With a double harbor, improved roads and in 1848 the railroad, Stamford became a prosperous manufacturing city as well as a bedroom town for New York City.

Notable buildings

Stamford Historical Society Museum, 1508 High Ridge Road (203-329-1183). A research and genealogy library, with local history and early redware.

Hoyt-Barnum House (c. 1699), 713 Bedford Street (203-329-1183). Restored blacksmith's house.

Stamford Museum and Nature Center, 39 Scofieldtown Road, Route 15 Exit 35 (203-322-1646). Country store, working farm, exhibits of farm tools, art, natural history, colonial and Native American culture.

Fort Stamford, Canfield Drive (203-977-4692). The site of the 1781 fort and lookout became the Goodbody estate in the early 1900s. Now a park, the Goodbody garden has been carefully restored.

Historic districts

Downtown Stamford Historic District, Atlantic, Main, Bank and Bedford Streets, and Summer Street between Broad and Main Streets and Summer Place. Though much changed, this area has been a hub since the stagecoach days and the years of the Revolution.

Long Ridge Village Historic District, Old Long Ridge Road, bounded by the New York State Line, and Rock Rimmn and Long Ridge Roads.

Revonah Manor Historic Distric, roughly bounded by Urban Street, East Avenue, and Fifth and Bedford Streets.

Stratford

Routes 1, 108, 110, 113, Merritt Parkway
  Incorporated 1639

Native Americans

Paugusetts. The Pequonnock living in Cupheag paid tribute to the Pequots (Cupheag means "harbor"). When the English pursued the Pequots in 1637 through Cupheag, the Pequonnocks joined the Pequots against the unwel-

come intruders. The Pequots were on their way to Sasaqua Swamp in Unquowa (Fairfield), which turned out to be their last stand. At this time what became Stratford included Bridgeport, Huntington, Monroe and Trumbull. Defeated in May of 1659, the Pequonnocks were granted rights to remain in their village of 150 wigwams at Golden Hill (now Bridgeport), and at another village on Coram Hill.

Historical notes

Cupheag. Sometimes Pequannocke. Named Stratford in 1643 after Stratford-on-Avon in England. The colonists built a palisade from the west side of the swamp to Watch-house Hill (now Academy) as protection from the Dutch, and from the warring Narragansetts and Mohegans.

Early industries were shipbuilding and oystering. In time, Stratford became a residential suburb of Bridgeport, with some manufacturing, including helicopters.

Ghost stories and legends

Just south of where Route 1 crosses the Housatonic on the Washington Bridge is the very spot, they say, where in 1649 a Milford man swam across the mighty river. He had been sentenced to a public lashing and chose to risk the racing currents of the Housatonic in an attempt to swim to safety rather than to submit to the court-ordered punishment. His crime? He had kissed his wife on the Sabbath. After his successful escape, his family

David Judson House, Stratford.

joined him in Stratford, where they happily remained. It is unknown whether he kissed her on subsequent Sabbaths.

Notable buildings

David Judson House (c. 1750), 967 Academy Hill (203-378-0630). Built by Captain David Judson on the site of the stone house his grandfather built in 1639. An excellent example of Georgian architecture, the Judson house is furnished with furniture made in Stratford and has on exhibit a collection of Chinese porcelain. The living room fireplace measures 7 x 10 feet and is equipped with two brick ovens. However, what makes the house interesting, and disturbing, are the slave quarters in the basement, a reminder of Connecticut's oft-forgotten past. The Captain Judson House is owned by the Stratford Historical Society.

Historic districts

Stratford Center Historic District, roughly bounded by East Broadway, Ferry Boulevard, the Housatonic River, the Connecticut Turnpike, and Birdseye and Main Streets. Many old houses are preserved in Stratford, particularly on Main Street/Route 1.

Trumbull

Routes 127, 111, Merritt Parkway
Incorporated 1797

Native Americans

Paugusetts. They called Tashua Hill "Tashe," which means "he lifts up."

Historical notes

What became Trumbull was surveyed and allotted around 1670. The area was at first called Old Farm, later Nichols Farm. A group of inhabitants formed the Village of Unity in 1725, and nineteen years later, joined with the Long Hill Parish to form the Society of North Stratford. However, they were still under the jurisdiction of Stratford.

In order to participate in government, North Stratford inhabitants had to make an overnight journey. For busy farmers, this was unacceptable, and they petitioned to form a separate town. In 1797 the Connecticut General Assembly granted town rights. The residents named their new town after the Revolutionary War hero, Governor Jonathan Trumbull.

Tashua Hill, 620 feet above sea level, was the most important observation point along the sound during the Revolutionary War. Men equipped with spyglasses watched for British from this high vantage point. At the first sighting, post riders were dispatched with the intelligence. In 1807 the Weston Meteor fell on Tashua Hill. It weighed 36.5 pounds and is now in the Peabody Museum in New Haven.

Nero Hawley, a freed slave, served in the Revolution. A brickmaker, his kiln was near the Pequonnock River. He is buried in Riverside Cemetery.

Geology

Tungsten and topaz were mined in Trumbull. Some specimens are exhibited in museums. Numerous other minerals were mined, including quarts, pyrite, ilmenite, tourmaline, hornblende and many others. The old Tungsten Mine and Topaz prospect, with the remains of kilns and dumps, is located in the woods off Old Mine Road, which is off Route 111, just past the intersection of Route 25 and Route 111. The area is now a town park, Old Mine Park.

Ghost stories and legends

Hannah Heneman, a resident of Trumbull, was a seeress. The *Connecticut Journal* of August 28, 1777, said of her, "… twenty years before her death, in a dream or vision; a venerable, comely person, whom she afterwards used to call her guardian angel and whom she had seen once before, appeared to her, and asked her age: she told him; upon which he replied, 'you will not live to one hundred years, but almost; you will live to be ninety-nine and then die.' And what is remarkable concerning her exit out of the world, she died the very day on which she was 99 years of age. The great age this person arrived to, together with those circumstances with respect to the time of her death are so very extraordinary, that it was thought proper to communicate them to the Public."

Historic districts

Nichols Farms Historic District, Center Road, 1681–1944 Huntington Turnpike, 5–34 Priscilla Place and 30–172 Shelton Road. This area is rich with interesting and carefully documented houses. The Historical Society is headquartered in a farmhouse (c. 1820) at 1856 Huntington Turnpike (203-377-6620). The Bunny Fountain, also on Huntington Road, was given by Gertrude Peet in memory of her husband, who was a post rider. On Shelton Road is the smallest Indian Reservation in the U. S., one of two Golden Hill Paugusett landholdings in Connecticut (not officially recognized by the federal government). It is a quarter of an acre.

Weston

Routes 53, 57
Incorporated 1787

Native Americans

Paugusetts. As late as the 1880s Paugusetts still camped at Devil's Den.

Historical notes

Originally part of Nor'field parish in Fairfield (1639), Weston became a separate ecclesiastical society in 1757, and was incorporated thirty years later.

When British General William Tryon was on his march to Danbury, word spread that he was going to take all boys prisoners. Already, boys thirteen and older had taken up arms and were away with their fathers, so it was very young boys who were endangered. The women gathered the rest of the children and took them to the ravine at Valley Forge and then into the wild Devil's Den area (now a nature preserve owned by the Nature Conservancy, 33 Pent Road, 203-226-4991). Here they kept the children hidden and safe and brought food up to them. Devil's Den is so named because of a large footprint on a rock. An early hoe factory operated at Valley Forge.

Weston produced charcoal and onions. The tumbling rivers provided water power for forges and foundries. The villages of Lyon's Plain and Valley Forge prospered. But, like so many Connecticut towns, the population declined after 1830, reaching a low of 670 in 1930. Early in the twentieth century, this pretty town was discovered by artists, writers, actors and musicians, and summer colonies began to spring up. After World War II, it became a commuter town.

Geology

Rough country, with rapidly falling rivers, most notably the Saugatuck and the Aspetuck. Just before sunrise on December 14, 1807, a large meteorite entered the atmosphere over Weston. This was the one of the first times such an event was recorded in the U.S. A thirty-pound fragment is now housed in Yale University's meteorite collection.

Historic districts

Aspetuck Historic District (also in Easton), roughly at Redding Road from the junction with Old Redding Road to Welles Hill Road, and Old Redding Road North past Aspetuck Road.

Bradley Edge Tool Company Historic District, roughly at Lyons Plains Road, north and south of the junction with White Birch Road.

Kettle Creek Historic District, roughly at Weston and Old Weston Roads north of Broad Street.

Norfield Historic District, roughly at the junction of Weston and Norfield Roads, northeast to Hedgerow Common.

Westport
Routes 1, 136, 57, 33
Incorporated 1835

Native Americans

Paugussetts. The Pequot Cockenoe de Long lived on what is now called Cockenoe Island, named in his honor. He taught the missionary John Eliot the Algonquin language.

Historical notes

Saugatuck. The first white settlers came to the east banks of the Saugatuck River in 1648. Their settlement was part of the West Parish of Fairfield and came to be known as Greens Farms. A later settlement on the west bank was, for nearly two centuries, part of Norwalk. The river became a busy commercial route. Commercial ships were based in Westport and the area prospered.

It was from Westport that the infamous smuggler and pirate, Thomas Newton, set sail to trade with the hated Dutch. For five years he conducted his business, accumulating vast wealth. A self-appointed vigilante, Dame Goody Johnson, decided to trap Newton, and in 1650 she succeeded in having him jailed for his dubious activities. He was was later released, however, and lived a long life enjoying his ill-acquired fortune, much to the irritation of not only Dame Johnson but much of Westport.

On April 25, 1777, British General William Tryon anchored twenty-six ships at the mouth of the Saugatuck River and disembarked his army of 2,000 well-armed men on Compo Beach (south of Route 136/Compo Road, the spot marked with two old cannons). From here they began their March to Danbury. Seventeen patriots managed to fire a shot at the powerful army before retreating. Another small skirmish took place at the Bennett House (at the corner of the Boston Post Road and Compo Road, where a marker has been placed).

When Tryon returned, after burning Danbury, he was met on Compo Beach by a swarm of gathering Americans. The Americans fired continuously on the British until they retreated to their ships. A Minute Man statue commemorates this event. Two years later, when the British burned Fairfield, the raging fire spread along the Greens Farms road in Westport.

In 1835 Daniel Nash and others successfully petitioned the General Assembly for town status, and parts of Norwalk, Fairfield and Weston were incorporated as Westport. During the forties, an influx of Irish and Italians came to build the railroad. By the beginning of the twentieth century, artists and writers began to settle in Westport, and by 1950, the town had become a residential suburb.

Notable buildings

Wheeler House (c. 1797), 23 Avery Place (203-222-1424). This house began as a traditional saltbox in 1797, when Captain Ebenezer Coley built it for his son. After a succession of owners, Morris Bradley purchased the house, and in the 1860s remodeled it into the popular Victorian Italianate villa style that we see it in today. Bradley added a flat roof and a cupola as well as a verandah. Behind the house is the cobblestone Bradley-Wheeler barn. Seven-sided, it is the only barn in Connecticut with an octagonal roof. It houses the Museum of Westport History at the Bradley-Wheeler Cobblestone Barn. Both buildings are listed on the national and state historic registers. The Society offers a highly informative guidemap.

Historic districts

Compo/Owenoke Historic District, roughly bounded by Gray's Circle, Compo Road South, and Long Island Sound. Scott and Zelda Fitzgerald spent a summer in the area in the 1920s. Until the time of the Civil War, the Wakeman family grew fields of onions. Most interesting are two houses which predate the Revolution, the John Bennett House at 96 South Compo Road (c. 1758), and the Wakeman House at 244 South Compo Road (c. 1758).

Mill Cove Historic District, between Compo Mill Cove and Long Island

Sound. The Sherwood family kept a mill here (John Sherwood's house is on Hillpoint Road across from the entrance to Old Mill Beach). The mill burned before 1900.

National Hall Historic District, Riverside Avenue, and Wilton and Post Roads.

Wilton

Routes 7, 33, 53, 106
Incorporated 1801

Native Americans
Siwanogs

Historical notes
Wilton was considered part of Norwalk in 1651, but the first house wasn't built until 1706. The village was granted parish privileges in 1726.

British General William Tryon marched through Wilton in April of 1777 after the Battle of Ridgefield. He and his men ransacked homes in the village and demanded food and supplies. A few homes were burned. Fortunately, many of the villagers had hidden their prized possessions before the British invaded.

The railroad came to Wilton in 1852, making the town easily accessible to city dwellers. Summer residents quickly flocked to this quiet agrarian community. After World War II, the population again swelled.

When Mark Twain lived in Stormfield in Redding, one of his favorite spots was the gorge of Knob Crook Brook, in Wilton.

Inventions, inventors and firsts
Ben Gilbert was a saver. He hated to throw anything away. By 1818, he had accumulated a huge quantity of horsehair. What to do with it? He invented a loom for weaving horse hair, and while his wife wove, he made hoops. He had invented the first flour sieve. Not content with this accomplishment, he went on to develop horsehair upholstery. But perhaps his greatest contribution was made when he wove twisted wire on his loom, and created wire cloth, from which modern sieves and window screens are made.

Geology
A ridge runs north and south between two valleys. Silver was reputedly mined here by the British before the Revolutionary War.

Notable buildings
Wilton has an active historical society which has preserved and maintains a number of interesting buildings, relatively close together. Lambert Corner, including Danbury and Westport Roads, has a complex containing the David Lambert House (c. 1724), which stands on its original site. The Lambert house was an early tavern and is pictured in Wallace Nutting's *Connecticut Beautiful.* Also in the complex are other landmark buildings saved from demolition, moved and restored. These include a saltbox or lean-to-style dwelling (c. 1829), an 1834 schoolhouse, the first railroad station in Wilton (c. 1852), and a post office (c. 1889).

The Sloan-Raymond-Fitch House, 249 Danbury Road (203-762-7257), is currently the society's headquarters. The house is a classic central chimney structure, built in 1757. Of particular interest is the large collection of Norwalk pottery, both earthenware and stoneware.

The society's newest house is the Betts-Sturges-Blackmar House, built in 1735. From Route 84, take Exit 3. Follow Route 7. The Raymond-Fitch House (Wilton Heritage Museum) is at the intersection of Routes 7 and 33. Staying on Route 7, you will come to the Betts-Sturges Blackmar House on your left. Continue on Route 7 to where Route 33 splits off, and you will come to Lambert Corners.

Historic districts

Cannondale Historic District, roughly bounded by Cannon, Danbury and Seeley Roads.

Georgetown Historic District (also in Redding), roughly bounded by Route 7, Portland Avenue, Route 107 and the Norwalk River.

Wilton Center Historic District, roughly bounded by the junction of Lovers Lane, and Belden Mill and Ridgefield Roads.

Hartford County

The county is 739 square miles, and has 29 towns: Avon, Berlin, Bloomfield, Bristol, Burlington, Canton, East Granby, East Hartford, East Windsor, Enfield, Farmington, Glastonbury, Granby, Hartford, Hartland, Manchester, Marlborough, New Britain, Newington, Plainville, Rocky Hill, Simsbury, South Windsor, Southington, Suffield, West Hartford, Wethersfield, Windsor and Windsor Locks.

Hartford County is graced with the state capitol, the Connecticut River, the Connecticut River Valley, and hills to the east and west. The northern towns bordering Massachusetts are still largely rural, but the most of the county is heavily populated. If you are serious about Connecticut history, a trip to Hartford is a must. Here you can visit the Historical Society, the Connecticut State Library and the Old State House. You will also want to see nearby Old Wethersfield.

Interstate Routes 91 and 84 cross Hartford County, plus the bypass routes, 291 and 384. For a good look at the county, take Route 5 from Enfield, near the Massachusetts border, and follow it down along the river,

through East and South Windsor and East Hartford. If you like, cross the river and continue on down through to Berlin on the Berlin Turnpike.

This is not a picturesque route—you will see strip malls, gas stations, big, boxy, flat-roofed store buildings and such, but interspersed are glimpses of old houses and an occasional open field. When you reach East Windsor Hill (in South Windsor), bear right and leave Route 5 for a stretch, so you can enjoy Main Street, with its fine old homes. Return to Route 5 in East Hartford, where the route itself is also Main Street.

Avon

Routes 10, 44, 202 (parts of 44 and 202 are the same)

Incorporated 1830

Native Americans

Tunxis

Historical notes

Originally part of Northington, the North Parish of Farmington. Avon became a separate and prosperous town after the opening of the Farmington Canal. In 1918 Theodate Pope Riddle, a survivor of the

Lusitania sinking, designed and built Avon Old Farms, a school for boys modeled after an English village. The buildings, constructed of locally quarried brownstone, hand-split slate and oak, were considered an outstanding architectural achievement at the time.

The Farmington (New Haven and Northampton) Canal runs south from the northern boundary with Simsbury, roughly parallel with Route 10.

Geology

River plain, bordered by mountains. An esker (glacial deposit made by a stream under ice), is located a mile from the Farmington town line, across the river and to the south.

Notable buildings

The brownstone buildings which now house the town hall were built by the Climax Fuse Company in 1884. They were purchased by the Ensign Bickford Fuse Company in 1907 and used for the manufacture of safety fuses until 1968.

Derrin House (c. 1747), 249 West Avon Road (860-678-7621). Recently leased from the state by the Avon Historical Society, this eighteenth-century house is in the process of restoration and open to the public.

Historic districts

Pine Grove Historic District, Route 167. Four nineteenth-century farmhouses, one eighteenth-century farmhouse, and a one-room nineteenth-century schoolhouse. The restored Schoolhouse 3 contains exhibits of life along the Farmington Canal (860-678-7621). The eight-grade Pine Grove Schoolhouse, in use from the 1830s to 1948, is also open to the public.

Berlin

Routes 5/15, 71, 71A, 364, 372
Incorporated 1785

Native Americans

Mattabessetts. Wangunks lived on the west banks of the Connecticut from south of Hartford to the Middletown area. Taramaugus, one of the Mattabesssetts, signed the deed selling the land to Sargent Richard Beckley of New Haven sometime before 1660.

Historical notes

Sargent Richard Beckley built a house in what came to be known as the Beckley Quarter of Wethersfield. Captain Andrew Belcher of Boston bought a piece of land from his father-in-law, Jonathan Gilbert, of Hartford. The northern part of Belcher's land, where he built his house, was The Great Swamp, and the southern piece was Meriden.

Twenty or twenty-five years after Beckley established himself, a group of families arrived from Farmington. The Beckley Quarter and the Great Swamp separated from Wethersfield and Middletown respectively and joined to become the Parish of Kensington, later incorporated as the town of Berlin, and named for Berlin, Prussia. Later still, the industrial New

Britain area became a separate town.

George Washington traveled through Berlin more than once. On June 29, 1775, he is believed to have stopped at the Beckley Tavern, in the Beckley Quarter, and planted three trees outside the inn. In his diary entry for November 10, 1789, he wrote, "Breakfasted at Worthington, in the township of Berlin, at the house of one Fuller." Berlin was on the New Haven–Hartford path, which opened in 1687.

Because of the quality of the local red clay, brick-making was an important industry well into the twentieth century.

Inventions, inventors and firsts

The Yankee peddler was born in Berlin. In 1740, the Pattison brothers, Edward and William, made household goods out of tin, the first in America, and sold them door to door in the neighborhood. They were so successful that they were soon traveling far and wide, with not only their own tin goods, but clocks from Eli Terry's Plymouth factory, pins, buttons, combs and whatnot.

They hired other salesmen and expanded their territory as far as 1,500 miles away. They traveled on foot, on horseback and in wagons, and established supply depots in distant cities so they could replenish their stock. At the time, this was the only large-scale industry in the state. They offered household goods, clocks, crockery, tools and hardware. The arrival of a Yankee peddler was cause for excitement. A family would gather around the itinerant merchant to hear the latest gossip and news and to view the tempting array of merchandise.

Historic districts

Worthington Ridge Historic District, roughly Worthington Ridge from Mill Street to Sunset Lane. It was here that the Pattison brothers lived and fashioned their tinwares, and here that George Washington stopped at the Fuller Tavern for breakfast.

Yankee peddlers spread Connecticut-made goods throughout the state and up and down the east coast. Illustration by Gretchen Geromin.

Bloomfield

Routes 178, 187, 189, 218
Incorporated 1835

Native Americans

Poquonocks

Historical notes

First settled in 1660 as part of Windsor. Organized in 1736 as the Parish of Wintonbury from the towns of Windsor, Farmington and Simsbury. Francis Gillette, the father of William, the famous thespian, named the town Bloomfield at its incorporation. Gillette's house was moved and is now at 545 Bloomfield Avenue. Chief Justice Oliver Ellsworth (1745–1807) had his first law office in Bloomfield, in a house built about 1768 at the northeast corner of Wintonbury and Woodland Avenues.

Agriculture, particularly tobacco, dominated Bloomfield life until the town became a densely populated suburb of Hartford. In 1970, the community was designated an All-American City in recognition of citizen participation in school integration.

Notable buildings

Old Farm Schoolhouse (c. 1796 and in use until 1922), Junction of Park Avenue and School Street.

Oliver Filley House (c. 1834), Mountain Road. In the process of restoration. Owned by the Wintonbury Historical Society (860-242-5613).

Bristol

Routes 6, 69, 72, 229
Incorporated 1785, as a city in 1911

Native Americans

Tunxis

Historical notes

In 1663, part of Farmington, "fforty acors of meddow Land" called "Poland" were granted to four men. In 1744, the parish of New Cambridge was organized. After several more grants and divisions, the town was incorporated as Bristol in 1785.

During the Revolution, an active minority of Tories lived in the Chippin Hill area. One of them, Moses Dunbar, joined the British in Long Island and received a captain's commission. In 1777 he was charged by the Patriots with high treason, convicted and hanged, for persuading other young men to follow his lead in enlisting in the King's army.

Bristol is best known for clocks, and was home to many clockmakers. The first clocks had fine, carved wooden works and found a ready market in the southern states. Gideon Roberts, who had a small shop on Fall Mountain in 1740, built his business by traveling great distances on horseback to sell his clocks. Within twenty years he and his sons had built a prosperous business and had as many as 400 clocks in process at once. Clocks soon became one of the most popular of the many Yankee peddler's wares.

A key development in clockmaking took place in 1818 when Joseph Ives substituted brass works, cut from the bottoms of kettles, for the traditional wooden works. This important invention solved the problem of warping in damp weather.

Chauncy Jerome, a cabinetmaker who learned clockmaking from Eli Terry, brought mass production techniques to clockmaking, and began fabricating his clock housings of brass. These developments—mass production, brass parts, Yankee peddlers—made clocks, once expensive luxuries affordable only by the rich, everyday household items available to all. By 1850, there were fifty clock works in Bristol.

Notable buildings

American Clock and Watch Museum (c. 1801), 100 Maple Street, off Route 6, I-84 Exit 31E/38W (860-583-6070). Befitting Bristol's clockmaking past, this museum houses more than 3,000 timepieces. Also on display is an outdoor sundial garden.

Carousel Museum of New England, 95 Riverside Avenue, I-84, Exit 31E/33W (860-585-5411). Antique and miniature carousels, plus a carving shop.

Historic districts

Endee Manor Historic District, roughly along Sherman, Mills and Putnam Streets.

Federal Hill Historic District, roughly bounded by Summer, Maple, Woodland, Goodwin and High Streets.

Main Street Historic District, roughly along Main Street from School Street to Summer Street, and adjacent areas of Prospect Street.

Burlington
Routes 4, 69, 179
Incorporated 1806

Native Americans
Tunxis

Historical notes

Like many Connecticut towns, Burlington has its antecedents in other towns. It was the West Woods section of Farmington. The first house was recorded in 1725. A group of Seventh Day Baptists, feeling persecuted in Rhode Island and seeking sanctuary and religious freedom, made the overland trek to settle in the remote forests of West Woods in 1740. In 1774, the Society of West Britain was organized, which with New Cambridge became Bristol in 1774. In 1806, West Britain became Burlington.

Connecticut's largest copper mine was on the Bristol/Burlington town line, with the greater part of the mine in Burlington. Eight shafts were sunk. From the years 1847 to 1854, $200,000 worth of low-grade copper ore was taken from the mine, but the operation was beset with financial and business difficulties and closed for good in 1895. In addition to copper, traces of silver were found, along with museum-quality chalcocite crystals.

Ghost stories and legends

Sightings of an ephemeral Green Lady have been reported in Burlington, Avon and Simsbury for more than a hundred years. The misty apparition is most closely associated with Burlington, where she emerges from a graveyard. Some say she lived in a house near a swamp in the 1800s and may have been drowned by her husband. This is one of those murky legends with multiple, vague accounts. Folklorist David Philips called her The Green Lady of Burlington in his book, *Legendary Connecticut.*

Historic districts

Hart's Corner Historic District, 274 Monce Road, 102 and 105 Stafford Road.

Canton

Routes 44, 179, 202 (much of 44 and 202 are the same)
Incorporated 1806

Native Americans

Massacoes. Chief Waguaheag lived near Cherry's Brook when the settlers arrived.

Historical notes

Part of Simsbury, settlement began in 1737, along Cherry's Brook, and at Suffrage (present-day Canton Center). Suffrage was so named because, according to all accounts, the earliest settlers suffered an unusual number of hardships and setbacks.

Canton, which may have been named for the city in China, was known for the hard drinking of its inhabitants. A popular cider house was across the way from the church, and a full barrel was kept close by for the indulgence of the thirsty parishioners. Early preachers gained stern reputations for their fiery sermons and constant battles against the cider stills, but their efforts were largely ignored, or so the story goes.

The making of resin, turpentine and pitch were successful early industries of Canton, but it was the axe factory of Samuel and David Collins and their cousin William Wells that brought renown to the town, and gave the manufacturing village of Collinsville its name. Until the cousins set up their axe factory, axes were made by blacksmiths, with the purchaser grinding his own blade, a task which took several hours.

The Collins Axe Factory was the first to make blades of tempered steel, and the first to use Lehigh coal. Huge grindstones, six feet in diameter and a foot thick, were brought to the factory from Nova Scotia. Business was so brisk that the turnpike was diverted to pass close to the factory, and a post office was set up in the new manufacturing village of Collinsville.

Interestingly, Samuel Collins hated the name and wrote in his diary, "The name has always been distasteful to me and my family. If I had been consulted and had consented to have my name used it would not have had any ville attached to it or been Frenchified at all. I would have called it Colinsford, like Torringford and Ashford, which are good Saxon names."

The Collinsville Axe Factory, instituting an enlightened policy for the time period, reduced the workday to ten hours. Happily, production remained steady, despite the shorter work time. Samuel Collins continued the Canton preachers' war on alcohol, and his firm bought up two nearby taverns and a drugstore in an attempt to prevent the sale of distilled products.

Ghost stories and legends

The Canton Tavern, on the Albany Turnpike (Route 44), was a busy stopping place during the Revolution. One dark night, a weary French paymaster stopped for bed and board on his way from Hartford to Saratoga. His saddlebags were laden with gold (or in some stories, silver) to pay French officers. He never made it to Saratoga, and when authorities investigated, they found his last known whereabouts to be the tavern. However, the tavern keeper assured them that the paymaster had left in perfectly good health.

Years later, the tavern burned to the ground, revealing a hidden skeleton, confirming to many that the innkeeper had indeed murdered his guest. Ever since the disappearance of the French paymaster, a ghostly headless horseman has been seen on the turnpike, always riding west towards Saratoga. In the early days, horses spooked at the sight of him. Today, headlights shine right through him as he gallops off.

Notable buildings

The Canton Historical Museum, 11 Front Street (860-693-2793). Exhibits and collections detailing the early history of Canton, especially Collinsville. Located in the former Collins Company Axe Factory building.

Historic districts

Collinsville Historic District, roughly bounded by Dunne Avenue, Collins Road, High Street, Cemetery Road and the Farmington River. This is an essentially intact nineteenth-century village built by David and Samuel Collins for their employees.

East Granby

Routes 20, 187, 189
Incorporated 1858

Native Americans

Massacoes. After John Griffin captured Manahannoose in 1648, and held him for burning Griffin's tar, Manahannoose signed a deed of "all the Lands in Massacoe" in order to secure his release. Tar was used by the colonists and sometimes burnt by them as a beacon. Manahannoose burned tar that John Griffin felt was his, and not Manahannoose's.

Historical notes

The General Assembly confirmed John Griffin's claim to Massacoe, recognizing him as the first to make pitch and tar "in these parts" and in 1663 granted him the lands "between Massacoh and Warranoake." The first house lots along Main Street, assigned in 1688, were not taken, and had to be reallotted five years later. The settlement was included in the town of

Simsbury. Later it became known as the Turkey Hill section of Granby. Finally, in 1858, East Granby became a town in its own right.

Agriculture was important from the settlement days. Dairies and tobacco farms flourished well into the twentieth century, and some continue today.

Geology

A basalt ridge runs through the center of town. Basalt, also called traprock, is an igneous rock, very dense and erosion-resistant.

Notable buildings

Farmington Canal (New Haven and Northampton Canal) runs south through town along the Granby border.

Old Newgate Prison (c. 1773) and Copper Mine (c. 1707), Newgate Road, I-91 Exit 40 (860-653-3563, 860-566-3005). This was America's first chartered copper mine. In 1737 and 1739, a blacksmith made Granby coppers, among the earliest coins made in the country. Today they are very rare and very collectible.

The castle-like Newgate Prison, named after the infamous Newgate Prison of London, was the first state-chartered prison in the nation. Until its inception, prisoners were incarcerated in local gaols. The dungeon cells were fifty feet below ground with simple bunks, covered with straw. It held captured Tories during the Revolution. The idea was to have the prisoners work the mines, but this proved unsatisfactory, as mining gave the pris-

oners access to weapons and a means of escape.

Billed as escape proof, Newgate's very first prisoner escaped almost immediately, as did the next several. At that time, the imposing stone structures had not been built, and the prison keepers relied on the underground caverns for security. After the escapes, the walls and towers were built over the subterranean prison. Conditions were harsh, damp and unhealthy, and Newgate closed in 1827.

Ezekiel Phelps House (c. 1744), 32 Holcomb Street. Original red stain remains on kitchen wainscoting, very rare in a house of this vintage. Also unusual for such an early house, the only summer beam—a heavy horizontal timber that usually supports the floor above—is in the attic floor.

Viets Tavern, 106 Newgate Road. The home of the first prison-keeper.

Historic districts

East Granby Historic District, Church Street and East Streets, Nicholson and Rainbow Roads, North Main, and School and South Main Streets. Collection of well-preserved farmsteads.

East Hartford

Routes 4, 5, and Silver Lane
Incorporated 1783

Native Americans

Podunks. The Podunks had several forts and villages along the eastern shores of the Connecticut River. Their territory included present-day East

Hartford, South Windsor, Manchester and East Windsor. However, they also enjoyed close ties to the Indians on the western side of the river.

The Podunks actually invited the English to settle in their midst. Waghinacut, a Podunk sagamore, walked with two companions, Jack Straw and Sagamore John, along the Connecticut Path to Boston where they met with Governor Winthrop. They described their lands in glowing terms to the unimpressed Governor. Straw spoke English and had been to England. (He had probably been captured and enslaved.) For a time he served Sir Walter Raleigh.

The reason the Podunks wanted the English to come was to ensure a balance of power. The Podunks feared the Dutch, who had settled at the mouth of the Connecticut and who were in alliance with the Pequots, an enemy of the Podunks. Winthrop declined the invitation, but the Podunks' hospitable offer led to the migration of Thomas Hooker and his followers two years later. The Podunks later regretted the arrival of the English. (See also Windsor, South Windsor and Manchester.)

When the preacher John Eliot arrived at the settlements on the western banks of the River in 1657, he invited the Podunks to come and hear his words. They were likely the first Connecticut Indians exposed to his preaching. Eliot, who had mastered the Indian languages, made it his mission to minister to them, and convert them to Christianity. After his sermon, he asked them if they accepted Jesus as their Savior. The sachems and old men scoffed and said no, the English had already taken their lands and now they wanted to make servants of them. Indeed, the General Court ruled a year later that the lands purchased from Tantinimo, a Podunk sachem, were in fact merely leased. In 1661, the court ruled that no individual could buy or rent land from the Indians.

By 1730, the Podunk population was greatly reduced. As late as 1747, the last of them were living on the banks of the Hockanum River in present-day East Hartford. By 1760, they were gone.

Historical notes

When Thomas Hooker and his followers settled on the western shores of the Connecticut River, they also laid claim to the eastern shores, so they could grow crops on the fertile flood plains. A few members of the band settled in present-day East Hartford, then part of Hartford.

Early settlers were industrious. Paper-making began in 1783, and East Hartford was an important paper-making center until late in the nineteenth century. The Pitkin family, among the earliest settlers and active for generations, operated an iron works, a powder mill, and a glass factory over the years.

In October 1782, Rochambeau and the French army encamped at Silver Lane while marching across Connecticut from and to Newport, Rhode Island, on the way to meet with Washington. Rochambeau himself stayed at Squire Elisha Pitkin's large unpainted, gambrel-roofed house, which stood at the corner of Pitkin Street and Roberts Lane.

The French soldiers stayed at various homes and inns and in tents, and their encampment brought revelry, dances and roasts. One French officer wrote of his stay on Silver Lane, "The inhabitants of Connecticut are the best people in the United States without any doubt. They have a lively curiosity and examine our troops and all our actions with evident astonishment. When they visited our camp the girls came without their mothers and entered our tents with the greatest confidence." But great confidence or not, things do happen. One of the local girls "had a child, Jamisie, the result of French gallantry."

Rochambeau's men were paid in silver. Kegs of it, for wages, were stored overnight at the house of James Forbes on Forbes Street. It was this silver—very rare in this country—that gave Silver Lane its name, and it is said that, now and then, a silver coin still turns up.

When President Monroe visited in 1817 he was entertained at the Wells Tavern. He thought that East Hartford's elm-lined Main Street was one of the most beautiful streets in America.

In the twentieth century, the aircraft industry began to dominate East Hartford. By the 1930s the Mutual Aircraft Club, Pratt & Whitney Aircraft Works, the Chance Voight Corporation, the Hamilton Standard Propeller Company, Rentschler Field (owned and operated by United Aircraft Corporation), and the Sikorsky Aircraft Corporation were all located near each other. Pratt & Whitney engines were used by famed airmen Byrd and Lindbergh.

Notable buildings

Center Burial Grounds (c. 1711), 941 Main Street, contains the graves of ninety-five Revolutionary War soldiers. There are examples of both Connecticut River Valley sandstone and Bolton granite in the headstones. Behind the cemetery is Fort Hill, where the Podunks had a stronghold in 1656.

Vintage Radio and Communications Museum of Connecticut, 1173 Main Street, I-84 Exit 56 (860-675-9916). History of radio from the 1920s to the 1970s. Sound effects, video viewing, library.

Selden Brewer House (c.1800), 165 Main Street, moved from original location in town. This was the homestead for the Brewer Tobacco Plantation.

Historic districts

Central Avenue/Center Cemetery Historic District, Center Avenue from Main Street to Elm Street and Center Cemetery.

Downtown Main Street Historic District, roughly bounded by Main Street, Governor Street, Chapman Place and Burnside Avenue.

Garvan-Carroll Historic District,

roughly bounded by South Prospect, Chapel and Main Streets.

East Windsor

Routes 5, 140, 191
Incorporated 1768

Native Americans

Podunks. The Podunk trail went through East Windsor to Agawam. It connected with the Nipmuck trail. (See also East Hartford.)

Historical notes

East Windsor and present-day South Windsor were both part of Windsor until 1768, when they were incorporated as East Windsor. South Windsor split off and incorporated in 1845. Many of the important events of the early town of East Windsor occurred in South Windsor. Settlement did not begin until the end of King Philip's War. Until then, East Windsor and present-day South Windsor and Ellington were used largely as pastures.

Warehouse Point, a village within East Windsor, was named for the warehouse built there in 1636 for the transfer of freight around the Enfield Rapids. Though great sailing ships navigated the Connecticut River as far north as Hartford, the river was too dangerous for the vessels to travel much farther. Instead, their cargoes were unloaded at Hartford onto ten-to eighteen-ton flatboats which were then poled upriver. However, it was impossible to pole boats heavier than twelve tons through the rapids, so they were unloaded at Warehouse Point.

Here the freight was stored until it could be placed on oxcarts and taken to Thompsonville, where it was reloaded onto flat boats and poled to Springfield.

Shade-grown tobacco was introduced in 1901 and became the predominant industry. Acres and acres were cultivated. Broad, level tobacco fields tented in gauzy netting stretched out along both sides of the roads, even the highways. Great drying sheds were built to cure the leaves which were considered superior cigar wrappers. Vestiges of the broadleaf tobacco industry remain to this day.

Geology

The first verified skeletal remains of a dinosaur were found at the bottom of a well by Solomon Ellsworth, Jr., in 1818. In blasting for the well, Mr. Ellsworth unfortunately blew apart some of the skeleton before he realized it was there. He thought it was human. It was a prosauropod dinosaur, Anchisaurus colurus, and is now in the Peabody Museum at Yale.

Notable buildings

Connecticut Fire Museum, 58 North Road, Route 140 (860-623-4732). Exhibits of fire trucks from 1850–1950, and a history of firefighting.

Connecticut Trolley Museum, 58 North Road, Route 140 (860-566-3005). Run by the Electric Railway Association at the same location as the Fire Museum, this museum shows trolley cars and steam and electric locomotives.

Enfield

Routes 5, 190, 191, 192, 220
Incorporated 1683 in Massachusetts,
as part of Connecticut in 1749

Native Americans

Agawams

Historical notes

Purchased from the sachem
Nottatuck for twenty-five pounds,
sterling. This tract included all the
lands from the Asnuntuck to the
Umquaatuck (at the foot of the falls)
and extended eight miles east. It was
part of Springfield Plantation. In
1679, the Pease brothers of Salem win-
tered in a hut which they built where
the present Enfield Street Cemetery
lies. The following spring they brought
their families to live in this new land,
and within three years, more than
thirty families had joined them.

With Woodstock and Suffield,
Enfield seceded from Massachusetts
and was admitted to Connecticut in
1749.

Enfield was home to a vibrant community of Shakers, the celibate followers of Mother Ann Lee. They established their community in Enfield in
1787. The Shaker Village remained
until 1915, when with the population
dwindled, the Shakers sold their land
to the state for a prison farm and
moved to Massachusetts.

It was also in Enfield that the Great
Awakening began, when the fiery and
renowned Reverend Jonathan
Edwards preached his "Sinners in the
hands of an angry God" sermon in
1741, setting off camptown meetings
and revivals throughout Connecticut
and New England.

Inventions, inventors and firsts

It was the Enfield Shakers who first
packaged garden seeds in envelopes
and forever changed the way seeds are
sold. Orin Thompson established the
first carpet mill in the U.S. in the
Thompsonville section of Enfield.

Geology

The Enfield Rapids are the famous
falls in the Connecticut River which
made navigation further north impossible without a bypass.

Historic districts

Bigelow-Hartford Carpet Mills Historic District, roughly bounded by
Lafayette Street, Hartford Avenue,
Alden Avenue, and Pleasant, High,
Spring, South and Prospect Streets.
Orin Thompson's Thompsonville Carpet Manufacturing Company,
founded here, eventually became, after a century of operations and
through multiple mergers, the
Bigelow-Sanford Carpet Company.

Enfield Historic District, 1106–1492
Enfield Street.

Enfield Shakers Historic District, at
Shaker, Taylor and Cybulski Roads.
Many of the Shaker buildings remain
standing. One wishes the state would
restore the village and open it to the
public.

Hazardville Historic District, Route
190 and 192. The Hazard Powder

Shaker Houses, Enfield. When John Barber did this picture, in 1836, the Shakers numbered 200.

Company was founded here in 1835. Ironically, the powder company and village were named for the founder, Colonel Augustus Hazard, rather than the hazardous nature of its business. The imposing two-story brick Hazardville Institute, at the junction of Routes 190 and 192, is undergoing a long and expensive restoration.

Farmington
Routes 4, 6, 10, 177
Incorporated 1645

Native Americans

The Tunxis, who had a fort at Little Meadow, were joined by dispossessed Indians from the river tribes such as those at Windsor and Middletown. As early as 1648, some of the Tunxis attended school, a number of them learned to read and write English, and many had adopted the clothing, names and some of the culture of the settlers. Nevertheless, they vigorously disputed colonial claims to their land.

In 1774, Elijah Wimpsey and Solomon Mossock, both native Ameri-cans, petitioned the General Assembly for a copy of the laws of Connecticut in an effort to defend their rights. Though the courts often agreed with their claims, they were unable to gain satisfaction. Finally, some of the Tunxis thought it best to move to New York where they would join the Mohawks. Eventually, however, most of them moved to Scatacook and on to Stockbridge, where they joined a growing band of displaced Native Americans. By 1804, only a few Tunxis remained in Farmington, and by 1850, they had all gone.

Historical notes

Farmington is called the "mother of towns" because from within her boundaries sprang seven other towns. In 1640, Hartford, Wethersfield, and Windsor sent Captain John Mason to explore Tunxis Sepus (meaning "at the bend of the little the river"), the wilderness inhabited by the Tunxis. He reported that the land was suitable for settlement. A small group of families then trekked westward from Hartford to build houses and create farms, and within a few years their town was incorporated as Farmington.

Almost from the start, there were troubles between the Indians and Europeans. The Colonial Records reported "a most horrid murder ... by some Indians," in the spring of 1657. For defense, seven of the houses along Main Street were fortified with double plank doors. Disputes over the ownership and use of the land continued.

Early citizens were active participants in the Revolution. General George Washington passed through six times and twice recorded dining in Farmington, though he neglected to name the inns that hosted him. Rochambeau encamped south of the village in 1781. The town was a busy thoroughfare for armies and a frequent stopping place.

After the Revolution, Farmington became prosperous. Industries included the manufacture of linen, leather goods, muskets, buttons and clocks. Candlemakers, cabinetmakers and carriage builders plied their trades. There were smiths of tin, silver and gold. Timothy Root produced 2,500 hats in his shop on Hatter's Lane in the years 1802 and 1803. The Farmington East India Company brought wealth and with it the construction of many large homes.

Then, in 1828, the Farmington Canal opened. By 1835, the Canal carried passengers and freight between New Haven and North Hampton and, despite numerous problems, brought increased trade and economic well-being. The Canal was an important, though often troubled, mode of transportation until it was superseded by the railroad. It ceased operation in 1847. (See also Granby and Plainville.)

Two years after the *Amistad* uprising (see New Haven), in March 1841, the Africans involved were sent to Farmington to live while waiting for funds to be raised for their voyage home. They lived with Austin F. Williams, an active abolitionist, who had a special building constructed for them. Later he built his own house on the property, and converted the Africans' quarters into a carriage house. A private residence, the Austin F. Williams house is at 127 Main Street.

Ghost stories and legends

Will Warren thought Sunday services were a bore and a waste of time and he refused to go to church. His Farmington neighbors were horrified at his waywardness and decided to punish him for his sins. They gave him a public flogging. Incensed and humiliated, Will tried to burn the town down in retaliation. The pious churchgoers, upset at the near loss of their homes, and Will's lack of repentance, set out to capture him. They pursued him over hill and dale, but he escaped into the mountains. A few sympathetic Indian women hid him in a boulder cave near the peak of Rattlesnake Mountain. Ever afterward, the cave has been called "Will Warren's Den."

Notable buildings

The Farmington Canal (New Haven and Northampton Canal), runs south from the northern boundary with Avon through town.

The Riverside Cemetery, on Garden Street, is on the site of an old Tunxis burial ground. In 1840, after many native American remains were discovered and disinterred, a red sandstone monument was erected with the inscription, "In memory of the Indian Race: Especially of the Tunxis Tribe, the ancient tenants of these grounds."

Beyond the monument is an open meadow where the Africans from the *Amistad* raised crops during their two-year stay in Farmington. One of them, Foone, is buried in the cemetery. He drowned while swimming in Pitkin Basin in August 1841. The Riverside Cemetery is part of the Freedom Trail.

Hill-Stead Museum (c. 1900), 35 Mountain Road, I-84 Exit 39 (860-677-9064, 860-677-4787). National Historic Landmark. Colonial Revival Style. Designed by noted architect Stanford White for the Cleveland iron mogul Alfred Pope and his daughter, Theodate Pope, who had attended nearby Miss Porter's School. Theodate contributed to the design of the house and went on to become the first woman architect in the U.S. The Popes were indefatigable collectors, and furnished the house with an extraordinary collection of impressionistic paintings, including works by Degas, Cassatt, Manet and Monet. The 150-acre property boasts a sunken garden designed by Beatrice Farrand. Today the Sunken Garden Poetry Festival is held on the grounds in the summer.

Stanley-Whitman House (c.1720), 37 High Street, I-84 Exit 39 (860-677-9222). National Historic Landmark. Built by Captain Judah Woodruff, Farmington's master builder, the house has been a tavern, a shop for journeymen shoemakers, and the town library. It is a sturdy, two-and-a-half story, central-chimney building with an overhang, a wonderful example of eighteenth-century architecture.

The Stanley-Whitman House.

Old Stone Schoolhouse (c. 1790), 93 Coppermine Road (860-677-0059). Restored one-room schoolhouse.

Day-Lewis Museum of Indian Artifacts, 158 Main Street (860-677-2754). Archaeological collection and dig site. Owned by Yale University.

Mendi *Amistad* Sites (860-678-1645). The Farmington Historical Society will, upon request, conduct a tour of *Amistad*-related sites.

Unionville Museum (c. 1917), 87 School Street (860-673-2231). One of the 6,000 free public libraries financed by Andrew Carnegie. Exhibits of the Unionville section of Farmington, where the Union Nut Company, founded in 1864, manufactured nuts and bolts.

Historic districts

Farmington Historic District, roughly bounded by Farmington Avenue, Mountain Road, Colton and Garden Streets, and Meadow Road. This area of town is graced with many historic homes and sites.

Glastonbury

Routes 17, 83, 94, 160 (scenic highway from the Roaring Brook Bridge west to the Connecticut River)

Incorporated 1693

Native Americans

Wangunks. Soweag, or Sequin as the English sometimes called him, was the sachem of Naubuc (Glastonbury). Soweag fell into disagreement with the planters of Wethersfield, and eventually moved to Mattabesett (Middletown). Many artifacts have been found within the bounds of Glastonbury.

Historical notes

Glastonbury was the first town in Connecticut to be split off from another town. Originally part of Wethersfield, this six-mile strip of land along the Connecticut River, extending three miles into the interior, was divided into thirty-four farms and used for grazing. More land was purchased from the Indians, and the bounds were extended.

The first house was built in Noag (South Glastonbury) before 1651, along the River near Tryon Street. In

time more houses were built and more people came from Wethersfield to live in Naubic, spurring the farmers to petition the General Assembly to form a separate town. Their petition was granted and the new town was named Glassenbury, a name which held until 1870, when it was changed to the present-day Glastonbury.

Glastonbury participated in the Revolution. Powder for the war effort was produced in Cotton Hollow until 1777, when the mill exploded. It was quickly rebuilt. Later, a massive fifty-foot dam was constructed, and behind it a smaller dam, providing power for a cotton and woolen mill. A row of workers' houses stood nearby.

Cotton Hollow bustled with activity in the early nineteenth century. By 1904, however, the mills stood empty and unused, and the high dam, which had been weakened by floods, was dynamited and destroyed. The crumbling stone ruins of the two mills and the remains of the abandoned little village can still be seen from Cotton Hollow Road, off Main Street, South Glastonbury.

Like many towns in eastern Connecticut, Glastonbury had its day as a manufacturing center. Cotton, wool and paper were produced. A glass factory (later excavated by Sturbridge Village) made green bottles. Beautiful building stone was quarried, including that used to build the Wadsworth Atheneum in Hartford. And, throughout the eighteenth and nineteenth centuries, ships were built in yards along the Connecticut River. Even heavy anchors were produced locally.

Later, commercial agriculture dominated Glastonbury's economy. J. H. Hale, the "peach king," created orchards on a scale until then inconceivable. In 1900, he produced $100,000 worth of peaches on his Glastonbury farms. Lucrative tobacco fields stretched out along the Connecticut River valley. Arbor Acres rose to international renown for its chickens.

Five remarkable sisters lived in Glastonbury at Kimberly House (now 1625 Main Street). Their mother, Hannah Hickock Smith, was a student of French, Italian and Latin and had a special glass house built so that she could read her foreign books undisturbed yet warmed by the sun. She penned one of the first anti-slavery petitions in the country, persuaded forty other Glastonbury women to sign it, and sent it to Congress, where it was presented by former President John Quincy Adams.

Her daughters, Hancy Zephaniah, Cyrinthia Sacretia, Laurilla Aleroyla, Julia Evelina and Abby Hadassah, were abolitionists like their mother, early feminists, and highly accomplished musicians, translators and artists. In 1873, the two youngest sisters refused to pay their taxes because they did not have the vote. The town confiscated their cows and sold them to pay the tax bill.

Inventions, inventors and firsts

The first shaving-soap manufacturer in America was started by J. B. Williams in 1842.

Ghost stories and legends

The famous (infamous?) Rattlesnake Hunt Club had its home in South Glastonbury. The members made annual expeditions into Meshomasic State Forest where they would capture numerous rattlers, a feat which garnered the club much attention. One member returned to a New York hotel with a bag of seven very lively snakes. They escaped, sending fear into the hearts of the other guests and the staff, but the nonplussed snake catcher single-handedly found and recaptured all the snakes. Did he knowingly let the serpents escape so that he could show off his heroism? One wonders.

Notable buildings

Welles-Shipman Ward House (c. 1755), 972 Main Street, South Glastonbury (860-633-6890). The interior and exterior of this architecturally interesting house have been much studied, sketched and photographed. It has elaborate paneling and molding in the parlors and an enormous kitchen fireplace.

Welles Chapman Tavern (c. 1776), 2400 Main Street (860-633-6890). A popular stagecoach stop and a landmark on the Hartford to New London route.

Museum on the Green (c. 1840), 1944 Main Street (860-633-6890).

Exhibits of local glass, silver, soaps, manuscripts, photographs and Native American culture.

John Hollister House, 14 Tryon Street. The oldest house in Glastonbury. Several Hollisters lived in this area. One built ships near the Ferry.

Historic districts

Curtisville Historic District, roughly Pratt Street from Naubuc Avenue to West of Main Street, also Parker Terrace and Parker Terrace Extension.

Glastonbury Historic District, roughly bounded by Main Street from Hebron Avenue to Talcott Road. Historical stewardship is taken seriously in this district. A walking tour reveals two dozen carefully preserved eighteenth- and nineteenth-century houses and churches.

South Glastonbury Historic District, High, Hopewell, Main and Water Streets. This includes the scenic Route 160. Take Water Street to Tryon Street and the oldest continuously operating ferry (see Rocky Hill).

J. B. Williams Co. Historic District, Hubbard, Williams and Willieb Streets.

Granby

Routes 20, 189, 202, 219
Incorporated 1786

Native Americans

Agawams

Historical notes

Granby was the Salmon Brook section of Simsbury, which was the eigh-teenth-century frontier against the Indians for the mother town of Windsor. Daniel Hayes, an early Granby pioneer, was captured by the Agawams and taken to Canada, from whence he escaped.

Agriculture, including subsistence farming, tobacco plantations, dairies and orchards, was the primary endeavor until the mid-twentieth century. The streams briefly supported some water-powered industry. Shoes, carriages and cards for woolen mills were produced.

Many towns, including Granby, pinned their hopes for prosperity on the construction of the Farmington Canal. The first shovelful of earth was ceremoniously dug at the Massachusetts border by Governor Wolcott on the July 4, 1825. The Governor broke the shovel, perhaps a portent of the bad luck, disasters and difficulties which befell and eventually doomed this ambitious project.

After a long and rancorous border dispute, Connecticut conceded a portion of Granby (and Suffield) to Massachusetts.

Notable buildings

Abijah Rowe House (c. 1732), 208 Salmon Brook Street/Route10/202 (860-653-9713). This is the oldest remaining structure left from the original Salmon Brook Settlement. It has been restored to its early nineteenth-century appearance and serves as headquarters for the Salmon Brook Historical Society. Also on site are the Weed-

Enders House (c. 1790), a small salt-box, and the Cooley School (c. 1870), the only remaining one-room school-house in Granby. Of particular interest are the extensive exhibits in the Colton-Hayes Tobacco Barn, including a rare Connecticut spinning wheel and recreations of a village store and meeting house.

Historic districts

Granby Center Historic District, 3–8 East Granby Road, 2 Park Road, 207–265 Salmon Brook Street South.

West Granby Historic District, Broad Hill, Hartland, West Granby and Simsbury Roads and Day Street South.

Hartford

Routes 44, 187

Incorporated 1635, city chartered in 1784

Native Americans

Siacog (also Suckiaug, or Sequin), related to the Hockanum and Podunks east of the river. Their sachem was Sequassen. The Siacog had a settlement in the South Meadow, until they were attacked by Uncas. They returned in 1650 and lived east of the Great Swamp in part of present-day Goodwin Park. There was a village at Soldiers Field (now Riverside Park).

At the present intersection of Grand and Broad Streets was Pesiponck, their sweating place. Here, they had made a little cave in the hillside which they would fill with heated rocks. When Pesiponck, the sweating place, was nice and warm from the hot rocks, the Siacogs would crowd together inside the cave for an hour or so. Afterwards, they would emerge refreshed.

Suckiaug, as Hartford was known, means "place of the dark earth." The name refers to the rich meadowlands. As their numbers and lands diminished, the Siacog likely joined the Tunxis to the west.

Historical notes

In 1614 the Dutchman, Adrian Block, sailed from Manhattan up the Connecticut River as far as the Enfield falls. He traded with the Indians along the way. Soon after, several English expeditions came down to the Connecticut River Valley from Plymouth to trade with the Indians and to ascertain the quality of the land.

In the early summer of 1633, the Dutch sent a party to Suckiaug and erected a fort and trading post on land they purchased from the Pequots. They called the post Fort Good Hope. Next, two English parties came down from Plymouth, one settling in present-day Wethersfield, the other in Windsor. Two years later, John Steel led a party of sixty from New Town (Cambridge) to settle in Hartford, followed by Thomas Hooker and his congregation the following spring.

The first home lots were laid out along the Siacog Paths, the Park River, and the Connecticut River (following the path which became Front Street, which vanished with urban renewal and the construction of Constitution

Plaza). In those earliest days, the houses were primitive, likely with thatched roofs, and rough log walls. A community bell was rung every morning an hour before dawn, a sort of colonial version of the alarm clock. Chimneys were inspected monthly, a vital measure of fire protection.

During the Revolution, George Washington passed through Hartford several times, and held meetings in the city. After the War, Hartford became an important shipping center, with wharves and warehouses along the riverfront. By the War of 1812, shipping was no longer a viable industry due to the embargo, but other businesses had begun to prosper and take its place in the economy.

Beginning with fire insurance, Hartford saw the insurance business develop within its borders, and the city quickly became the insurance capital of the world. Samuel Colt, who invented his rapid-fire gun by carving a wooden model while at sea, capitalized on the public's desire for firearms, and built a huge factory, surrounded by homes for workers, and a dam to contain the river in time of floods. Fuller Brush, Columbia bicycles, and Royal and Underwood typewriters grew to become key industries.

The literary arts flourished in Hartford. The Hartford Wits, a group of irreverent poets, was popular immediately following the Revolution. In 1764, the bookseller/stationer Thomas

Underwood typewriter from an early magazine story extolling the virtues of the machine.

Green commenced publication of the Connecticut Courant. The paper, consisting of four pages, was published on Mondays, and contained primarily foreign and national news. Green served as editor, publisher and printer.

In 1768, Green moved to New Haven and left the paper in the hands of his partner, Ebenezer Watson. For a time, Israel Putnam was a correspondent for the paper. The Courant published Noah Webster's *Blue Backed Speller*. When Watson died, his widow Elizabeth took over, becoming the first woman editor in the country. Under her guidance, the newspaper also published a few more books. Today, The Hartford Courant is the oldest newspaper in the nation.

Mark Twain and Harriet Beecher Stowe lived in Nook Farm, in the Forest Street section of Hartford, and produced much of their best work there.

Inventions, inventors and firsts

Hartford has been the birthplace of many firsts and inventions, too numerous to list entirely in this book. Here are a few:

First FM station in the world was WDRC, which began broadcasting in Hartford in 1939.

Amelia Simmons wrote the first American cookbook, *American Cookery, or the art of dressing viands, fish, poultry and vegetables.* It was published in Hartford in 1796.

The American School for the Deaf, the oldest institution of its kind, was founded by the Rev. Thomas H. Gallaudet on Asylum Hill in 1817. It later moved to North Main Street in West Hartford.

The first periodical for young people, *The Children's Magazine,* was established in Hartford in 1789.

Ghost stories and legends

One of the most enduring legends of Connecticut is that of the Charter Oak. In 1687 Sir Edmund Andros set out for Hartford to execute a royal order to annex Connecticut as part of the New England Colony. Since the Connecticut Colony had previously been granted a liberal charter by King Charles II, making the colony independent, Andros was not exactly a welcome guest. Nevertheless, he arrived in Hartford, stayed at Zachary Sanford's tavern (on the site of the present-day Traveler's Insurance Company), and then met with the Assembly. He demanded that the Assembly surrender the Charter from King Charles II.

The Charter Oak had long served as a council tree for the local Indians. It was destroyed by a gale in 1856 and the wood was made into chairs and other souvenirs.

"The tradition is," Benjamin Trumbull wrote in his 1818 History of Connecticut, "the charter was brought and laid on the table, where the assembly were sitting. By this time, great numbers of people were assembled ... the lights were instantly extinguished, and one Captain Wadsworth, of Hartford, ... carried off the charter, and secreted it a large hollow tree, fronting the house of the Hon. Samuel Wylys ... The candles were officiously relighted; but the patent was gone, and no discovery of it, or of the person who had conveyed it away."

The tree, a mighty white oak, was said to have been used as a council tree by the Siawogs. It fell during a late summer storm in 1856 and its wood was used for chairs, gavels, a table and other articles, many now in museums.

Notable buildings and locales

Although there is much of historical interest to see in Hartford, the old houses have vanished, and driving through the city, or speeding along one of the Interstates, one can only imagine how Hartford looked in years past. North of the train station stood a brick kiln (1637); Thomas Hooker's house was on the site of the modern Aetna Insurance Company; a great covered bridge, 974 feet long, spanned the Connecticut River from 1818–1895, when it was destroyed by fire; and before the arrival of the Europeans, paths crisscrossed Suckiaug, one along modern Main Street.

Bushnell Memorial Hall (c. 1930), 166 Capitol Avenue, I-91 or I-84 Capitol Area Exit (860-246-6807). Designed by Harvey Corbett for members of the Bushnell family, the interior and exterior appearance of this imposing brick-and-granite auditorium was controversial at the time of its erection. Numerous operatic and classical performances have been conducted within the Bushnell's walls. The Bushnell was the site of the earliest rock concerts to appear in Hartford.

Bushnell Park & Carousel, at Jewell Street, I-91 or I-84 Capitol Area Exit (860-246-7739, 860-249-2201). The carousel (c. 1914), made by Stein & Goldstein, boasts forty-eight hand-carved horses and a Wurlitzer organ (c. 1925).

Bushnell Park (c. 1853) and Central Park (c. 1853), were the first planned public parks in the U.S. The noted landscape designer and Hartford native, Frederick Law Olmsted, advised his friend, the Reverend Horace Bushnell, on the development of the park. The land was purchased for the park in 1854. The citizens of Hartford voted 1,005 to 682 in favor of the purchase. Today the millstream, or Park River, is buried underground.

The success of Bushnell park inspired the Park Movement of the nineteenth century. Hartford led the way with the creation of an extensive park system, which encompassed Colt Park, Elizabeth Park, Goodwin Park, Keney Park, Pope Park and Riverside Park.

Buckley Bridge (c. 1904). Though Hartford had nine stone arch bridges,

Imlay's Mill in what is now Bushnell Park.

none spanned the Connecticut River until Senator Morgan Buckley spearheaded the effort to build one. He wanted the bridge to be constructed along classic lines, and sought the advice of well-known experts.

Beginning in 1900, Chief Engineer Graves amassed over a hundred photographs of bridges from all over the world so that the best design could be determined. A Boston architect named Wheelwright was engaged. Finally, and with much fanfare, the Buckley Bridge was built. It has nine arches, with spans from 68 to 119 feet, and is still beautiful, almost a century after completion.

Butler-McCook Homestead (c. 1782), 396 Main Street, I-91 Exit 29A (860-522-1806). A rare, remaining eighteenth-century house in Hartford. Two and a half stories, center hall, end chimney.

Congregation Beth Israel, the first synagogue in Hartford. Organized in 1847, built in 1876, and expanded in 1898, the building is now the home of the Charter Oak Cultural Center.

Charter Oak Cultural Center (c. 1876), 21 Charter Oak Avenue (860-249-1207). Hartford's first synagogue, now an arts center and gallery. The architecture is being carefully preserved.

Connecticut Historical Society. 1 Elizabeth Street, I-84 Exit 46 (860-236-5621). Research library and exhibits on Connecticut history. If Connecticut history intrigues you, and you want to know more, this is the place to visit. The Society has also published books on Connecticut history.

Elizabeth Park Rose Gardens (c. 1904), Prospect Avenue, I-84 Exit 44. The first municipal rose garden in the country. For a time neglected, the Rose Gardens have been rejuvenated. Even if you are not a rosarian or gardener, a trip to Elizabeth Park in June will be memorable.

Hartford Ancient Burying Ground, corner of Gold and Main Streets (behind the church), I-84 Asylum Avenue exit (860-249-1207). Thomas Hooker and other early settlers are buried here. Interesting stones (no rubbings please!).

Nook Farm was the center of Hartford's literary flowering, and was home to Mark Twain, Harriet Beecher Stowe, Charles Dudley Warner and William Gillette.

The Harriet Beecher Stowe House, Farmington Avenue at Forest Street, I-84 Exit 46 (860-525-9317) and the Mark Twain House, 351 Farmington Avenue, at Woodland Street, I-84 Exit 46 (860-493-6411), are worth a literary pilgrimage. Both have been carefully restored and furnished. Beecher's house is an example of "scientific household management" developed by her sister Catherine. Twain's residence is a splendidly ornate brick house with a marvelous conservatory.

Old State House (c. 1796), 800 Main Street, I-91 Exit 31 or I-84 Exit 52 (860-522-6766). This is the oldest state house in the nation. It is on the square where the first meeting house in Hartford was built. Here the famous Amistad and Prudence Crandall trials were conducted and here the first constitution was written. Meticulously restored.

The First State House. Moved from its original site in 1796. Later a tenement. Destroyed in 1910.

Wadsworth Atheneum (c. 1842), 600 Main Street, I-91 Exit 29A, I-84E Exit 48B, I-84W Exit 54 (860-247-9111, 860-278-2670). The oldest continuously operating art museum in the country. Houses 50,000 works spanning 5,000 years. Of particular interest to students of Connecticut history is Wallace Nutting's collection of furniture.

Historic districts

Hartford has many officially designated historic districts in various states of restoration.

Ann Street Historic District, Allyn, Ann, Asylum, Church, Hicks and Pearl Streets.

Buckingham Square Historic District, Main and Buckingham Streets, Linden Place, Capitol Avenue, 248–250 Hudson Street.

Capen-Clark Historic District, Capen, Clark, Elmer, Barbour, Martin and Main Streets.

Clay Hill Historic District, roughly bounded by Main, Mather, Garden and Walnut Streets, plus 8 Florence Street.

Colt Industrial District, Huyshope, Van Block, Curcumbe, and Van Dyke Avenues, Colt Park.

Congress Street Historic District, Congress Street, 54–56–58 Maple Avenue.

Department Store Historic District, 884–956 Main Street and 36 Talcott Street.

Elm Street Historic District, 71–166 Capitol Avenue, 55–97 Elm Street, and 20–30 Trinity Street.

Frog Hollow Historic District, Capitol Avenue between Oak Street and Park Terrace, Hillside Avenue, Hamilton and Summit Streets.

Goodwin Block Historic District, 219–275 Asylum Street, 5–17 Hayes Street 210–228 Pearl Street.

Hartford Golf Club Historic District (also in West Hartford), Simsbury Road, Bloomfield and Albany Avenues, Norwood Road, Mohawk and Mohegan Drives.

Jefferson-Seymour District, roughly bounded by Jefferson, Seymour, Wadsworth and Buckingham Streets.

Lewis Street District, 1–33, 24–36 Lewis Street, 8–28 Trumbull Street and 60 Gold Street.

Little Hollywood Historic District, Farmington Avenue, Owen Frederick and Dennison Streets.

Main Street Historic District No. 2, West Main Street, North Central Row, East Prospect Street and North Atheneum Square.

Parkside Historic District, 176–230 Wethersfield Avenue.

Pratt Street Historic District, 31–101 and 32–110 Pratt Street, 196–260 Trumbull Street.

Prospect Avenue Historic District (also in West Hartford), roughly bounded by Albany Avenue, North Branch of Park River, Elizabeth, and Fern Streets, Prospect and Asylum Avenues and Sycamore Road.

Sigourney Square Historic District, Sargeant, Ashley and May Streets, 216–232 Garden Street.

South Green Historic District, Wethersfield Avenue, Alden, Dean, Main, Morris, Stonington and Wyllys Streets.

Upper Albany Historic District, roughly bounded by Holcomb and Vine Streets, Homestead Avenue, and Woodland and Ridgefield Streets.

West End North Historic District (also in West Hartford, roughly bounded by Farmington Avenue,

Lorraine, Elizabeth, and Highland Streets.

West End South Historic District (also in West Hartford), roughly bounded by Farmington Avenue, Whitney and South Whitney Streets, West Boulevard and Prospect Avenue.

Hartland
Routes 20, 181
Incorporated 1761

Native Americans
Agawams

Historical notes
Hart(ford)land was in the "North East Part" of the Western Lands. Though named in 1733, it was twenty years before the first settler came to live, and that was John Kendell of Granby, who wanted to escape his debts. He remained only a year. Thomas Giddings from Lyme arrived in 1754 and became the first permanent resident.

Despite the rough terrain, more settlers arrived and Hartland became a farming town as well as home to a sawmill, a gristmill, and blacksmith, tannery, calico and print shops. On Barkhamsted Road, on Center Hill, Anson Tiffany operated his doll factory. The Red Lion Inn was an important stopping place near the Massachusetts border for travelers carrying freight on their way to Hartford and Farmington.

In 1811, Titus Hayes led the "First Exodus" to Ohio. The "Year With No Summer," 1816, when there was frost even in July and August, saw another exodus, and the population continued to decline virtually every year until well into the twentieth century.

In the late 1930s, Hartland Hollow, an area of abandoned farms in the valley of the East Branch of the Farmington River, was flooded to create the Barkhamsted Reservoir for metropolitan Hartford. Much of Hartland is now owned by the state, including the Tunxis State Forest and the People's Forest. Though part of Hartford County, Hartland is in Litchfield Hills and is very rural in nature.

Notable buildings

Gaylord House (c. 1845), Route 20, West Hartland (860-379-9722). Built by the noted architect Elias Gilman, this six-room, two-story house has been restored to its original splendor. Exhibits of furniture and tools.

Manchester

Routes 6/44, 83
Incorporated 1823

Native Americans

Podunks. The Podunks, whose large forts or villages were near the mouth of the Hockanum in East Hartford and the Podunk River in South Windsor, had several smaller villages in Manchester. The primary Manchester village was on present day Olcutt Street about where Verplanck School is located. Other villages were on present-day West Center Street, Hillstown Road and Bush Hill.

The Indian paths, deep furrows through the woods, were adopted by the Europeans. The Great Path, which led from Boston to the Connecticut River, lay under Spencer Street, West Center Street, East Center Street and part of East Middle Turnpike. There was also a path from the village at the mouth of the Hockanum in East Hartford to Snipsic Lake, upon which Tolland Turnpike was built. Other probable paths were on Hillstown road, Hackmatack and Keeney Streets and Love Lane. The wood of the Osage Orange trees, which grew near Tolland Turnpike in Buckland, was prized for bows.

Historical notes

Manchester was part of East Hartford, known at first as the Five Mile Tract and later as Orford Parrish. George Washington stopped at Woodbridge Tavern (Manchester Green), and his diary notation suggests relief that he had left the rugged hill country to the northeast. The Woodbridge Tavern sported a famous lion with a twisted-tail sign. Nearby was the equally well known Pitkin Tavern.

With level, sandy lands, Manchester was an early center of industry and commerce. Paper, blankets repeating rifles (invented by Christopher Spence), glass and powder were produced. The Cheney Brothers, an artistic and innovative bunch, founded the great silk mills that gave Manchester its nickname "Silk City."

Over the years, various attempts were

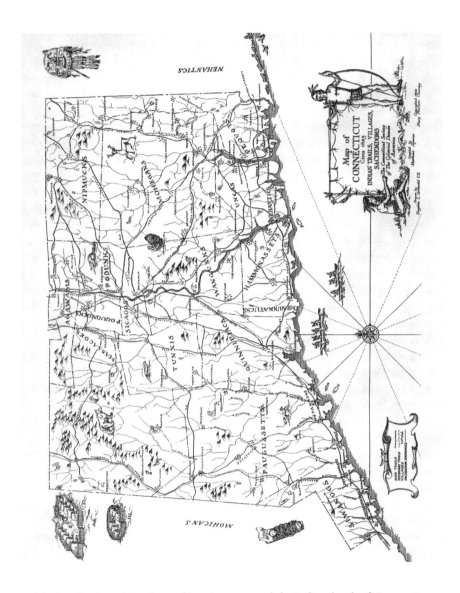

Mathias Speiss, a Manchester historian, mapped the Indian lands of Connecticut. His work is still considered valid.

made to mine copper in the mountains above Highland Park, but the venture was never very productive. The Podunks frequented springs in this area, perhaps for the minerals.

Manchester was served by turnpikes and later trolleys, railroads and highways. It continues as a commercial center for surrounding towns.

Geology

Three skeletons of Early Jurassic prosauropod dinosaurs were discovered in the Wolcott sandstone quarry, a mile north of the Buckland railroad station. The skeletons are at the Peabody Museum in New Haven. The first skeleton, Ammosaurus major, was found in 1884. Anchisaurus polyselus and a juvenile Ammosaurus major were discovered in 1892. The Anchisaurus polyselus was discovered in a stone which had already been cut into a block. The block contained only half of the skeleton but it was suspected that the other half was in a block used in building the Hop Brook Bridge in South Manchester. When the bridge was destroyed 85 years later, scientists from the Peabody Museum were on hand. They indeed found the missing half of the right femur and reunited it with the rest of the skeleton in the museum. Next time you drive past the signs for Buckland Mall while speeding along Route 84, you might want to imagine, for a moment, the thirteen-foot dinosaurs who once roamed this area.

Notable buildings

Cheney Homestead (c. 1780), 106 Hartford Road, I-84 Exit 60, I-384 Exit 3 (860-643-5588). The ancestral home of the legendary Cheneys, this white clapboard house can be seen from Route 384 W.

Little Theatre of Manchester (c. 1867), Cheney Hall, 177 Hartford Road, I-384 Exit 3 (860-645-6743). Built by the Cheney family, the hall was the site of dramatic performances, dances, concerts and lectures. Horace Greeley spoke at the dedication ceremonies. Susan B. Anthony campaigned for women's rights here.

Apel's Opera House (c. 1880). Boxing matches, burlesque shows, opera, and amateur dramatic performances entertained the citizens of north Manchester towards the close of the nineteenth century. Today, one would never guess this brick building's rich cultural past. It stands beside the railroad tracks at the corner of Oakland Street and Apel Place.

Pitkin glass factory, junction of Parker and Academy Street. This beautiful stone ruin, which has been fenced in to prevent trespassers and vandalism, seems more like the remains of an English castle than a glass factory.

The Pitkins of East Hartford and Orford Parrish supplied quantities of powder during the Revolution. In repayment for their work, they were granted a twenty-five year monopoly on glassmaking in 1783. Because local sand was not of a suitable quality, sand was brought by barge up the Connecticut River from New Jersey, and then transported overland by oxen to the glass works. After the silica was melted in a furnace, it was blown into beautiful green and brown bottles.

Beset by financial difficulties, and competition from cheaper bottles imported into the state, the Pitkin glass factory suspended operations once the monopoly ran out. Other glass factories opened in Manchester and elsewhere.

Historic districts

Cheney Brothers Historic District, bounded by Hartford Road, Laurel, Spruce and Campfield Streets. Mill buildings, mansions, the original homestead. A drive or walk through this area is a glance at Manchester's heyday. The eight Cheney brothers were the first Americans to master the difficult art of silk weaving. They built their first mill in South Manchester in 1838, and for the next 80 years, they and their descendants grew their business to national dominance.

They lived in mansions amongst their workers for whom they built homes, a fire department, library, theater, and other amenities. Inevitably, this part of town became known as Cheneyville. Except for the Homestead (see notable buildings above), the houses cannot be visited, but the grounds and architecture are still worth a look.

Brick arched tunnels ran from the houses to the Cheneys' church, enabling the women in the family to visit one another and attend services without facing inclement weather or muddying their skirts. Heat generated by the mills was piped into the mansions, an early form of both recycling and central heat.

Main Street Historic District, roughly Main Street from Center Street to Florida Street. Manchester has an unusually wide, hillside Main Street with a park near the summit.

Marlborough

Routes 66
Incorporated 1803

Native Americans

Podunks, Wangunks

Historical notes

Marlborough was split from from Colchester, Hebron and Glastonbury. An early tavern, Saddler's Ordinary (called an "ordinary" because it was authorized by a town ordinance), built about 1653, was close to Lake Terramuggus on the Path to Monhege, between the Thames and Connecticut Rivers.

The Marlborough Tavern, owned by one or both of the Buell brothers, William and Timothy, opened possibly as early as 1740. By 1765 the tavern was run by Timothy's son Elizah, and by 1800 the busy New London and Hartford Turnpike was bringing a steady stream of stage coaches. George Washington passed by the Tavern on his way from Hartford to Lebanon in 1781. Tradition has it that he stopped for a glass of toddy in the tap room.

Over the years, Presidents Monroe, Madison, and Jackson, and Governors John Dempsey and Ella Grasso were entertained in the Marlborough Tavern.

Industries included two cotton mills near Lake Terramuggus, which produced blue slave cloth for the South, a foundry, the repair and manufacture of muskets, grain mills and sawmills. Manufacturing peaked in 1840, and the last mill closed in 1904 when it burned.

Inventions, inventors and firsts

In 1882, Mary Hall was the first woman admitted to the bar in Connecticut. Two years later, she was made one of the first female notaries of the public. Hall specialized in probate law, wrote historical pieces about her hometown, and founded the Goodwill Club of Hartford to "amuse, instruct and befriend … boys." Mary Hall owned Grasmere (Marlborough Tavern), from 1893 until her death in 1928.

Notable buildings

Colonel Elisha Buell House (c. 1740), which is also the Marlborough Tavern, junction of South Main Street and Route 66. The tavern has undergone many alterations but is still in business. Joseph Giggey of the Marlborough Historical Society has done extensive research on its history.

New Britain

Routes 71
Incorporated1850, as a city in 1870; the town and city were consolidated in 1905

Native Americans
Wangunks, Tunxis

Historical notes

The daughter of Berlin, and the granddaughter of Farmington, New Britain was first settled in 1686. More settlers followed and formed the Great Swamp Settlement further south of the original settlement. The fine pastureland attracted colonists.

In 1800, New Britain turned toward manufacturing, when James North and Joseph Shipman began making sleigh bells in a barn. Yankee peddlers not only sold these bells far and wide, they dressed their own horses in them. Peddlers tinkled and jingled wherever they went, creating demand for the bells. In the process, they also created the quintessential Currier & Ives image that we have of early America. North and Shipman dissolved their partnership, but each continued in business, and many of their helpers set up in business for themselves too.

Soon, the peddlers were demanding more than bells for their customers, and hardware, a natural outgrowth of the sleigh-bell industry, became a mainstay of New Britain businesses. After the panic of 1837, many of these small companies consolidated in or-

New Britain was a small but growing industrial town when this picture was made.

der to survive, and from these consolidated firms grew huge factories which produced hardware, rules, carpenters' tools, levels, locks, washing machines, household utensils, and various other items. New Britain was nicknamed "Hardware City" around the world. Who would guess today that it all began with the manufacture of sleigh bells?

The blacksmith Elihu Burritt, born in 1810, brought renown to New Britain when he advocated for international peace and worked to promote interest in The League of Universal Brotherhood. As a fifteen-year-old blacksmith's apprentice, Burritt taught himself Greek and Latin. By the time he was thirty, he had a good working knowledge of fifty languages. Called the "learned blacksmith," he wrote books and pamphlets and traveled to Europe with his message. He served as an official of the Peace Congress from 1848 to 1851.

New Britain's factories began to attract immigrants about the middle of the nineteenth century. Irish, followed by Germans, then by Slavs at the beginning of the twentieth century came to the city to find work and begin new lives. By the 1930s, New Britain's populace was so international in makeup that people said you needed a passport to visit. Later, people from South and Central America arrived, to add yet other cultures to New Britain's mix.

Inventions, inventors and firsts

Central Connecticut State University began as Teacher's College of Connecticut in 1850. It was the first normal school in the state and one of the first in the country.

Notable buildings

New Britain Industrial Museum, 185 Main Street, Route 9 Exit 35 (860-229-0257). After urban renewal and the development of highways, little of old New Britain remains. Still, for those interested in industrial history, a trip to this museum is worthwhile. Included are changing exhibits of such noted manufacturers of "Hardware City" as the Stanley Works, Fafnir Bearing, American Hardware, and Landers, Frary and Crace.

New Britain Museum of American Art, 56 Lexington Street, I-84 Exit 35 (860-229-02570). This is the oldest museum in the U.S. devoted exclusively to American art. The collection includes works by Cassatt, Wyeth and O'Keefe, and a large number of works by American impressionists.

Art League Barn (c. 1870), 30 Cedar Street (860-229-1484). Victorian Civil-War-era barn, now an art school and gallery.

Ezra Belden Homestead (c. 1746), 530 East Street. The the oldest extant house in New Britain, inhabited by the eighth generation of the original owners' family.

Historic districts

City Hall/Monument District, 13–35 West Main Street, Central Park.

Walnut Hill District, an irregular pattern roughly bounded by Winthrup, Arch and Lake Streets, and Walnut Hill Park. Frederick Law Olmstead designed ninety-acre Walnut Hill Park.

Newington
Routes 5/15, 173, 174, 175
Incorporated 1871

Native Americans
Mattabesett

Historical notes
Purchased from Soweag, a Mattabesett sachem, as part of the Wethersfield tract. By 1636 the area was used by Wethersfield residents as a resource for pipe staves and building materials,

and as pastureland. It was called Pipesstave Swamp and Cow Plains. Pipe staves were sent to Wethersfield and transshipped to the West Indies, where they were made into pipes or huge casks. In 1671, Land-Mile-in-Breadth, as it was then known, was divided amongst 71 Wethersfield citizens. Six years later, settlement began with the erection of a sawmill and the residence of John Slead of Farmington in the Saw Mill House.

Captain Martin Kellogg served the colony as an interpreter and agent for the Indians. When he was a boy, he lived with his family in Deerfield, where he was captured by Indians in 1704. While in captivity in Canada, he learned the native tongue. Because of this facility, some Stockbridge Indians were sent to him, and he acted as their teacher. Kellogg's Newington house is no longer standing.

In 1721, the General Assembly gave Newington its name, and in 1754 it determined its boundaries. The town participated in the Revolution.

By the twentieth century, Newington was known for its medical establishments: the Cedarcrest Sanatorium on Cedar Mountain, which treated tuberculosis patients, the Newington Home for Crippled Children (now Newington Children's Hospital), and the VA hospital.

Notable buildings
Enoch Kelsey House (c. 1799), 1702 Main Street, Route 287 and Routes 5/15, Route 287 exit (860-666-7118).

Enoch Kelsey House, Newington.

Enoch Kelsey was a farmer and a tin-smith. The house contains unusual painted wall decorations done free-hand (not with stencils). The house was moved from its original location on Kelsey Street in 1979.

Kellogg-Eddy House (c. 1808), 679 Willard Avenue, Routes 5/15, Route 175 exit (860-666-7118). Ornate detailing and fancy woodwork.

The Metropolitan Museum in New York obtained the paneling from the Charles Churchill mansion (c. 1763) for the American wing. The house had fallen into ruin and the fire department had obtained permission to destroy it, which it did in 1930.

Historic districts

Newington Junction, North Historic District, 55–108 Willard Avenue, South Historic District, 268–303 West Willard Avenue, and West Historic District, 269–303 West Willard Avenue. These three related districts feature interesting architecture, including the Kellogg-Eddy House.

Plainville
Routes 10, 177, 372
Incorporated 1869

Native Americans
Tunxis

Historical notes
The Great Plains of Farmington became Plainville after the Long Level section of the Farmington Canal was built. Thirty-six feet wide, four feet deep and with a ten-foot-wide tow path, the Canal was dug entirely by hand. It opened in 1828 and brought with it a lively spell of prosperity. Nearly every house in town was turned into a tavern. Warehouses and factories were built. And residents optimistically dreamed of the day when Plainville would rival the city of Hartford.

But prosperity was brief. The canal suffered from washouts, floods, droughts, breaks, collapse and financial instability, and lasted only twenty years. The taverns closed and reverted to private homes, or in many cases, disappeared, but little Plainville, though never a rival to the capitol city, remained a manufacturing town.

Notable buildings
Plainville Historic Center (c. 1890), former Town Hall, 29 Pierce Street, I-84 Exit 34 (860-747-6577). Exhibits on the canal, Native Americans and life in the 1820s.

Asahel Hooker House (c. 1774), 135 Redstone Hill. This is the oldest remaining house in Plainville. There is a massive boulder in the cellar, which the builders were unable to move. The house was the workshop of a tinsmith as well as a residence.

Stockinette Knitting Mill (c. 1877), 58 West Main Street. This was the shipping room for the Plainville Manufacturing Company, which produced union suits.

Historic markers and districts

Underground Railroad Stop, 109 East Main Street, the home site of abolitionist John Norton. Red sandstone stagecoach milestones, corner of Betsy Road and East Street and south of the east corner of New Britain and Farmington Avenues.

New Haven District Campground. Off Route 177.

Farmington Canal (New Haven and Northampton Canal) runs roughly south through town along the Boston and Main Railway. Markers indicate the course of the canal through Plainville. A quarter mile of the canal has been restored along Route 177, Norton Park (860-747-6577).

Rocky Hill

Routes 3, 99, 160
Incorporated 1842

Native Americans

Wangunks

Historical notes

Part of Wethersfield, named for the trap rock ridge that rises in the north-east. In 1722, the village was known as the Stepney Parrish of Wethersfield.

Rocky Hill's fortunes were closely tied to the river. The Rocky Hill/Glastonbury ferry commenced operations in 1655, and has continued without interruption to the present. (A trip on this ferry, though today it also carries automobiles, is a nice way to experience a bit of Connecticut history. From Rocky Hill, take Route 160, Ferry Lane. From South Glastonbury, take Main Street to Tryon Street.) Because the course of the Connecticut River changed, Rocky Hill became Wethersfield's primary port. It was a hub of shipbuilding and trade, and grew famous for its eateries. The streets were dotted with the imposing houses of ship captains.

Once, shad were so plentiful in the river they were caught by the barrelful and considered fit only for the most indigent to eat. Today, many consider the fish a delicacy, especially the roe. When the shad are running, usually in June, Rocky Hill is filled with activity.

Inventions, inventors and firsts

The pewtersmith Thomas Danforth, who built his house in 1783 at the corner of Main and Ferry, is credited with creating the first chain stores. He kept his own shop well stocked and provided pewter ware for the Yankee peddlers who traversed the countryside. Not content with this success, he set his sons up with stores, and, by 1818, the family had outlets in Philadelphia, Atlanta and Savannah.

Geology

Dinosaur State Park, 400 West Street, I-91 Exit 23 (860-529-8423). Dinosaur tracks have been found in the Connecticut River Valley since 1802, but none so numerous as those discovered by highway workmen in 1966. Twelve feet below the surface, the men found a layer of rock with hundreds of 185-million-year-old footprints, from ten to sixteen inches long. Work was halted so that scientists could examine the find. Two thousand footprints from the Jurassic era were eventually discovered. This important site has been preserved as a state park. The most abundant tracks are those of the theropod, Eubrontes. You can make a cast if you bring your own plaster.

Simsbury

Routes 10, 167, 185, 187, 202, 309
Incorporated 1670

Native Americans

Massacoes

Historical notes

Fire has played an unusual role in Simsbury. The earliest industry, established in 1642, was the manufacture of tar, turpentine and pitch. The Massacoes, the local Indians, burned the enterprise down five years after its inception, and were sternly ordered to deed their lands to the colonists in reparation.

During King Philip's War, in the spring of 1676, the town was set on fire and forty houses plus outbuildings were destroyed, more damage than any other town in Connecticut suffered. Fortunately, the inhabitants had already fled to Hartford and Windsor. Tradition has it that King Philip directed the burning and watched the conflagration from a cave (now King Philip's Cave) on Talcott Mountain (off Route 185).

Later, in 1825, the first carpet factory was established in what came to be known as Tarriffville, on Route 187 (because tariffs were levied by Congress on imported carpets), and a village grew up around the factory.

The Thompsonville Manufacturing Company took over the carpet factory in 1840 and employed nearly 200 men. But in 1867, fire struck again, destroying the mill, much of the village, and all but four of the workers' houses. Later, various firms, including briefly the Hartford Silk Company, occupied the mill.

Massacoh was part of Windsor and became Simsbury in 1670. Parts of Simsbury became or were added to East Granby, Granby, Canton and Bloomfield.

Inventions, inventors and firsts

The first copper coin minted in the colonies was made by John Higley in 1737. The coins were stamped, "I am good Copper," and "Value me as You Will." Copper had been mined in Simsbury since 1705. In 1744, Higley manufactured the first half-ton of steel produced in the U.S. His furnace was on Hopmeadow Street.

The Ensign-Bickford Company, established in Granby in 1836, but moved to Simsbury in 1839, produced the first safety fuses for blasting.

Ghost stories and legends

Women who lived alone, who grew herbs, or who were self-suffcient aroused suspicion in colonial minds, and Debby Griffen was no exception. Folks attributed all sorts of powers and strange doings to her. Still, when the meeting house was found in disarray, and a valuable cup missing, no one suspected her. The pious men of the town set up a watch around the meeting house the very next night and hoped to catch the thief. Who should come along but Debby Griffen! Before anyone could accost her, she slipped through the keyhole of the meeting house door. Minutes later, she emerged with a silver plate. The men chased her, and as she reached Three Cornered Pond, one of the men shot her so that you could see straight through her. Griffen fell and disappeared into the pond. Some say that on certain nights, even now, you can see the silver plate glistening in the watery depths. A reproduction of the meeting house, complete with the keyhole, can be seen at Massacoh Plantation (see below).

Notable buildings

Captain Elisha Phelps House (c. 1771), 800 Hopmeadow Street, in the Simsbury Center Historic District. For many years, the ballroom in this house was the largest room in town, except for the church. Balls, parties and meetings were held here. For a time it was the Canal Hotel, reflecting the optimism and hopes the town had for the Farmington Canal. In 1792 the local lodge of the Free and Accepted Masons was organized and held its first meetings in the house, much to the worry and consternation of quite a few Simsbury townfolk.

Robert and Julia Darling House (c. 1927), 720 Hopmeadow Road (Cannon Medical Building). Terra cotta hip roof, six chimneys, casement windows, and a porte cochere make this former residence unique.

Heublein Tower, Talcott Mountain State Park (860-566-2305). The first lookout tower for public use was built by Daniel Wadsworth on Talcott Mountain in 1810. Part of Wadsworth's estate, Monte Video, the tower inspired John Greenleaf Whittier's poem of the same name. Destroyed in 1840 by strong winds, three more lookout towers were built on this high ridge, one in 1848, which burned in 1864, a second in 1867, lost in 1889, and a third, the Heublein tower, which was built in 1914 and stands today. The tower was originally part of the Heublein family estate, where the successful hotelier and restaurateur Gilbert Heublein entertained friends. Heublein is credited with inventing the pre-mixed bottled cocktail.

Historic districts

East Weatogue Historic District, roughly, properties on East Weatogue Street, from just north of Riverside Drive to Hartford Road, and Folly Farm.

Simsbury Center Historic District, roughly, Hopmeadow Street from West Street to Massaco Street. The District includes the Massacoh Plantation. 800 Hopmeadow Street (Route 10) 860-658-2500. Victorian carriage house (c.1880), peddler's cart, one-room schoolhouse (c. 1740), 1795 Hendrick Cottage and Herb Garden, and other exhibits.

Tariffville Historic District, roughly bounded by Winthrop Street, Main Street, Mountain Road, Laurel Hill Road and Elm Street. This is where the tax-free carpets were made.

Terry's Plain Historic District, roughly bounded by Pharos, Quarry and Terry's Plains Roads, and the Farmington River.

South Windsor

Routes 5, 30, 74, 194
Incorporated 1845

Native Americans

Podunks. The meadows along the Connecticut River, particularly between the Podunk and Scantic Rivers, were camping grounds for the Podunks. Near the East Hartford/ South Windsor town line was a large Podunk fort, the largest known. For years, farmers tilling the fertile meadows along the river have turned up native artifacts.

Historical notes

South Windsor was included in the lands purchased by settlers from Dorchester in 1636. Originally a section of Windsor, present-day South

Windsor separated as part of East Windsor in 1768, and then separated from East Windsor in 1845.

The John Bissell Ferry, in East Windsor Hill, was the first ferry across the Connecticut River. It was in operation from 1641 to 1917.

Inventions, inventors and firsts

Mrs. Prout made the first American cigars. South Windsor native John Fitch, itinerant clock-maker and peddler, invented the first steamboat. Built in 1785 with steam-powered side paddle wheels, Fitch's boat traveled an astonishing eighty miles per day. It successfully completed its maiden voyage down the Delaware River in 1787. Fitch was granted a patent in 1791. Nevertheless, he was unable to elicit interest in his invention either in this country or abroad, and was in fact ridiculed. Dejected, he committed suicide. A monument was erected in his honor on King Street.

Eli Terry, the inventor of the inexpensive Yankee Clock, was also South Windsor born. The Reverend Timothy Edwards was the first pastor and the father of Jonathan Edwards. President Grant's ancestral home was in the

A version of Fitch's steamboat with a screw propeller.

East Windsor Hill section of South Windsor.

Like the other towns in this region, shade tobacco for cigar wrappers was an important crop. Netted fields and long sheds dotted the relatively flat and stoneless countryside.

Geology

Sand, Sandstone. In the old Wapping area is one of the largest active sand dunes in the state.

Notable buildings

Wood Memorial Library, 783 Main Street, I-91 to Bissell Bridge to Route 5, to Main Street (860-289-4178). Interesting collection of Native American artifacts, particularly Podunk artifacts unearthed in the meadows by local farmers.

Historic districts

East Windsor Hill District, roughly bounded by Scantic River, John Fitch Boulevard, Sullivan Avenue and the Connecticut River. This tiny section of South Windsor is rich with architectural gems and history.

Windsor Farms Historic District, Main Street, roughly bounded by Strong Road, US 5, 1-291 and the Connecticut River.

Southington

Routes 10, 120, 229, 364
Incorporated 1779

Native Americans

Tunxis

Historical notes

At first Samuel Woodroof used the area that became Southington as a hunting and fishing ground. In 1698, however, he and his wife Rachel and their six children moved to the valley and built themselves a house. Over the next dozen years more families arrived, some coming from New Haven and Wallingford.

Early industries included the manufacture of tinware, buttons, Britannia tumblers, combs, grindstones and cement. The completion of the Farmington Canal encouraged more industry. Fortunately for Southington, the failure of the canal was soon followed by the arrival of the railroad, built along the towpath of the canal, and the city was able to continue as a center of manufacturing.

The route of the Farmington (New Haven and Northampton) Canal and the Boston and Maine Railway runs roughly south through town.

Inventions, inventors and firsts

The first bolt-threading machinery was invented in the Marion section of town by Martin Barnes and Micah Rugg, two blacksmiths. With their invention, production increased from 60 bolts a day to 500 bolts a day.

Geology

The Great Unconformity. Exposed layers of rock from 400 million and 200 million years ago. To see this rare geologic formation, take the dirt road off Mount Vernon Road, just north of Roaring Brook Drive. The Unconformity is a fifteen-minute hike in, on a moderately difficult trail, along Roaring Brook.

Notable buildings

Southington boasts many notable historic houses and historic industrial complexes. The town has created two historic trails highlighting these buildings. One house of particular note is the Dr. Henry Skelton House (c. 1748–1760), 889 South Main Street, in the Plantsville section of town. Wedgewood potteries in England produced blue and mulberry plates with images of the original house. Skelton was an Englishman who bought large tracts of land in Plantsville and built this house before moving first to Woodbury, and later, Watertown. He was a surgeon during the Revolutionary War.

Jonathan Root House (c. 1720), corner of North Main and Mill Streets. Now used as office space, this house was a tavern during the Revolutionary War.

H.D. Smith Hardware Building (c. 1882), 24 West Street. Brick with gingerbread trim.

South End School House (c. 1863), South End Road, near Country Club Circle (860-621-4811). The first schoolhouse was built on this site in 1793. The present one-room schoolhouse has been carefully restored.

Historic districts

Marion Historic District (also in Cheshire), along Marion Avenue and the Meriden-Waterbury Turnpike. Homes and buildings from the eighteenth, nineteenth and early twentieth centuries.

Meriden Avenue/Oakland Road Historic District, roughly Oakland Road, between Meriden and Berlin Avenues, and Meriden Avenue between Oakland Road and Delhunty Road.

Plantsville Historic District, roughly bounded by Prospect and Summer Streets, Quinnipiac River, Grove Street, South Main Street, West Main Street and West Street. Homes and buildings from the nineteenth and early twentieth centuries.

Southington Center Historic District, roughly North Main Street, north from Vermont Avenue, and Berlin Street from Main Street to Academy Lane. Homes and buildings from the eighteenth, nineteenth and early twentieth centuries.

Suffield

Routes 75, 159, 168, 187, 190
Incorporated 1749

Native Americans

Agawams

Historical notes

Originated as a township of Massachusetts in 1670. Spelled Southfield, the town, along with Enfield and Woodstock, was discovered to lie actually within the boundaries of the Connecticut Charter. However, due to a surveying error, the towns were governed by the Massachusetts Colony.

Connecticut taxes were lower and the government freer, so the citizens of the three towns agitated for repatriation to the Nutmeg State. As a compromise, Massachusetts was given the small piece of land between Granby and Suffield, which appears as an indentation on the boundary line between the two states.

Early records show that some of Suffield's settlers were captured during the attack on Deerfield, and never returned. The purchase of a slave is documented in the 1671 account book of Colonel Pynchon.

Tobacco first became an important crop in 1753. For decades, vast acres were devoted to growing shade tobacco under great, white nets. The leaves were picked and dried in long sheds, and were considered the finest available domestic wrappings for cigars.

Inventions, inventors and firsts

In 1810, Simeon Viets opened the first cigar factory in the U.S. Located on the corner of Rately Road, the factory assured "quality control." Viets hired a Cuban to teach local women how to roll the cigars, and sent peddlers all over the countryside to sell them.

Dr. Sylvestor Graham, who was born in West Suffield, created the graham cracker in 1840. He promoted his crackers as a healthy antidote to the gluttony of the day.

Notable buildings

In October 1920, about one hundred of the oldest houses were marked with the dates they were constructed and the names of the builders. The earliest were the central-chimney houses, built before 1760, followed by the central-hall/end-chimney houses, constructed after 1760. Houses built in the last decade of the eighteenth century tended to have Palladian windows, and those built from 1795 to 1830 usually had semicircular attic windows. Driving through Suffield, it is fun to note these changing architectural fashions.

Hatheway House (c. 1761–1794), 55 South Main Street, Route 75, I-91 Exit 40 (860-668-0055, 860-247-8996). Formal gardens surrounding an eighteenth-century mansion.

Historic districts

Hastings Hill Historic District, 987–1308 Hill Street, 1242 Spruce Street, and 1085–1162 Russell Avenue.

Suffield Historic District, vicinity of North and South Main Streets, Suffield and South Streets, and Russell and Mapleton Avenues.

West Hartford

Routes 44, 185, 189, 218
Incorporated 1854

Native Americans

Siacog

Historical notes

The West Division of Hartford. In 1679 Stephen Hosmer built a sawmill on Trout Brook, west of present-day North Main Street, and became the first settler. His house was likely near or on the site of 183 North Main Street. Within a few years, he was joined by others, and in 1711 the West Division became a parish. In 1780, a group of Quakers purchased an acre for a meeting house on South Quaker Lane. Tradition holds that when John Greenleaf Whittier came to Hartford to edit *The New England Review* in 1830, he served as an elder in the Quaker church.

Industries included blacksmith shops, tanneries, boot and shoe shops. Brickyards and the Goodwin potteries took advantage of the fine clay in the south end of West Division. In 1828 Samuel Talcott built a woolen mill on Quaker Lane, also in the south end, which was fast becoming the manufacturing center of town. A creamery followed when the mill closed.

Notable buildings

West Hartford has many surviving eighteenth-century houses, particularly in its designated historic districts.

Noah Webster House/Museum of West Hartford History, 227 South Main Street, I-84 Exit 41 (860-521-5362). Birthplace and childhood home of Noah Webster. Exhibits include Webster's *American Dictionary* and the *Blue Back Speller*. The speller, published by the *Connecticut Courant*, sold over a million copies and standardized American spelling, a feat the British had not yet accomplished. Also on exhibit is an interesting collection of Connecticut redware and period furniture.

Sarah Whitman-Hooker Homestead (c. 1739), 1236 New Britain Avenue, I-84 Exit 41 (860-523-5887). Sarah Whitman was born in the Whitman House at 208 North Main Street. She married Thomas Hart Hooker, who died in Boston during the Revolutionary War.

After Hooker's death, and after the fall of Ticonderoga, three British officers were held for a year in Sarah's house. She kept a slave named Bristol about whom we know little except that he planted an elm tree in the front lawn. Later the house was the Sheaf of Wheat Tavern.

Historic districts

Prospect Avenue Historic District (also in Hartford), roughly bounded by Albany Avenue, the North Branch of the Park River, Elizabeth and Fern Streets, Prospect and Asylum Avenues and Sycamore Road.

West End North Historic District (also in Hartford), roughly bounded by Farmington Avenue, Lorraine, Elizabeth and Highland Streets.

West End South Historic District (also in Hartford), roughly bounded by Farmington Avenue, Whitney and South Whitney Streets, West Boulevard and Prospect Avenue.

Wethersfield

Routes 3, 5/15, 99, 175, 287
Incorporated 1636

Native Americans

Siacog. Sowheag, the father of Sequassen, was the chief sachem of the Siacog. Wethersfield was called Pyquag.

Historical notes

The town of Wethersfield claims to be the oldest town in the state, and indeed the Connecticut Code of 1650 proclaims, "the most ancient Towne … for the River is determined by the Courte to bee Weathersfield." In 1634, ten "adventurers" led by John Oldham came overland from Massachusetts to found a settlement. The men spent a harsh and difficult winter trying to survive and to prepare for the arrival of their families. They were likely assisted by the Indians. The following year, their families joined them. At first the settlement was called Watertown, but in 1636 the court named it Wythersfield. The first house lots were on Broad Street, with Oldham's on the east side of the north end. But calamity struck. DeForest, whose *History of the Indians of Connecticut,* published in 1852 and still considered authoritative, explained:

"A disaster now fell upon the little village of Wethersfield, up the Connecticut River, which the inhabitants of that place seem to have provoked by their own violence and rapacity. About the beginning of their settle-ment, a large tract of land was sold them by Sequin or Sowheag, on condition that he might reside near them and under their protection. The bargain was agreed to, and Sowheag built his wigwam near the houses of the settlers; but in a little while, the latter, for some reason now unknown, quarreled with him and drove him out of the neighborhood. Finding himself thus unworthily treated, and not being strong enough to revenge his own wrongs, he turned to the Pequots, who were probably his ancient enemies, and engaged them to make an attack upon the ungrateful settlement.

"Some time in April 1637, a horse-man who was riding near Wethersfield, discovered a large body of Indian warriors cautiously approaching the place. Without a moment's delay, he turned his horse's head and galloped back to the village to give the alarm. Some women whom he met and informed of their danger, instead of flying, began to ask incredulously, what Pequots he talked about, and how the Pequots should come there; but the horseman, thinking his time too precious to be wasted in disputing the matter, left them and galloped on.

"The sudden approach of the savage warriors dispelled the women's doubts, and they attempted to escape; but three of them were taken. Two were girls, who allowed themselves to be carried away without resistance. The other struggled against her captors so stoutly, biting and kicking them, that one of the Indians became exasperated and dashed out her brains. The Pequots pushed on, surprised many of the people at work in the fields, killed two other women and six men, destroyed twenty cows, and inflicted considerable injury upon the other property of the settlers."

This incident led to a precipitous meeting of the General Court in Hartford—and to the Pequot War. The two girls were ransomed by the Dutch and returned to Wethersfield.

The village grew. Ship building and trade became key industries. In fact the first ship built in Connecticut was the "Shipp Tryall," constructed at Wethersfield Cove in 1648. Merchants exported beaver and deer skins, brick, onions, pipe staves, salt beef, fish, corn, pork, horses and garden seeds to the West Indies and imported sugar, wool, rum and cotton.

Fortunes were made. Great, gambrel-roofed warehouses were built. (One from 1660 still stands at Cove Park and is maintained by the Historical Society.) Then, in 1692 a flood swept away six of the warehouses and changed the course of the River. Rocky Hill, further south, benefited greatly from this change.

Washington was in Wethersfield several times and even had a pair of shoes made by a local cobbler. His longest stay in Connecticut was at the Webb House (see below), from May 19th to May 24th 1781, when he held a conference in the south parlor.

Wethersfield became known for its onion fields and later its seeds. Washington Irving wrote of the "plantations of onions" in his Knickerbocker History of New York, claiming that the the Dutch could not look in the Wethersfield direction without their eyes watering.

Ghost stories and legends

There were witches in Old Wethersfield, or so people believed during the witchcraft hysteria that swept New England in the mid-seventeenth century. Three of the accused were condemned and hanged: Mary Johnson, who confessed her "familiarity with the devil," and John Carrington and his wife, who were convicted of witchcraft.

Notable buildings

Buttolph-Williams House (c. 1710), 249 Broad Street, I-91 Exit 26 (860-529-0460, 860-529-0612). A hewn overhang, small casement windows, and narrow clapboards make this house distinctive. Elizabeth Speare used it as the setting for her Newbury Award-winning novel, *The Witch of Blackbird Pond.*

Webb-Dean-Stevens Houses, 203–215 Main Street, I-91 Exit 26 (860-529-0612). Three historic houses, close together. The Joseph Webb House (c. 1751) was built by a prosperous merchant. This is where Washington stayed for five days and conducted strategic war meetings. The Silas Deane House (c. 1766), was the home of the prominent lawyer. The Isaac Stevens House (c.1788), was the home of a leather worker and saddler.

The Wethersfield Historical Society, I-91 Exit 26 (860-529-7656), owns and maintains several historic buildings. The Old Academy (c. 1804), 150 Main Street, houses the Society's archives and library. The Wethersfield Historical Society Museum, Keeney Memorial Cultural Center (c. 1893), 200 Main Street, has exhibits and houses the visitors center. The Hurlburt-Dunham House (c. 1804), 212 Main Street, was built for John Hurlburt, who was captain of the first Connecticut ship to sail around the world, 1796–1798. And the Cove Warehouse (c. 1690), Main Street at Cove Park, is the only warehouse remaining from the golden years of Wethersfield seafaring endeavors.

Historic districts

Old Wethersfield Historic District, bounded by Hartford, the Railroad Tracks, I-91 and Rocky Hill. In addition to the houses which are open to the public, Old Wethersfield has many carefully preserved private buildings of interest. A drive through Old Wethersfield will give you a taste of Connecticut's colonial history, but a walk is even better.

At 26–28 Marsh Road is the site of Mary Rowlandson's house. The current house on the site was built for a sea captain, and in 1868 became the Shepardson Tavern.

Rowlandson's account of her eleven weeks as a captive of the Narragansetts during King Philip's war was first published in 1682. It became a bestseller and remains the best-known captivity narrative to this day.

At 22 Garden Street is the largest cucumber magnolia tree in the state (c. 1860).

The Ancient Burying Ground (c. 1637) contains the graves of the Pequot victims, the freed slave Quash Gomer (1799), and the Beadle family, who were murdered by William Beadle in 1782. The burial ground is on the site of an older Indian burial ground.

Windsor

Routes 75, 140, 159, 178, 305
Incorporated 1635

Native Americans

Matianuck was the Indian name for the Windsor locale. The English claims covered such a vast area that lands of several tribes were encompassed. There were Matianucks, west of the Connecticut River between Hartford and the Farmington River, Poquonocks, in the north, the Tunxis on the Tunxis River (Farmington River), Podunks on the east shores of the Connecticut River, and to the north of the Podunks, the Scantics. The tribes were related and friendly to one another.

Historical notes

Windsor calls itself "The first permanent English settlement in Connecticut." After being invited to settle by the Podunks, who sought to strengthen their position against the Pequots and their allies, the Dutch, a company of English came down from

Plymouth by sea, sailed up the Connecticut River, and disembarked in 1633. They established a trading post near where the Farmington River meets the Connecticut River. Two years later, a larger group of settlers followed an ancient Indian path down from Dorchester and settled in Windsor. These two groups did not always have amicable relations. The first winter the settlers experienced knee-deep snow and the Connecticut River froze.

After the Pequot attack on Wethersfield, the colonists organized an army of ninety men. Captain John Mason of Windsor lead them in a counterattack, and burned the Pequot encampment in Mystic (known as the Pequot, or Mystic, Massacre; see Groton and Wethersfield).

At the outbreak of the Pequot War in 1637, the settlers built the Palisado, which ran about a quarter of a mile along the present Palisado Road. The land inside the Palisado was divided into small parcels, with the interior free for a meeting house. After the war, they returned to their far-flung houses outside the fort. The Palisado was used again during King Philip's War when fleeing colonists from Simsbury sought refuge within it.

Tobacco became an important crop. The first tobacco was grown from Virginia seed in 1640. In 1900, the first shade-grown tobacco was planted.

The rich local clays were used for brick-making sometime before 1670.

Today, there are many extant eighteenth- and nineteenth-century brick houses in Windsor.

The original town of Windsor included Windsor itself, towns on both sides of the River, present-day Windsor Locks, Granby, East Granby, Simsbury, the southern part of Suffield, part of Bloomfield, East Windsor, South Windsor, Ellington and the northern part of Vernon.

The first river crossings were by canoe, but in 1648–1649 John Bissell was appointed ferryman by the courts. His ferry was located 300 yards or so north of the Ellsworth Homestead, and crossed the river to East Windsor Hill.

Arsenic and Old Lace, the Broadway play, is based on the murders committed at Mrs. Amy Archer-Gilligan's convalescent home on Prospect Street. Archer-Gillegan was alleged to have killed at least sixty-four people with arsenic and was convicted of five of these murders in 1916. Her conviction was later overturned, but she spent the rest of her life institutionalized.

Ghost stories and legends

Pirate's gold in Windsor? The legend persists that Captain Kidd sailed the *San Antonio* up the Connecticut and hid his gold on Clark's Island. The rumored treasure has never been found, but mysterious sightings of his ship have been reported on foggy nights.

Notable buildings

Luddy/Taylor Connecticut Valley Tobacco Museum, Northwest Park, I-91 Exit 38 (860-285-1888). Artifacts and history of the Connecticut River Valley tobacco farms.

Joseph Rainey House, 299 Palisado Avenue. Rainey was the first African-American elected to the U.S. House of Representatives. He served the state of South Carolina for five terms from 1870–1879 and petitioned for civil-rights legislation. He bought this property in 1874 and used it as a summer residence for the rest of his life.

Palisado Cemetery, Palisado Avenue. Nancy Toney, a former slave of the Chaffee/Loomis family, is buried here. She was considered too old for emancipation when slavery was outlawed in Connecticut in 1848. She remained with the family until her death in 1857. She is thought to be the last of a group of elderly slaves in similar circumstances. Her grave is at the rear of the cemetery.

Oliver Ellsworth Homestead, 778 Palisado Avenue, I-91 Exit 39 (860-688-8717). John Adams called Oliver Ellsworth "the firmest pillar of Washington's administration." The house was built by his father, and was called Elmwood after the thirteen elms that Oliver planted. A cedar, which was believed to be the oldest tree in Connecticut, grew in the north part of the yard. It had been used by the Indians as a council tree. It was destroyed in 1877.

Windsor Historical Society, 96 Palisado Avenue/Route 159 (860-688-3813). The Society owns two houses, which are open to the public. The Walter Fyler House (c. 1640) is one of the oldest remaining frame houses in Connecticut, though there have been additions to it. The Dr. Hezekiah Chaffee House (c. 1765), is a three-story brick Georgian colonial.

Historic district

Though Windsor does not have an official historic district, it does have many well-preserved and carefully re-stored buildings, particularly on Palisado Avenue and Windsor Avenue.

Windsor Locks
Routes 75, 140
Incorporated 1854

Native Americans

Podunks

Historical notes

Windsor Locks was the Pine Meadow section of ancient Windsor. After the Pequot War, it was purchased from Tehano or Nehano. In 1663, Henry Denslow became the first settler.

George Washington passed through on Old Country Road in the autumn of 1789 and wrote of the area, "Between Windsor and Suffield you pass through level, barren and uncultivated plain for miles." Driving through Windsor Locks today, one can only think that times have changed, and wonder what George would say should he see the area now.

When construction began on the Northampton to New Haven (Farmington) Canal, in an attempt to overcome the barrier to transportation on the Connecticut River imposed by the Enfield Rapids, Hartford businessmen became alarmed. To compete, they commissioned the Enfield Canal, which would bypass the rapids and eliminate six miles of portage. This canal was completed in 1829, and ran along the Connecticut River from Windsor Locks North to Thompsonville. When the railroad usurped the river as a carrier of moving freight, the canal was used for water power, and Windsor Locks industry thrived.

Eighteenth-century industries included grist, saw, fulling and paper mills. A gin distillery was established in 1811. Later, yarn and knitting factories sprung up. Tobacco-sorting establishments played an important role.

In 1941, Bradley Field opened as a military airbase. Commercial airlines began flying out of Bradley six years later.

Inventions, inventors and firsts

Ella Grasso of Windsor Locks was the first woman to be elected Governor of Connecticut.

Ghost stories and legends

In 1777, the Hessian soldier Hendrick Rodemore, living in a cabin on the Denslow Farm as a hired hand, set up the first Christmas tree in the U.S. Though it would be more than sixty years before Queen Victoria popularized the custom in the English-speaking world, it was here in Windsor Locks that a decorated and illuminated fir tree was first seen.

Notable buildings

New England Air Museum, Bradley International Airport, Route 75, I-91 Exit 40 (860-623-3305). Exhibits of 75 aircraft from 1909 to the present.

Noden-Reed Park Museum, 58 West Street, I-91 Exit 41 or 42 (860-627-9212). An 1840 farmhouse and rare brick barn on the site of Samuel Denslow's 1762 farm.

Litchfield County

The county is 921 square miles, and has 26 towns: Barkhamsted, Bethlehem, Bridgewater, Canaan, Colebrook, Cornwall, Goshen, Harwinton, Kent, Litchfield, Morris, New Hartford, New Milford, Norfolk, North Canaan, Plymouth, Roxbury, Salisbury, Sharon, Thomaston, Torrington, Warren, Washington, Watertown, Winchester and Woodbury.

Litchfield County is what we imagine when we think of New England. It is postcard-pretty, with wooded hills, winding roads, farms and lovely town greens. Dominated by the state's highest terrain, the county also boasts the states highest peak, at 2,380 feet, Mount Frissel in Salisbury. Litchfield County contains many art galleries, gardens and carefully restored homes as well as historic sites.

Although the county is not served by an Interstate road, the multi-lane Route 8 runs south from Winsted through Torrington, Harwinton, Thomaston, Watertown and on down to Route 95 in Fairfield County.

Litchfield is rich with scenic roads. There's Route 41, which you can pick up at the Massachusetts line in Joyceville in Salisbury, and wind south through Sharon to the New York State line. The stretch of Route 44 which goes through Salisbury is also worth exploring. If you take Route 4 from Sharon and go east to Route 7, which skirts the Housatonic River, and drive south through Kent, you will be able to enjoy two of the state's three remaining covered bridges.

An advertisement luring vacationers to the Litchfield hills.

Barkhamsted

Routes 20, 44, 179, 181, 219
Incorporated 1779

Native Americans

Mohicans. See legends below.

Historical notes

Barkhamsted, named for the English town, was Windsor's share of the Western Lands in Litchfield County. One hundred and eight people from Windsor were granted parcels in 1732. Because the country was so rugged, settlement was slow. Early industries included the manufacture of axes, boots, bricks, chairs, lumber, saddles, scythes, shovels, spades, wooden ware and chemicals for the textile industry. Even before settlement, timber was harvested from the forests, particularly pine. By 1845, a million board feet per year were shipped to the West Indies.

In the late 1800s the population declined precipitously, as citizens moved west to better farmlands or to cities, and as local industry declined.

In the 1840s, Masons held secret meetings near the town green. This was during the time of much national foment against the Masonic Temple. During the clandestine meetings, it was the duty of one young man, "Little Johnny" Merrill, to keep watch. At the first sign of anti-Masonic mobs, he was to beat his drum in alarm.

In the 1930s parts of the town were flooded by the Metropolitan District Commission to create reservoirs.

Inventions, inventors and firsts

A Cheshire cabinetmaker, Lambert Hitchcock, built his chair factory in the Riverton section of town in 1818. At first, using production-line techniques, he made chair parts for South Carolina factories, but it was not long before he was making complete chairs in his own distinctive style, with wooden, cane, or rush seats, and gold stencils of flowers and fruit baskets. Hitchcock was likely the first to manufacture the Boston Rocker.

Hitchcock provided employment for many families, hiring men as carpenters, children to paint the chairs and women to do the decorating. Soon the busy factory area became known as Hitchcocksville. Despite cash-flow problems, the enterprise continued to grow, and Hitchcock himself became famous and entered politics.

Falling on difficult times, the business was dissolved in 1848. By 1901, the building was abandoned. It stood empty and in disrepair for nearly five decades. The name Hitchcocksville was dropped, erased from maps, and this area of Barkhampsted was officially called Riverton. Then, along came the dreamer, John Tarrant Kenney, who decided to revive the chair-making enterprise.

Today Hitchcock chairs are manufactured in a modern plant in New Hartford. And Riverton's legacy of chairs has been memorialized in the Hitchcock Museum, in the Old Union Church. Lambert Hitchcock's home and factory have become showrooms for Hitchcock chairs.

Ghost stories and legends

The Lighthouse Legend has persisted, often embellished in the retelling, for more than a hundred years. In 1740, Molly Barber, daughter of a wealthy Wethersfield family, fell in love with a man her father considered unacceptable as a husband. He forbade the marriage, and to be certain that his daughter would not disobey, he kept her close to home. Angry and frustrated, Molly told her father that if she couldn't marry the man she loved, she would marry the first who asked her, regardless of who or what he was.

At that time there was a Narragansett from Block Island working in her father's gardens. His name was James Chaugham. Whether from love, or merely to carry out her threat to her father, Molly and James eloped. They escaped over Talcott Mountain to an Indian village near the Tunxis River, where they stayed for a month with the sachem Tomo. Here Molly learned and adopted the Indian way of living. When her father's search party arrived at the village, they did not recognize her, and left.

Still, Molly and James worried that they would be caught, and Molly especially feared her father's terrible temper. So they slipped away to the wilderness of Ragged Mountain, where they built a cabin and raised a family. One by one their children grew up,

and most of them married and built cabins of their own nearby. The wilderness became a small village. The inhabitants, like Molly and James, were a mixture of European, Native American, and also African American, though most predominantly Native American.

Eventually, a stagecoach line came close by the village. Stages rumbled past on the route from Hartford to Albany. Because the lights of the village were the first signs of life after many dark and forested miles, and a tavern was just five miles further ahead in New Hartford, the drivers called the village the Barkhampsted Lighthouse. By the 1860s, the village was abandoned.

Interestingly, archaeologist Kenneth Feder has discovered much truth in this legend, and from his work we learn that there was indeed an interesting "village of outcasts" in Barkhampsted. He has also located descendants of Molly and James.

Bethlehem

Highways 61, 132
Incorporated 1787

Native Americans

Paugussetts

Historical notes

Purchased from Nunawague and five other chiefs in order to enlarge Woodbury in 1710, the nearly 18,000 acres of the North Purchase included Bethlem, as it was then known, and Judea (now Washington). Bethlem remained agrarian, with most farms located on hilltops, until the beginning of the twentieth century. Industries, fueled by water power, included cotton and wool mills, a straw hat and bonnet factory, as well as the manufacture of leather goods.

Inventions, inventors and firsts

The Reverend Joseph Bellamy was "called" to preach during "winter privileges" in 1738, and remained to found what was essentially the first seminary in his home. His students included Aaron Burr and Jonathan Edwards II.

(Winter privileges meant you didn't have to travel to services in another town during the bad weather in winter. A pastor would come to your locale to preach. It was winter privileges that led to the formation of many new towns.)

Historic district

Bethlehem Green Historic District, bound by parts of North Main, South Main, and East Streets, West Road and Munger Lane.

Bridgewater

Routes 67, 133
Incorporated 1856

Native Americans

Paugusetts

Historical notes

Originally the Shepaug Neck part of New Milford. Bridgewater was settled in the mid-eighteenth century, with the first school district formed in 1858.

Farmers grew tobacco, and raised sheep and dairy cows. From 1823 to 1870, hatmaking was an important industry.

Ghost stories and legends

The entrepreneur Charles Thompson established a mail-order business in the 1860s. A marketing wizard, he used premiums as enticements for his products. His most successful premiums were dolls, which were coveted by little girls all over the country. His business grew so large that the post office had to grow too, quickly becoming a first-class post office.

This was in the time when postmasters made a commission on the sale of stamps. But the postmaster and Thompson were not friends, and their feuds were the stuff of town gossip. Nevertheless, the postmaster profited so handsomely from the sale of stamps that he was able to build himself a pretentious house, which townsfolk called "the house that Thompson built."

Like many entrepreneurs, Thompson's reach sometimes exceeded his grasp. One time, when his credit was low, he needed half of a carload of lanterns to fill an order. Fearing he wouldn't be able to obtain enough, he placed orders for five carloads from various manufacturers. And all five arrived! Ever the marketing genius, he lit the lanterns. The horizon glowed for miles around, drawing customers from far and wide. He sold all five carloads.

Canaan
Routes 7, 63, 126
Incorporated 1739

Native Americans
Mohicans

Historical notes
The town of Canaan was promoted as a "land flowing with milk and honey" during the land auction held in New London in 1738. Because of these glowing promises, Canaan brought record prices—sixty pounds per land right. It is and was true that the river valleys are fertile, but much of the town lies along thin-soiled and rocky mountain ridges, a surprise and a disappointment for the buyers.

Iron ore, limestone and the forests were important natural resources, and numerous mines and iron furnaces flourished. The woods hold ruins of furnaces. Canaan is known as Falls Village because of its proximity to the Great Falls of the Housatonic (Housatonic means "place beyond the mountains"). Here a power-company dam was built in 1913.

Captain Gershom Hewitt of Canaan, during the Revolution, secured the plans of Fort Ticonderoga for Colonel Ethan Allen through a ruse. This aided Allen in his attack on the fort. Hewitt is buried in the Lower Cemetery on Sand road.

Inventions, inventors and firsts
The coldest temperature on record in Connecticut was −32°F in Falls Village on February 16, 1943.

Ghost stories and legends
The Knickerbocker Tavern (no longer standing, but was at the Junction of Route 7 and Sand Road) was an overnight stop for passengers on the Albany stage. It became the source of many wild tales and stories, because it was also the place of entertainment for the local men who worked in the woods lumbering, in the mines or at the forges. The "Red Eye Infantry" as they were called, would revel long into the night, while exhausted travelers longed for a moment of quiet and sleep.

Notable buildings
Beebe Hill School House, Beebe Hill Road. Traditional one-room school house.

South Canaan Meeting House (c. 1804), Routes 7 and 63. Greek Revival-style meeting house.

Historic district
Falls Village Historic District, roughly bounded by Beebe Hill Road, Railroad and Water Streets and Brewster Road. As described in the official records of the U.S. Department of the Interior: "Falls Village is a community created in mid-nineteenth century as a station stop on the Housatonic Railroad. The depot, the inn, the banks, the street layout and the houses today maintain their nineteenth-century integrity, giving a faithful picture of the community's organization a century and a half ago. The buildings include some excellent, unaltered examples of the Greek Revival, Italianate, Second Empire and Queen Anne styles of architecture."

Colebrook

Routes 8, 182, 182A, 183
Incorporated 1779

Native Americans

Mohicans

Historical notes

Colebrook was the last town in Connecticut to be settled (not incorporated) by Europeans. This was in 1765. Because wood and hence charcoal were so plentiful, Colebrook had several furnaces. Iron ore was brought by oxen from the Salisbury mines to be worked in these furnaces. Cannons were made for the Revolution. A cannon captured at Bunker Hill and now on display in Quebec is said to have come from Colebrook.

Industry included mills, tanneries, a scythe factory and the manufacture of wooden ware. The population declined after the Civil War. Today, Colebrook is home to many summer residents.

Inventions, inventors and firsts

Ebenezer Jenkins invented "elastic steel." This was used for clock and coach springs, hoops for hoop skirts, and fish hooks.

Historic districts

Phelps Farms Historic District. This postcard village, on Route 183, is considered by many to be the best preserved post-Revolutionary settlement in the state. It includes eighteenth-century houses, a church, and an old tavern, which once served travelers on the New Haven Turnpike.

Colebrook Center Historic District, roughly the junction of Rockwell, Colebrook, Schoolhouse and Smith Hill roads and Route 183.

Cornwall

Routes 4, 7, 45, 125, 128
Incorporated 1740

Native Americans

Mohicans. Mohawk hunting grounds. The local Indians used the summit of Mohawk Mountain as a lookout so they could watch for the feared Mohawks. (The site is now Mohawk Mountain State Park, on East Street). There was a path from Bantam to Weataug that crossed Cornwall Hollow from southeast to northeast.

Historical notes

Cornwall was sold at an auction in Fairfield in 1738. Prior to the sale, in 1731, 300 acres were set aside for Yale. The first church was "gathered" in 1740.

Schools have played an important role in the history of Cornwall. In 1817, Edwin W. Dwight encountered a "dusky skinned youth weeping on the steps of Yale College." The lad was crying because he could not be admitted to the college and so could not obtain an education. Dwight was thus inspired to found the Foreign Mission School. One of his early students was Henry Obookiah, a Hawaiian stowaway and "pagan priest" who died before completing his studies, but whose arrival initiated a long connection between the Sandwich Islands and

Cornwall. The Foreign Mission School educated Native Americans and Hawaiians to become missionaries to their own people.

One student was Ta-wah, or David C. Carter. Carter's grandparents, Nathaniel and Sarah Carter, lived in Dudleytown, also called Owlsbury, overlooking Cornwall, but decided to leave Connecticut and settle in New York. Here three of their children were captured by Cherokees. Two of the captured children, girls, were ransomed and returned home. But the boy, Nathan, Ta-wah's father, chose instead to remain with his captors, and was adopted as a member of the Cherokee tribe. He married a Cherokee woman and raised a family. After attending the foreign Mission School, Ta-wah became an advocate for Indian rights, a jurist and editor.

In 1826, two Native American men, students of Edwin Dwight's, married two white women from town, causing cries of outrage amongst the citizenry, and the Foreign Mission School was forced to close its doors. The Rumsey School for boys was later founded on the site of the Foreign Mission School.

Agriculture was the predominant enterprise during the early years, but like other towns in Litchfield County with an abundance of wood, iron furnaces gained in importance. In 1833, the Cornwall Iron Company began operations, and with the advent of the Housatonic Railroad eleven years later, prosperity was brought to the town.

Matthew Lyon, of Dublin, came to this country in 1765 at the age of 19. A colorful figure, he was the subject of much colonial gossip. Lyon arrived penniless, his one guinea having been stolen by the captain of the ship he sailed on. Worse, the captain sold him to Jabez Bacon of Woodbury who, in turn, sold him to Hugh Hanna of Litchfield for a pair of stags. Eventually, he bought his freedom and moved to Cornwall.

He fought with Ethan Allen at Ticonderoga and was the instigator of numerous military exploits during the Revolution. Afterwards, his career took many turns, and he served in Congress for both the states of Vermont and Kentucky, served time in jail, and in fact, was elected to office while incarcerated.

Inventions, inventors and firsts

Cream Hill Agricultural School (Route 128) was founded in 1845 by Dr. Samuel Gold and his son T. S. Gold. This was one of the first agricultural schools in the country. T. S. Gold went on to become the father of modern agriculture in Connecticut. He founded or helped to found the Agricultural College at Storrs, the Experiment Station, and the State Board of Agriculture.

Ghost stories and legends

Dudleytown, or Owlsbury as it was called, is now little more than overgrown cellar holes and rubble on a wooded hilltop plateau overlooking Cornwall Bridge, but this abandoned village has generated many stories and myths. Part of the Mohawk hunting grounds, the densely wooded plateau was settled in 1738, by a Thomas Griffiths, who was quickly joined by other families. The Dudleys arrived in 1747.

The Dudley brothers were descended from a line of supposedly cursed ancestors, the first of whom to experience the curse, the Duke of Northumberland, was beheaded by King Henry VIII in 1533. Nevertheless, in Owlsbury's infant years, the Dudley brothers seemed to have left the curse behind. The citizens built roads, a school, houses and barns. At night, the eerie shrieks of owls pierced the nocturnal quiet, but otherwise nothing unusual occurred. Many of Owlsbury's leading citizens went out into the world where they enjoyed successful careers.

But gradually, almost imperceptibly, mishap befell one household after another—madness, smallpox, fire, death, too many, in fact, to be anything other than the Dudley Curse. By the beginning of the twentieth century, the town was all but abandoned, and today, the remains can only be reached by hiking Dark Entry Road, or Dudleytown Road, mere trails off Route 7. The ghost town is now part of Dark Entry Forest Wildlife Preserve.

Notable buildings

West Cornwall Covered Bridge, which crosses the Housatonic on Route 128, has been preserved as a state landmark. Also, the Cornwall Bridge Railroad Station, at the junction of Poppleswamp Brook Road and Kent Road.

Goshen

Routes 4, 63, 272
Incorporated 1739

Native Americans

Mohicans. At the junction of Route 4 and Lover's Lane is the site of an Old Indian Stockade, which the Mohicans built as protection against the Mohawks.

Historical notes

Early businesses included the Harvey Brooks Pottery Shop (c. 1818–1867), grist mills, sawmills, tanneries and blacksmith shops as well as dairies and cheese making. The Harvey Brooks Pottery Shop is now at Sturbridge Village, but the local historical society has an extensive collection of the redware produced by Brooks. Another Goshen potter, Captain John Norton, moved to Vermont in 1798 and began producing both redware and salt-glazed pottery.

Inventions, inventors and firsts

Goshen was home to various dairy-related firsts. A grazing town, early settlers included the Norton family, who among other things created the first cheese factory in 1810, were the first to ship cheese in round casks and containers (in 1792), and developed the first aspired, or "pineapple" cheese. Using the pulp from annatto seeds, the Nortons

Central Goshen in August of 1835. The cow-filled dirt road is now Route 63. The building in the right-hand corner with the cupola was the Academy. It now houses the Goshen Historical Society.

"painted" or colored their cheeses yellow. This was the first cheese that was not white, and brought higher prices. Yellow cheese is still popular today.

Geology

Most of the town is 1,000 feet or higher above sea level. Ivy Mountain, 1,642 feet above sea level, offers views as far east of the Connecticut River as Bolton Mountains, and as far as the Catskills, on the west.

There is a rock shelter, sometimes called Indian cave, which can be found by following Route 272 along Hall Meadow Brook. A half mile in on the first road to the right, a short distance in from the road, is the cave.

Historic districts

Goshen Historic District, routes 4 and 63 and Gifford Road.

West Goshen Historic District, roughly bounded by Route 4, Beach, Mill, and Milton Streets and Thompson Road.

Harwinton

Routes 4, 72, 118, 222
Incorporated 1737

Native Americans

Tunxis

Historical notes

Named for Hartford (Har), Windsor (Win) and Farmington (ton) in 1732, Harwinton was conveniently located on the Hartford-Litchfield Turnpike. Primarily agricultural, many farmers supplemented their incomes by harnessing the available waterpower and making tinware, bricks, pitchforks, hats, cutlery, whetstones, barrels and clocks.

One native son, Collis P. Huntington, grew up to be a peddler, traversing the highways and byways selling his wares. As a favor to a clockmaker friend, he headed west to collect some debts. There he remained to build the Southern Pacific Railroad.

Ghost stories and legends

Joseph Merriman found an abundance of lead, so the oft-told tale goes, and melted it to make bullets. However, when he went back again for more lead to replenish his bullets, he could not find the lode. Later, during the Revolutionary War, several hundred men and boys gathered under the direction of three clergymen and searched for three days to find the reputed lead deposits, but in vain.

Then, years later, a Mr. Tyler was walking in the forests when he came upon an enormous lead boulder. He lifted the "great lead rock" to his shoulders to carry it out of the woods, but "the invisible hand of an unknown enemy pounced upon him with such a blow that he fled in terror" and dropped his treasure. A strong wind blew and the skies darkened as if a great storm were brewing. When Mr. Tyler recovered himself, and went back to the forest, the boulder was gone.

From 1812 to 1817, a concerted effort was made to find the legendary lead. Many scientists visited and took samples. But not a trace of lead was ever found. There is, interestingly, a stream called Leadmine Brook, so named at least as early as 1732.

Historic districts

Burlington-Harmony Hill Roads Historic District, Harmony Hill, Locust Grove and Burlington Roads. Rural, eighteenth-century character, with houses close to the road. Both Washington and Lafayette dined at the Abijah Catlin Second House (c. 1765) when it served as an inn.

Litchfield-South Roads Historic District, roughly Litchfield Road from Bridge park to Harwinton Heights Roads and South Road from Litchfield Road to South Cemetery. Six Federal style houses are among the oldest surviving buildings in this area and have served as the heart of the town since the first settlement.

Kent

Routes 7, 341
Incorporated 1739

Native Americans

Mohicans, circa 1625. With increasing pressure from the advancing colonists and the disruption it caused, many surviving Native Americans became wanderers. Some of these wanderers banded together to form new tribes. One of the largest, and for a time the most successful, of these tribes were the Scatacooks, gathered together by Gideon Mauwehu. Mauwehu and his followers lived intermittently in Derby, New Milford and New York state.

One day, on a hunting expedition, Mauwehu ascended a mountain along the Housatonic River and realized that the country was uninhabited—no Europeans. Immediately, he returned home, packed up, and led his family and followers to the peaceful western banks of the Housatonic, where their settlement was called Schaghitcoke (Scatacook). Mauwehu invited friends and acquaintances from Potatuck, New Milford, and the Hudson River to join him, and many came. When Weraumaug, the sachem of the New Milford tribe, died, most of his followers joined the Scatacook settlement.

But they enjoyed their solitude for a mere decade, before the European settlements began cropping up in 1738. In 1742, Moravian missionaries arrived to convert the Scatacooks. Mauwehu and over a hundred of his followers were baptized. The Moravians, active but unpopular missionaries in the colony, preached temperance and peace. This made their success with the Scatacooks a matter of contention with the Kentish settlers, who saw the Scatacooks as customers for their rum and a source of income.

The Legislature ordered the Moravians to take an oath of allegiance before they could preach to the Indians. As oath-taking and military service were both contrary to their beliefs, they refused, and left with many of their converts to live in Pennsylvania. This move proved disastrous, and many of the old Scatacooks grew sick and died. Those who survived returned to their home in Kent.

Nevertheless, by the eve of the Revolution, many of the Scatacooks had died or had moved away. Some joined their friends in Stockbridge. In April 1786, Joseph Mauwehu, Gideon's son, signed a petition complaining that their children had no schools, their hunting grounds had been taken, they had lost their fishing rights at the falls of the Housatonic, and many of their number were poor and ill.

For the next hundred years, a series of "purchases" and "sales" to satisfy debts reduced the land of the Scatacooks to a few tillable acres and stoney hill country. By the autumn of 1849, there were only 30 or 40 people living in Schaghitcoke. A hundred years later, the WPA guide reported, unsympathetically, "a dozen half-breed Indians still reside as wards of the state" at Schaghitcoke.

Today, Schaghitcoke is one of only five remaining tracts of tribal lands in the state of Connecticut. It is still located on the western banks of the Housatonic, on Route 7.

Historical notes

The sale of Kent took place in Windham in 1738, with bids starting at fifty pounds a share. Most of the purchasers were from Colchester. Others were from Norwalk and Fairfield. The town was named Kent, but the early settlement was called Flanders.

George Washington's expense account for Saturday, March 3, 1781, lists "Getting a horse out of Bulls Falls, $215. Shoeing horse, $34.00." Apparently, a horse belonging to either Washington himself, or one of his companions, took a tumble into the Housatonic at the fording place near Bull's Iron Works. This is where Bull's Bridge now spans the river.

Iron mining and smelting were important industries. The Kent Iron

Mines were east of South Kent. There was a furnace on Forge Brook, at the entrance to Macedonia State Park, and another at East Kent. By 1845, three blast furnaces turned out 3,000 tons of iron a year. Two hundred and eighty hands were employed in these operations. There were also blacksmith shops, a general store, tanneries, sawmills, a trading post and schools.

Today, Kent boasts numerous art galleries, and is home to many summer residents.

Geology
Two-hundred-foot waterfall in Kent Falls State Park, on Route 7, a mile and a half north of North Kent.

Notable buildings
Bull's Bridge, Route 7. This picturesque covered bridge crosses the Housatonic into New York.

Sloane-Stanley Museum, Route 7 (860-927-3849). Includes the ruins of a nineteenth-century furnace and houses Eric Sloane's extensive and beautiful collection of tools.

Historic districts
Flanders Historic District, Route 7, Cobble Road, Cobble Lane and Studio Hill road. Many fine old houses.

Litchfield
Routes 118, 202, 209, 254
Incorporated 1719

Native Americans
Tunxis

Historical notes
Purchased from the Tunxis in 1667 by William Lewis and Samuel Steele of Farmington (and known as Matetucke). Later, in 1714 a quit-claim was issued to John Marsh for these "Greenwoods" for fifteen pounds. Ownership was also claimed by a joint committee of Hartford and Windsor, who paid fifteen pounds in 1715 or 1716 to the Potatucks for what they called Bantam. Once these issues were resolved, settlement began. In 1751, Litchfield was named the county seat.

George Washington passed through Litchfield several times, and slept in Litchfield once or twice. In his journal for Thursday and Friday, May 24, 25, 1781 he writes, " … on my return to New Windsor—dined at Farmington and lodged at Litchfield." His likely accommodations were either at the tavern kept by Samuel Sheldon on North Street, or also on North Street, at the Kilbourn house, kept by Captain William Stanton. His aide, Benjamin Talmidge, also had a house in Litchfield.

As the crossroads of important and major stage routes to New York and elsewhere in New England, Litchfield became a hub of commerce. It served as a supply depot during the Revolutionary War as well as host to General Washington. By 1810, it was the fourth largest town in Connecticut.

However, when the railroad came to Connecticut, Litchfield was bypassed. The town never enjoyed the access to water power that enabled other towns to develop industry. With the decline of the stages, the population dropped. The town managed, however, to preserve many of its fine and commodious homes, and enjoyed a "golden age" as a center of ideas and culture.

Harriet Beecher Stowe, her brother Henry Ward Beecher, and Ethan Allen were all born in Litchfield.

Inventions, inventors and firsts

The Litchfield Law School, founded in 1784 by Judge Tapping Reeve, was the first law school in the U.S. Reeve ran the school until his retirement in 1820, when it was run by Judge James Gould. The school closed in 1833. Aaron Burr and Noah Webster were among the thousand pupils who attended the Litchfield Law School. The Tapping Reeve House and Law School are on South Street.

Geology

Bantam Lake, on the western edges of Litchfield, is the largest natural lake in Connecticut.

Ghost stories and legends

In the back of Wolcott's Orchard, on South Street, the women of Litchfield gathered around a hot fire. They had in their possession the leaden statue of King George III, stolen from Bowling Green, New York, and they were about to consign him to the heat of the flames and melt him down until there was nothing of his shape but a great molten pool of lead. From the melted King they fashioned bullets for the Continental Army, their husbands, and brothers and sons. The mold for the bullets is on exhibit in the Historical Society Museum. The Oliver Wolcott House is on South Street.

Notable buildings

Litchfield Historical Society Museum, 7 South Street/Route 202 (860-567-4501). Research library. Changing exhibits.

Historic districts

Litchfield Historic District, the village green and North and South Streets. Coterminous with village and borough boundaries.

Milton Center Historic District, roughly bounded by Milton, Shearshop, Headquarters, Sawmill and Blue Swamp Roads.

Morris

Routes 61, 109, 209
Incorporated 1859

Native Americans

Potatucks. The Potatucks frequented the shores of Bantam Lake, and used the area as a camping ground. There is some evidence of skirmishes with the Mohawks.

Historical notes

Purchased from the Bantam tribe of the Pootatucks. Settled as the South Farms section of Litchfield, and incorporated as a separate parish in 1767. In the mid-nineteenth century it separated from Litchfield and renamed for James Morris, a prominent resident and educator.

Primarily a dairy town, a few mills and industries developed along the rivers. However, by the close of the nineteenth century, Morris had become a town of gentlemen farmers, and by the 1930s, two thirds of the taxpayers were non-residents. A thriving summer colony grew up around Bantam Lake.

Geology

Rolling hills. Most of Bantam Lake lies within Morris. The largest naturally formed lake in Connecticut, Bantam Lake covers 1,200 acres. Mount Tom is on the western boundary of Morris.

Notable buildings

Mount Tom Tower (also in Litchfield and Washington), off Route 202 SE of Woodville. A stone tower at the summit of 1,325-foot Mount Tom straddles three towns.

Historic districts

Town Hall and District School Number 6, 12 South Street.

New Hartford

Routes 44, 202, 219
Incorporated 1738

Native Americans

West Hill Pond was a camping ground.

Historical notes

New Hartford was part of the Western Lands divided up for the creation of new towns and settlement by the General Assembly in 1732. One hundred eighty-two taxpayers from Hartford became the first proprietors of the town. In addition to farming, various industries sprang up, and by the beginning of the nineteenth century New Hartford was primarily industrial. Fine cotton duck for sails and for

the military, levels, rules and planes were produced. Two rail lines served the busy community.

However, at the turn of the century, the cotton mills left. By the Depression, other industries had left or failed. In 1936, the Greenwood Dam broke, causing devastation and flooding. In time, even the rail lines were torn up.

Gradually, the town recovered. New industries, including the modern Hitchcock Chair factory, are located within New Hartford's borders.

Inventions, inventors and firsts

Elias Howe, a mechanic in Greenwood's Cotton Mill, built the first practical sewing machine in the cellar of the Old New Hartford House. It was patented in 1846. Walter Hunt of New York had discovered the principle twelve years earlier, but Howe made the same discovery independently and put it to use. The first woman to operate the machine was a New Hartford school teacher.

Geology

Soapstone, quarried in the Nepaug State Forest, was used by the Indians to fashion bowls. Tipping Rock, a glacial boulder on the Tunxis Trail, weighs about twelve tons. It is twenty-eight feet in circumference. Nevertheless, it is balanced such that it can easily be "tipped." Also of geologic interest on the Tunxis Trail is Table Rock. Looking very much like a giant's table, ten or twelve people can fit together underneath it.

Ghost stories and legends

Like many towns, New Hartford consisted of several villages. Satan's Kingdom, just past the Farmington River Gorge, was toward the end of the eighteenth century home to a mixed gathering of Native Americans, African Americans, and renegade whites. The residents were perceived as lawless outcasts by residents in surrounding villages, though they pretty much kept to themselves.

Notable buildings

Gillette's Grist Mill (c. 1776), Maple Hollow Road.

Bakerville Blacksmith Shop, Route 202.

Historic districts

Pine Meadow Historic District, roughly bounded by the Farmington River and Wicket, North Ten, Church and Main Streets.

New Milford

Routes 7, 37, 67, 109, 202
Incorporated 1712

Native Americans

Potatucks. Called this valley Weantinock. Chief Waramaug built a long house, 20 by 100 feet in dimension, on a hilltop. Reputedly, artisans from many neighboring tribes came to help in the creation of this house, Chief Waramaug's Palace, bringing the best bark for the construction, and contributing their artistic skills to decorating the interior with vivid images of birds, animals, reptiles and amphibians. In the main council room of the Palace, the artists painted pictures of their Chief, his family and council members.

When the chief died, passing mourners each dropped a stone at his grave site, creating a monument. The monument vanished when a later mansion was built there, with the main fireplace located exactly where the great chief lay.

The "Cove" or "Eel Rocks" near the Great Falls of the Housatonic was a favorite Indian fishing place and camping ground even after the arrival of Europeans. The falls stopped the spawning salmon from swimming further upstream, and so the fish were plentiful. Goodyear Island, in the middle of the river, was a trading post at the falls, where the Indians and Europeans traded with each other. Once the dam was constructed in Derby, lower down the river, the fish no longer swam this far upstream, and the catch diminished.

Historical notes

Purchased from the Potatuck Indians in 1703. John Noble and his eight-year-old daughter Sarah tramped through the woods from Westfield, Massachusetts, to settle in 1707. According to tradition, Noble left his daughter in the care of the local Indian women while he was away on business for a month.

Roger Sherman settled in New Milford in 1748 and spent his young manhood here. He is the only man to sign all four of the Articles of Association, in 1774, the Declaration of Independence, in 1776, the Articles of Confederation, in 1777, and the Constitution of the United States, in 1787. While in New Milford, he worked as a shoemaker, surveyor, merchant and lawyer. There is a bronze tablet marking the site of his home on Route 7, at the Town Hall.

The southern portion of the Housatonic Railroad opened in 1840. New Milford became a center of industry and commerce for the region. New Milford covers the largest area of any town in Connecticut.

Geology

Hill country. The Housatonic runs north to south, cutting a deep valley through the limestone. Limestone and mica were quarried. Beryl, tourmaline garnets, acquamarines and other minerals have been found. Along Route 7 is Tory's Hole, a limestone cave. Further along Route 7 is another cave at Strait's Rocks.

Ghost stories and legends

Lillinoah, the daughter of Chief Waramaug, rescued a European man and nursed him back to health. While she was caring for the man, they fell in love, and the Chief, after a lot of persuasion, granted the young couple permission to marry. The man, whose name has been lost, wanted to go back to his own people, he said, to assure them of his safety, before wedding his beloved. He was gone a long time and the princess pined for him and, after

awhile, despaired of his return. The Chief, worried about his daughter's great sadness, suggested to his aid, Eagle Feather, that he should marry Lillinoah.

Distraught at the loss of her love, and the prospect of marrying another, Lillinoah grabbed a canoe and plunged into the treacherous river. Suddenly she saw her lover, standing high above on a premonitory. She raised her arms up to him in a plea for help. Without hesitation, he jumped to her rescue. The canoe capsized and the lovers were dashed against the rocks of the waterfall, where they died in each other's arms. The place is known as Lover's Leap.

Notable buildings

Lover's Leap Bridge, south of New Milford on Pumpkin Hill Road.

Historic districts

New Milford Center Historic District, roughly bounded by Bennet and Elm Streets, Center Cemetery, East, South Main and Mill Streets, and the Railroad.

Norfolk

Routes 44, 182, 272
Incorporated 1758

Native Americans

Mohicans

Historical notes

This was the last town in Litchfield County where land was auctioned off (in 1738), but only one person, Timothy Hotford, purchased a right. Further sale was suspended in 1750, but four years later, the sale was continued in Middletown, and ordered to continue until the whole was sold.

The early farmers cleared land, planted crops, and to serve their own needs, built blacksmith shops, gristmills and sawmills. In the early nineteenth century, the Blackberry River was harnessed for the manufacture of linseed oil, woolens, cheese boxes, scythes, hoes and men's hats. Although these industries declined in importance, the arrival of the Connecticut Western Railroad in 1871 insured prosperity.

Joseph Battell, who owned a local store, was with his energy and entrepreneurship especially responsible for the economic success of Norfolk. His ability to attract wealthy customers from afar, and promote the secluded beauty of the forests and hills, influenced financiers, industrialists and writers to build their summer estates in Norfolk.

Mr. and Mrs. Carl Stoeckel established the Litchfield County Choral Union and the Norfolk Music Festival in 1899. The annual concerts attracted internationally renowned performers, and lasted until 1925. Today, the tradition is carried on by the Yale Summer School of Music and Art, which hosts concerts in the Music Shed of the Stoeckel estate.

Geology
Haystack Mountain looms over the hilly town.

Ghost stories and legends
According to oral tradition, Thomas Day and his son, who had a forge on the south side of the river, made iron from Salisbury ore. At their forge, they produced links for the huge iron chain that was stretched across the Hudson to prevent the British from sailing upriver. Accounts differ on how successful the chain was.

Historic districts
Norfolk Historic District, roughly bounded by Greenwoods Road, West Litchfield Road, Mountain Road and Westside Road.

North Canaan
Routes 7, 44
Incorporated 1858

Native Americans
Mohicans

Historical notes
Originally part of Canaan, North Canaan ironically (and somewhat confusingly) includes the early village of Canaan. Canaan was a popular crossroads town in the era of stagecoach travel, with busy routes to Albany, Hartford and New Haven passing through.

Industry included the manufacture of pig iron, and numerous lime quarries. Most of the quarries were in the East Canaan section of town. The marble for the state capitol in Hartford came from the Allyndale Quarries in the northeast part of town. Items as large as two-ton ship anchors and as small as nails were made at the forge of Squire Samuel Forbes. Ethan Allen worked as Forbes's bookkeeper.

The Housatonic Railroad arrived in 1841, followed by the Western Connecticut Railroad in 1871, ensuring that the village of Canaan would continue as a busy hub. In the heyday of rail transportation, a dozen passenger trains stopped at the Canaan Union Depot daily, as well as freight trains, including two milk trains carrying Borden's products.

Geology

Limestone quarries. Minerals found include amphibole, actinolite, apatite, calcite, pyrite, dendrite, serpentine, talc, and tremolite.

The Blackberry and Housatonic Rivers both wind through North Canaan.

Ghost stories and legends

There is a tradition that Hessian soldiers were confined in the dungeon of the Douglas Tavern, a mile outside the village, after General Burgoyne's surrender. The tavern later became part of the Canaan Golf Club.

Notable buildings

Beckley Furnace (1837–1918), Lower Road, off Route 44, parallel to the Blackberry River, is one of the better preserved sites. Remains of a forty-foot-tall blast furnace. Further downstream, also on Lower Road, are the sites of the Forbes Furnace (1821–1880), and Canaan 3, the Furnace in the Field.

Samuel Forbes House (c. 1752), 89 Lower Road (across the bridge from the furnaces).

Canaan Union Station (c. 1872), is the oldest station in continuous operation in the U.S. It was erected as a station and hotel by the Housatonic Railroad. It currently serves an excursion line, and houses several shops.

Lawrence Tavern (c. 1751), Elm Street. Built by Isaac Lawrence as a tavern for travelers passing through from Hartford and Litchfield to Albany. He inscribed the front stone step with the names of his first wife and his eleven children. The house is a private residence owned by his descendants.

Historic district

Canaan Village Historic District, roughly bounded by West Main, Bragg, and Orchard Streets and Granite Avenue. This former railroad hub has been thoughtfully preserved.

Plymouth

Routes 6, 72, 262
Incorporated 1795

Native Americans

Tunxis. The area between Naugatuck and Waterville was known as Mattatuck. "Indian Heaven" is the area east of the Reynolds Bridge area of Thomaston. Three fourths of a mile from Buttermilk Falls is Jack's Cave. As late as 1830, this cave was inhabited by three elderly Indians, the leader of whom was Jack. The cave has a 10 by 20-foot passage. Inside is a solid rock "sleeping room." According to tradition, an ancient Indian trail from Farmington to the Naugatuck passed by the cave. Another cave, Indian Jack's East Cave or Charlie Krugh's Cave, is east of here. You cannot see the caves from the road, but must get out and hike a short piece of the Mattatuck Trail, entering from Allentown Road and heading south.

Historical notes

As early as 1657, the Tunxis sold rights to hunters who mistakenly thought that they had discovered a lead mine. It was more than seventy years, however, before others followed to settle. The parish was known as Northbury and was part of Waterbury, and later part of Watertown. The town was named Plymouth because one of the first settlers, Henry Cook, was the grandson of one of the Pilgrims. He lived in the part of Plymouth that later became Thomaston.

Inventions, inventors and firsts

Eli Terry moved from his birthplace (then East Windsor, now South Windsor), and set up shop in Plymouth after apprenticing with the clockmaker Daniel Burnap. Terry secured a patent on the Equation Clock in 1797. He sold his business to one of his apprentices, and went into partnership with Seth Thomas and Silas Hoadley. Their goal was to produce a total of 4,000 clocks, 500 at a time. To accomplish this, Terry produced in 1802 the first interchangeable clock parts. He often went out on horseback himself to peddle these clocks. In 1810, he sold his interest in this endeavor, and moved to the western side of town which later became Thomaston. Here, in 1814, he patented the first shelf clock.

Terry's son, Eli Terry, Jr., who was born in Plymouth, set up his own clockmaking shop two miles east of Plymouth Center. This part of town, on the Pequabuck River, was soon called Terryville after his factory, and became the industrial center. Another son, James, pioneered in the manufacture of silk, and then took over the Eagle Lock Company which developed the cabinet lock. A third son, Andrew, founded one of the first malleable iron foundries. Eli Terry, Sr., moved to Terryville himself in 1838.

Notable buildings

The Lock Museum of America, 130 Main Street/Route 6 (860-589-6359) Terryville was once known as "Lock Town of America" because there were over forty lock manufacturers located here. The Eagle Lock Company was across the street, on the site of the present shopping mall. The Museum boasts a collection of more than 22,000 locks, keys and associated items.

Historic districts

East Plymouth Historic District, East Plymouth and Marsh Road.

Roxbury

Routes 67, 199
Incorporated 1796

Native Americans

Paugusetts. At Roxbury Station (Route 67), is Pulpit Rock. Here it is said that John Eliot preached to the Indians.

Historical notes

The first European to explore Shepaug was Captain John Minor from Stratford. Minor was a surveyor, missionary and interpreter to the Indians. He settled in Pomperaug (Woodbury). The area east of the Shepaug River was settled as the Upper Farms of Woodbury. Lower Farms, or Shepaug, was settled somewhat later and in 1731 the settlers were granted permission to hire their own minister "for the difficult parts of the year." In 1743, Shepaug's petition to be a separate society called Roxbury was granted by the General Assembly. Fifty-three years later Roxbury was incorporated as a town.

Ethan Allen's cousins, Remember Baker and Seth Warner, were born in Roxbury, and served under Allen as Green Mountain Boys in Vermont.

Geology

Mountainous. The gorge of the Shepaug River is to the west. Mining was an important factor in the early economy of Roxbury. Mine Hill, where much of the activity took place, is northwest of Roxbury Station (Route 67 to Mine Hill Road, to Hodge Road). The first mine was opened in 1750 in hopes of finding silver, but title to the mine was the subject of much contentious litigation.

A rich vein of spathic iron was discovered, and a furnace was built. Spathic iron was particularly valuable in the production of steel. The ore vein, along a fault line, was approximately eight feet in width and was opened a distance of a mile. The American Smelting Company operated the mine for four decades, averaging ten tons of pig iron a day. Afterwards, the Columbia School of Mines used the mine for demonstrations.

There were also granite quarries in the vicinity which supplied stone for churches and other buildings in surrounding towns. The area is rich in minerals, including siderite, garnets, zircon, pyrite, quartz, malachite, magnetite and others.

The ruins of the furnaces are crumbling in the woods, and the area is riddled with dangerous mine shafts. This was a rich hunting ground for collectors until an amateur collector was seriously injured in a 1972 fall. An open garnet mine was worked near Roxbury Falls, close to the Southbury line.

Historic districts

Roxbury Center Historic District, Route 67, Weller's Bridge, South and Church Streets.

Salisbury

Routes 7, 41, 44, 112
Incorporated 1741

Native Americans

Mohicans. Near the close of King Philip's War, in 1676, Major John

Talcott hotly pursued a large band of Indians for three days as they fled westward. When he reached their encampment in the northeast corner of Weatogue (Salisbury), he and his men attacked, killing many.

As European settlement encroached on the native people's lands, refugees from various quarters—River Indians from Windsor, Mohicans from the Hudson, and others—gathered together in the rugged mountains in the remote northwest corner of Connecticut. European settlement in the area came late, around 1720, and was sparse. At that time, there were seventy wigwams in the village of Weatogue.

Relations between the two peoples remained good, until more settlers arrived, and more "purchases" were made. The Indians complained that some of the lands that were taken had never been sold, and they received sympathy and support from several of their white neighbors. However, the General Assembly found the "purchases" to be valid. These complaints continued for a number of years, but with little hope of a favorable resolution. Therefore, many of the Indians left for Stockbridge. By 1774, only nine Indians remained in Salisbury.

Historical notes

Originally known as Weatogue. The first purchase was made by two Dutchmen from New York, Lawrence Knickerbocker and Johannes Diksman, who gave twenty pounds to Sakowanahook, Konaguin and "all of the nation of the Mohokandos (Mohicans)," in exchange for more than half of present-day Salisbury. This was on January 31, 1721. Five years later, Connecticut settlers purchased from Metoxon, the sachem, the western part of Salisbury up to within two miles of the Housatonic River, and much of Sharon. In 1738, Thomas Lamb made a purchase of Metoxon. By that time, he had already been working a forge at Lime Rock (Route 112) for four years.

Quarries, mining and the associated forges were key components of Salisbury's growth. Ore from Salisbury provided the raw material for surrounding towns as well as for the locals. Lamb's early Lime Rock forge was operated by Barnum Richardson well into the nineteenth century.

West of Lime Rock, in Lakeville (Route 41), a small forge was erected in 1748. Twenty years later, the property was purchased by Ethan Allen, John Haseltine and Samuel Forbes, who remodeled it into a blast furnace so they could produce cast iron rather than wrought iron. This was the earliest important blast furnace in Connecticut. They sold out to Richard Smith of Boston before the Revolutionary War.

During the war, Congress took over operations, and the plant became one of the principal arsenals for the Continental armies. Sixty workmen cast cannons, cannon-balls, shells, kettles and other supplies. The guns for the

U.S.S. Constellation were forged in Lakeville.

Another furnace was located at Mt. Riga. It was here that the anchor for the U.S. S. Constitution was made. It took six yoke of oxen to transport it to the Hudson. The Salisbury furnaces also supplied the army during the War of 1812 and played a vital role in the development of the railroad.

Most of the iron came from mines at Ore Hill (north side of Route 44, now a pond). There were other nearby mines in operation, including the Chatfield Mine (Route 112) which opened in 1732 and didn't close until 1921, the Davis Mine, in Lakeville itself, and other mines near the lake, now filled with water. In the earliest days, ore was transported in bags by horse from the mines to the furnaces. There was a well-worn path from the mines at Ore Hill to Furnace Village (present Lakeville).

The iron industry lasted until the first years of the twentieth century. After the Depression, many of the factory buildings and workers' houses were converted into artists' studios and homes.

Salisbury is sometimes called the "Mother of Vermont" because so many of its citizens, such as General Ethan Allen, Governor Thomas Chittenden, and Chief Justice Nathaniel Chipman went from Salisbury to settle the state of Vermont. The Constitution of Vermont was drafted in Lakeville.

Inventions, inventors and firsts

First tax supported library in America was organized in Salisbury in 1803.

Caleb Bingham, a pioneer writer of textbooks, was born in Salisbury in 1757. His *English Grammar* was the second published in the United States while his *American Preceptor* enjoyed sixty-four editions. Bingham moved to Boston in 1784 where he opened a girls' school, and later ran a bookstore at 44 Cornhill Street. The bookstore served as an educational center, and it was here that the idea of free primary school was first publicly discussed. In 1796 he published the first copy-slips for teachers.

Ghost stories and legends

There have been persistent tales of a strange race of people living in squalor along the sides of Mount Riga for hundreds of years. One Depression-era guide says, quite seriously and with little sympathy, "Along the lower slopes of Mt. Riga, tucked away in shallow mountain coves, are the cabins of 'The Raggies,' a 'lost' people about whom little is known. The ancestry of the Raggies may possibly be traced to Hessian deserters who worked the woodland forges at the top of Mt. Riga, or to the early woodsmen, who, when there was no longer use for charcoal, still stayed on, knowing no trade and having no means to move from the area. They live in squalor, intermarry, and twelve or fourteen are often crowded together in a two-room shack. Sanitation is entirely inadequate: sink drains flow into springs of drinking water unrestrained ... Canned woodchuck is a favorite dish ... A local woman has taught the people to 'put up' the meat of Johnny Chuck, to can brook suckers and preserve the berries that grow on the rocky slopes."

Supernatural powers, witchcraft and diabolical acts were early attributed to the Raggies. In November of 1802, three houses in Sage's Ravine were mysteriously bombarded with rock and mortar. A total of fifty-six windowpanes were smashed. Worried townspeople set up a watch to determine the source of the flying stones, but no source could be discerned. In fact, the rocks and mortar were not of a local type. The strange event was blamed on the Raggies' otherworldly skills.

Geology

The highest elevations in the state are in Salisbury, where Mount Frissel reaches 2,380 feet and Mount Riga and Bear Mountain loom over the town. The remains of an old blast furnace (1808–1860) are on Mount Riga.

Notable buildings

Holley House (c. 1808), Millerton Road/Route 44, Lakeville (860-435-2878). Small complex including heritage gardens, a restored house museum, the Salisbury Cannon Museum and exhibits.

Historic districts

Lakeville Historic District, bounded by Millerton Road/Route 44, Sharon Road, Allen Street and Holley Street. Remaining buildings of the Holly iron works, and the site of the 1762 Blast Furnace (at the outlet of Lake Wononskopomoc), as well as the Holley House museum.

Lime Rock Historic District, roughly bounded by White Hollow, Elm, Lime Rock, Norton Hill and Furnace Roads. The area's first forge was built here in 1735.

Sharon

Routes 4, 7, 41
Incorporated 1739

Native Americans

Mohicans (see also Salisbury). The Indians, refugees from several tribes, lived mostly in the northwestern parts of Sharon. Their principal village was on the plain between the base of Poconnuck (Indian Mountain) and Wequadnach (Wequagnock, or Indian Pond).

The Indians made complaints about the disposition of their lands, and the General Assembly appointed numerous committees to look into the matter, eventually "giving" the Indians fifty acres, though even this small parcel did not come into their possession. By 1752, all of the Indians were gone.

Then, in the autumn of 1754, Timotheus, who had lived in the Indian village, reappeared. He visited the local farmers' houses and complained indignantly that his people had not even been granted the land that the General Assembly had ruled was theirs. One day, sitting in the kitchen of Jonathan Pettis, speaking as had become his custom, of the wrongs done to his people, he grew agitated and said, "I vow it is my land and you know it. I swear it is my land, and I will have it."

Henceforth, there were nocturnal disturbances in the settlement. Thomas Jones, who had come recently to live near where the Indians had had their village, heard men's voices outside his house at night, and some nights the walls of his house were beaten with clubs and hatchets. Jones was alarmed. Neighbors came to sit guard with him, three or four a night, for three weeks.

One Sabbath night, while a group of armed men were gathered in the cabin, an Indian lifted the blanket that served as a front door and poked his head in. One of the men said quietly, "shoot," but another said, "better to wait and get a good aim." The Indian withdrew and the men pressed their faces to the wall and watched him through a large crack.

The man who had said to wait, John Palmer, now shot and missed. He grabbed another gun, and shot again, this time through the window. The Indian seemed to stumble and fall, and the men rushed from the cabin. Nothing. No one. Then, up ahead, they saw a man in a white blanket, and Palmer shot a third time, and missed.

One of the men told Joseph Jackson that he should go into the house and stand guard while the others remained outside. Briefly, he did as was suggested, and went into the house, but then, impatient, he ran back out. He encountered a man in loose blue clothing. In the darkness, he fleetingly mistook the man for John Gray. But, Gray was close beside him, and so he ran after the stranger, convinced that he was an Indian. The night ended without bloodshed.

An angry Jones sent an account to the General Assembly with affidavits from the others attached. Timotheus accepted two pounds ten shillings of New York currency and eight pounds of Connecticut tenor in exchange for a quit claim of his rights. He left Sharon for good. In 1774, only one Indian remained. A century later, Andrew Hotchkiss established his factory, Hotchkiss and Sons, on the site of an Indian burial ground on the Webotuck River in Sharon Valley.

Historical notes

Sharon was named from the Hebrew Plain of Sharon. The town was sold at auction in New Haven in 1738. There were forty-nine purchasers, sixteen of whom moved to Sharon to live. Most of these were from Colchester and Lebanon.

In addition to farming, early industries included a blast furnace in Sharon Valley, a wrought iron manufactory at

Skinner Pond, mining, gray iron foundries where the Burnham cookstove was made, a satinet factory, hat shop, tailor shop, tanneries and clock shop. Mousetraps were produced in large quantities by the Jewett Manufacturing Company. Hotchkiss and Sons produced currycombs, and later exploding shells, which were invented by Andrew Hotchkiss.

All of these industries, except some farming, have vanished. The town became a summer colony in the first quarter of the twentieth century, and continues as a summer residence to this day.

Notable buildings
Gay- Hoyt House (c. 1775), 18 Main Street, on the Green (860-364-5688). Pretty brick village farmhouse, with an interesting collection of furniture.

Sharon Clock Tower. An imposing ornamental clock tower, built of local stone, put up as a memorial.

Historic districts
Sharon Historic District, roughly Main Street from Low Road to a junction with Mitchelltown, Amenia, Union and West Woods Roads. The Sharon Green (Route 41) is considered by many to be one of the prettiest greens in Connecticut.

Sharon Valley Historic District, junction of Sharon Valley and Sharon Valley Station Roads. This was the site of the Hotchkiss iron works. A lime kiln remains on the west side of Sharon Station Road.

Thomaston
Routes 6, 109, 222, 254
Incorporated 1875

Native Americans
Tunxis. Tunxis means "fast-flowing little stream."

Historical notes
Originally part of the Mattatuck Plantation. The present-day Thomaston/Plymouth area was set off as the Northbury Parish in 1739. In 1789, Northbury joined with Westbury to form Watertown. Then, in 1795, the old Northbury section separated from Watertown and became known as Plymouth. The Thomaston section was called Plymouth Hollow. This is the area where Seth Thomas built his clock factory in 1813, and which by 1856 he was calling Thomas Town. When this area was separated from the mother town of Plymouth in 1875, and incorporated as a town in its own right, it was named Thomaston.

Seth Thomas was instrumental in bringing the railroad to Plymouth Hollow so that he could obtain a good supply of brass from Waterbury. Eli Terry, his former partner, who later sold his share of the business and retired, developed his famous "patented shelf clock" while working in Thomaston in 1810.

Ghost stories and legends
When Abi Blakeslee Humaston heard that the British were about to

make a second food raid, she whipped up a supply of sausages using red flannel and turnips as the main ingredients. The hungry British seized the Yankee treat and unwittingly carried them off for a much-anticipated meal. There is no record of their reaction to the dining experience.

Torrington

Routes 4, 183, 202, 272
Incorporated 1740, chartered as a city in 1923

Native Americans

Mohicans. Last chief, Paugnut. An Indian fort was located northwest of the city, heading towards Goshen, on the left, about three fourths of a mile past the junction of Route 4 and Pothier Road.

Historical notes

Once called Mast Swamp, because of the abundant stand of pines cut down and used for ship's masts, and the swamp where the city was eventually built, the town was officially named Torrington for Great Torrington in Devonshire, England. It was part of the Western Lands owned by Windsor.

All the voters took an oath of fidelity in 1774, and despite a population of only 843, 169 men participated in the militia. During the Revolution the women met once a week in one of the taverns to discuss the news. Many of the families were impoverished during the war effort and had little to eat.

The Naugatuck River, and smaller rushing streams, provided power for industry, and Torrington became a center for the manufacture of brass, woolen cloth, hooks and eyes, needles, tacks and millwork.

John Brown, the noted abolitionist, was born on Pothier Road, a mile from the junction of Route 4. The house burned in 1918, leaving only a cellar hole, but the property is maintained by the John Brown Association and is part of the Connecticut Freedom Trail. Brown was five generations descended from Peter Brown, a Mayflower passenger. His father was an abolitionist.

Brown proposed the idea of "forcible emancipation" of slaves and in 1859, he and twenty men captured the national arsenal at Harper's Ferry. Rob-

Anything you could need or want for your "sea shore cottage" you could purchase at the Hartford and Torrington shops of Bruce, Filley & Company.

ert E. Lee apprehended Brown, who was convicted of treason and hanged in December of that year. Abolition was an early cause in Torrington. On August 18, 1798, Abijah Holbrook freed his slaves, Jacob Prince and Ginne Prince, husband and wife.

Inventions, inventors and firsts

Gail Borden was granted a patent for the "process of evaporating milk in a vacuum," in 1856. A year later, he was producing condensed milk commercially at his now-vanished factory at Burr Pond.

Israel Coe produced the first machine-made brass kettles in his Torrington plant, and initiated a thriving manufacturing business.

Notable buildings

Hotchkiss-Fyler House (c. 1900), 192 Main Street, Route 8 Exit 44 (860-482-8260). Victorian mansion with adjoining museum. Fine example of the intricate woodwork of the period. Adjacent to the mansion is the history museum, with a permanent exhibit of Torrington's past.

Historic district

Downtown Torrington Historic District, roughly bounded by Church and Alvord Streets, Center Cemetery, Willow Street, East Main Street, Litchfield Street and Prospect Street.

Torringford Street Historic District, Torringford Street from main Street North to West Hill Street.

Warren
Routes 45, 341
Incorporated 1786

Native Americans

Mohicans, their hunting grounds.

Historical notes

Settled in 1737 as part of Kent. In 1750, the parish of East Greenwich was organized, and the area was known by that name until thirty-six years later when it was incorporated as a town. Agriculture, particularly the production of butter and cheese, plus the iron industry, were the primary occupations of the town. However, as these occupations declined, residents emigrated west. Nearly 3,000 people left Warren during a fifty-year period beginning in 1772. By the 1930s there were only 300 residents. Many roads were abandoned and fields reverted back to forest.

Ghost stories and legends

It was said that Rhoda Paine, the first white child born in Warren, was so strong that as a woman she could lift a full barrel of cider into a cart.

Notable buildings

The one-room brick schoolhouse was built in 1774 from locally made bricks. It was in continuous use for 140 years. In 1929 it was moved to the center of town and has been restored and furnished with historical artifacts.

Washington
Routes 47, 109, 199, 202
Incorporated 1779

Native Americans
Paugusetts. Probably hunting grounds. Possibly also Mohican.

Historical notes
The eastern part of town was the Parish of Judea of Woodbury. The western section was the Parish of New Preston of New Milford. The parishes were joined together and named for General George Washington, who passed through several times. His diary entry for Friday, May 25, 1781 reads, "Breakfasted at Squire Cogswells …" The Cogswell Tavern was a hip-roofed house, built in 1762, and kept by Major William Cogswell and his wife Anna Whittlesey Cogswell. It was near the village of New Preston.

Quarries, ironworks and agriculture were early industries. A quartz vein containing rare minerals, including blue blades of cyanite, tourmaline and andalusite, was mined near the Shepaug River. Marble and white clay were also mined.

The naturalist W. Hamilton Gibson spent his summers at Washington Depot near the Gorge of Mallory Brook (Route 47). Washington was also the boyhood home of Horace Bushnell, and Mount Bushnell was named for him.

Washington is now primarily a residential town, with a summer colony, private schools and retail shops.

Notable buildings
Institute for American Indian Studies, 38 Curtis Road, off Route 199, I-84 Exit 15 (860-868-0518). Re-creation of a seventeenth-century Algonkian village, artifacts and art. If you are interested in Connecticut's Native American past, you should visit this museum.

Gunn Historical Museum (1781), corner of Wykeham Road & Route 47, I-84 Exit 15 (860-868-7756). Local history, period furnishings.

Historic districts
Calhoun-Ives Historic District, 79–262 Calhoun Street and 11 and 12 Ives Road.

New Preston Hill Historic District, New Preston Hill, Findley and Gunn Hill Roads.

Sunny Ridge Historic District, 2–20 Nettleton Hollow Road, 145 Old Litchfield Road, 6 Romford Road and 10–32 Sunny Ridge Road.

Washington Green Historic District, roughly along Ferry Bridge, Green Hill, Kirby, Roxbury, Wykeham and Woodbury Roads, Parsonage Lane and The Green.

Watertown
Routes 6, 262, 63, 73
Incorporated 1780

Native Americans
Paugasuck. The land on both sides of the Naugatuck River, which included present-day Watertown, was called Mattatuck, meaning "badly wooded" (that is, heavily forested).

Historical notes

Watertown, the northeastern corner of Waterbury, was known as Wooster and Wooster Swamp. Here Edward Wooster of Derby gathered or possibly grew hops. In 1738 the Ecclesiastical Society of Westbury was formed, and 42 years later, when the town was sectioned off from Waterbury and incorporated, the name was changed to Watertown.

Watertown was famous for its "Connecticut Red" oxen and for merino sheep. The Oakville section (along Route 73, northwest of Waterbury) was a bustling manufacturing village. Here, the Oakville Pin Factory, one of the first in the nation, produced pins. Other goods included wire and pruning shears. Sawmills, tanneries and grist mills were important to the early economy of Watertown. Later, silk, shellac, gold beads, silver spoons, brass buttons, leather goods and rayon were important products.

Nathaniel Wheeler, a sewing machine pioneer and native son, manufactured the lock-stitch sewing machine in Watertown in 1850 before moving his concern to Bridgeport.

Revolutionary War poet John Trumbull was born in 1750 in a house on Main Street (now vanished), 140 feet northeast of the memorial fountain. Reputed to be a phenomenal scholar at an early age, he passed an exam for entrance to Yale when only seven, but deferred attendance until he was thirteen. Trumbull became one of the Hartford Wits and was best known for his satirical poem "M'Fingal."

Ghost stories and legends

James Bishop, proprietor of the Bishop Tavern (originally on the Litchfield-New Haven Turnpike at the foot of Academy Hill, but later moved to Echo Lake Road), was famous for mowing his fifty-acre field of hay in a single day. When he thought the time was right, he sent runners to surrounding towns with notification of the mowing day. Few men or boys resisted the call, and at dawn they lined up, scythes at the ready. A horn blared the signal to begin. Men with rakes followed close behind those with scythes, and by evening, the meadow was dotted with great haystacks. Bishop served the volunteers five meals and lots of cider, rum and other drinks.

One year, Bishop got it into his head to transport the hay down to New Haven in a single load. He had a huge wagon built. Roads were widened, bridges shored up, and a few trees cut down. A small building was even moved! When everything was ready, twelve yokes of oxen were hitched to the loaded wagon, their yokes festooned with crimson streamers. Musicians sat astride the oxen, and played peppy tunes. Bishop, accompanied by other outriders, rode in front of the wagon in a fancy coach drawn by two grays. Crowds cheered and waved at the procession as it lumbered along the route to New Haven. All this for a giant load of hay!

Winchester

Routes 8, 20, 183, 263

Incorporated 1771, borough of Winsted incorporated as a city in 1858

Native Americans

Several tribes probably used this area as a summer residence. An Indian chipping ground, where projectile points were manufactured, was located near Highland Lake, about three miles from the center of Winsted, and a quarter mile west of the lake shore.

Historical notes

Part of the lands granted to Hartford by the Connecticut General Assembly for "plantations … or villages" and divided in 1732. Because the land was so rough and thick with hemlock, pine and mountain laurel (hence the name Green Woods), settlement did not begin until mid century. Four forges were built between 1795 and 1812 to manufacture refined bar iron.

In 1785 land was purchased for the Winchester Center green and for a meeting house. The whipping post was out front. By 1810, however, Winchester Center was eclipsed by Winsted, in the eastern part of town. The name comes from combining Winchester and Barkhamsted.

Winchester/Winsted manufactured scythes, thread, clocks, leather for bookbinding and pins. The Gilbert Clock Company, derived from the earlier Hoadleys and Whitings Clock Company, founded in 1807, was renowned for the fine craftsmanship and precision of the clocks they made.

Widow Hannah Averit arrived in Winchester with her seven children shortly after the death of her husband in 1765. Penniless, she had come to the lands that her husband had purchased in the wilds. Hannah Averit was the only woman to sign the oath of fidelity to the State of Connecticut.

Jonathan Coe, III, was an outspoken abolitionist. His house, which stood on the right side of Coe Street, near the junction with Marshall Street, was a station on the underground railroad.

Inventions, inventors and firsts

Ribbon candy was invented in a local candy store in the late 1880s.

Ghost stories and legends

One winter evening, while Caleb Beach and his family sat at the dinner table, they heard the sounds of weaving coming from the loom room. When they got up from the table to see who was there, the room was empty, but the door was wide open. Looking out, they saw the fresh tracks of a cloven hoof in the snow and "a slight mark as if a forked tail had been drawn across the powdery surface." A woman of the parish, suspected of the devilish visit, was whipped for witchcraft.

Other stories come from the "Green Woods" of Winchester, of tame trout, talking owls, five legged cows, and the mysterious Winchester Wild Man. The first reported sighting of the frightening, very large, hairy and elusive Wild Man was in 1895, and sporadic reports have continued well into the twentieth century.

Notable buildings

The Solomon Rockwell House (c. 1813), 225 Prospect Street, located off Route 44 (860-379-8433), looks more like a southern mansion than a home in New England. The door casings, fireplaces and stairways were elaborately carved with a penknife. Solomon Rockwell owned an iron foundry. The house is the headquarters of the Winchester Historical Society and houses a museum.

The Winchester Center Kerosene Lamp Museum & Lighting Emporium, 100 Old Waterbury Turnpike/ Route 263 (860-379-2612), houses an idiosyncratic collection of lamps mostly made between 1850 and 1880. The museum is on the green in a building that was once a grist mill.

Historic districts

The Winchester Green area, Routes 44 and 8 and Main Street.

The West End Commercial District on the North side of Main Street between Union and Elm Streets.

Woodbury

Routes 6, 47, 64, 132, 317
Incorporated 1673

Native Americans

Potatuck. The Europeans called Woodbury Pomeraug Plantation, after Chief Pomeraug, who sold the lands. The first deed was supposedly lost (if it ever existed) but was referred to in five subsequent deeds. The

Potatucks retained a tract of land, the Potatuck Reservation, but by 1758 their numbers had declined to such an extent that they left to join others elsewhere. Castle Rock, on the west bank of the Pomeraug River south of the center of town, according to tradition was used as a fortress by Chief Pomeraug. Chief Pomeraug is believed to be buried on the west side of Main Street/Route 6.

Near the Nonnewaug Falls, on the Nonnewaug River, is said to be the last resting ground of Chief Nonnewaug. The Falls, which drop 100 feet, are off Route 61, just after the Bethlehem/ Woodbury town line.

Historical notes

Purchased by several Stratford families in 1659, possibly because of religious dissension. In the spring 1673, fifteen families settled in the Pomeraug Valley, laying their house lots along both sides of the Indian trail. Much of the original town was later set off to form Washington, Southbury, Roxbury and Middlebury. Fearing attacks from Indians, a number of the settlers built palisades around their houses. In 1675, during King Philip's War, many returned to Stratford for refuge, but were ordered back to Woodbury by the General Court in 1678.

Primarily agricultural, the woods were harvested as fuel for the metal industries in neighboring towns. Shears, knives and so-called German silver were made in Woodbury.

Ghost stories and legends

The beautiful red-headed Moll Cramer had a special way with horses. Her husband, Bill, kept horses and raced them, and if a horse was too small or young for a man, Moll took the reins. She always won. She was a sight—long red trusses flowing behind her, her horse in the lead—and men's heads turned in admiration. Bill grew wildly jealous, and finally arranged it so that Moll couldn't race. He lost every one of his races thereafter. Moll missed the racing and worked in the stable cleaning tack to be near her beloved horses. She worked to keep herself strong, hoping to take the reins once again. Bill ignored her.

One day, when a drunken blacksmith came to shoe a small horse, Moll objected. The drunk shoed the horse anyway, and as Moll had feared and predicted, the horse threw the shoe during the race and injured his foot. Bill blamed Moll, said she had cast a spell, called her a witch, and in a rage, he beat her face with a whip.

Moll did the in those days unthinkable, and left her belligerent husband. She built herself a brush hut on Good Mountain. Bill continued to lose races, went into debt and sold his horses. One by one, as the horses were sold, they'd escape and run to Moll. People began to say that she was a witch, that she had powers.

Moll cut her hair short like a man, and tried one last time to race, but no one would let her. Filled with sorrow, she returned to her cabin. People said

that in all their memories, it had never stormed on Good Mountain, but now, fierce storms seemed to emanate from the spot where Moll kept her cabin. People called her the Beautiful Witch of Woodbury, and they feared her.

Good Mountain was too harsh for gardening, and so Moll begged for food, just a little, enough to keep a bit of flesh on her bones. If you refused her, bad luck was sure to follow. Children and animals loved her, though, and found their way to her mountain hut, until one day she simply disappeared.

Notable buildings

Glebe House & Gertrude Jekyll Garden (c. 1740), Hollow Road, I-84 Exit 15 (203-263-2855). This gambrel-roofed house served as a parsonage for the Episcopal Reverend John Rutgers Marshall, who, because of his religious beliefs, was suspected of British sympathies and kept under surveillance during the Revolution. The only extant Jekyll Garden in the U.S. is at Glebe House.

Jabez Bacon House (1762), Hollow Road, near the junction with Route 6. Large gambrel-roofed mansion. Bacon owned ships and warehouses, profiteered during the Revolutionary War, and kept slaves. It is said that he was the first millionare in America.

Canfield Corner Pharmacy (c. 1875), Intersection of Routes 6 and 47. Oldest continuously operating pharmacy in Connecticut. Mary Tyrrell, the pharmacist, is a wealth of information about local town history. After you have had a soda at the original soda fountain, you can walk around the park, and view the many eighteenth- and nineteenth-century houses. Number 100 was built circa 1770, number 50 in 1791.

Hurd House (1675), Hollow Road (203-266-0305). This is the oldest structure on its original site in Litchfield County. Hurd was the town miller. In the eighteenth century, the blacksmith Michael Skelly lived and worked here with his family. In addition to the Hurd House, the Historical Society has restored the No. 2 South Center Distric School (c. 1867) and the brick Archives Building (c. 1888). Brochures for self-guided walking tours are available.

Historic districts

Both sides of Main Street/Route 6 for two miles, and including radiating roads. Also both sides of Main Street from the Woodbury/Southbury town line to Middle Quarter.

The Hotchkissville Historic District is roughly bounded by West Wood, Paper Mill, Weekeepeemee, Washington and Jack's Bridge Roads.

Middlesex County

The county is 373 square miles and has 15 towns: Chester, Clinton, Cromwell, Deep River, Durham, East Haddam, East Hampton, Essex, Haddam, Killingworth, Middlefield, Middletown, Old Saybrook, Portland and Westbrook.

The Connecticut River, its mouth, and a stretch of the Connecticut shore enrich Middlesex County. From the sandstone quarries in Portland, at the northern extremity of the county, to the harbor of Old Saybrook, this, the smallest county in the state, has a varied landscape.

The limited-access Route 9 crosses Middlesex County in its entirety, from Cromwell south to Old Saybrook where it connects with Interstate 95. For an afternoon glimpse of the county and its history, pick up Route 154 in Haddam near the Middletown line and follow it through Haddam, Chester, Deep River, Essex and Old Saybrook.

You could also take Route 17 through Portland from the Glastonbury line. Leave Route 17 for 17A to enjoy one of the best up-close drives along the Connecticut River. Route 17 will then reconnect with 17A. Follow it across the bridge to Middletown and on through Durham, where you can either continue on to New Haven County or take Route 79 to Route 146 through Killingworth and Chester.

Chester
Routes 148, 154
Incorporated 1836

Native Americans
Known as Pataconk or Pattyquonck in the seventeenth century.

Historical notes
Settled by families from Saybrook in 1740, water power from the streams in town powered saw mills and grist mills. After the Revolution, ship building became an important industry. Sheep raising, the manufacture of tools, wire goods and manicure sets, and the quarrying of granite were also important industries. The Chester Ferry, which began in 1769, is still in operation. Today, this once industrial town bills itself as the "left bank of the Connecticut River."

Inventions, inventors and firsts
Samuel Silliman developed three types of inkwells, the "School

Inkstand," the "Desk Inkstand," and most importantly, the "Soldiers' Pocket Inkwell." In an era before the ballpoint pen, Silliman's pocket inkwell enabled Civil War soldiers to carry writing implements without fear of ink spills. Perhaps it is his inkwell that is responsible for the abundance of letters that were written home from the battlefield.

Clinton

Routes 1, 81
Incorporated 1838

Native Americans

Hammonasset, headed by the sachem Sebequanash ("the man who weeps"). By the time the English arrived in 1633 the Hammonassetts were few in number. When the Mohegan sachem Uncas married the daughter of Sebequanash, the area came under his control.

Historical notes

Originally the southern part of Killingworth. Although most households in Clinton/Killingworth supported the Revolution, two men were sent to the New London gaol for transporting Tories to Long Island. Several other men were locked up in Willington, but were released when they changed their minds and were sympathetic to the cause.

Visitors included George Washington twice, probably Lafayette, said to have dined in Clinton, the Old Leatherman (see Haddam), and

Madam Knight. Benjamin Franklin was a frequent visitor.

The legend is that Franklin was riding through town when his horse suddenly turned in at the home of the Reverend Jared Eliot. It turned out that Eliot had previously owned the horse, who may have been just a bit homesick. The men struck up a conversation and became friends. Eliot was an experimental farmer and physician.

Madam Knight wrote, "wee put forward with all speed and about seven at night came to Killingworth and were tollerably well with Travillers fare and Lodged there that night." This was strong praise from the woman whose account of her trip is primarily a list of complaints and criticisms of the accommodations she encountered.

Shipping and shipbuilding commenced in 1700. There were three boat yards on the Indian River, which goes through the center of town. Four or five ships were built in a year.

Witch hazel was gathered in the back woods and distilled. Later the Pond Extract Company consolidated several small operations, though individuals continued to gather witch hazel from the woods.

Notable buildings

Stanton House (c. 1790), 63 East Main Street, I-95 Exit 63 (860-669-2132). Classes for Yale were first conducted on this site. Parts of the original seventeenth-century building, where the Reverend Pierson taught

Collegiate School classes, were incorporated into the Stanton House. The ell of the house was the Adam Stanton store. It is outfitted with shelves, drawers and counters. Collections of eighteenth- and nineteenth-century furnishings and antique dinnerware are exhibited.

Historic districts

Clinton Village Historic District, along Cemetery Road, Church, East Main and Liberty Streets, Old Post Road and Waterside Lane.

Cromwell

Routes 3, 99, 372
Incorporated 1851

Native Americans

Wangunks

Historical notes

Originally the Upper Houses area of Middletown, settled in 1650. Shipbuilding was the chief industry. One of the first steamboats, the *Oliver Cromwell,* was built here by William C. Redfield. Redfield also conceived of the idea of pulling barges with tugboats on the Hudson River. And he was one of the first to dream of a railroad connection to the west.

A. N. Pierson, a Swedish immigrant, founded the Pierson Nurseries in 1871. By the 1930s, the three-hundred-acre Pierson Nursery had thirty acres under glass, and produced ten million roses, giving Cromwell the nickname of the Rose Town. Other cut flowers were also grown. The nursery continues today as one of the world's largest.

Notable buildings

Frisbie House (c. 1853), 395 Main Street (860-635-0501). This ornate house was built for John Stevens, who manufactured cast-iron goods, mostly toys. His firm, the J&E Stevens Company, manufactured the first mechanical bank in 1869.

Historic districts

Main Street Historic District, roughly bounded by Prospect Hill Road, Main, Wall and West Streets, Stevens and New Lanes, and Nooks Hill Road.

Middletown Upper Houses Historic District (Upper Houses River Port), Route 99.

Deep River

Routes 80, 145, 154
Incorporated 1859 as Saybrook. The name was changed to Deep River in 1947.

Native Americans

Hammonassetts

Historical notes

Deep River was originally Saybrook. In 1665 the Saybrook lands east of the Connecticut River were set off as Lyme and Old Lyme. The western lands, from the Connecticut River to Killingworth and from the Sound to Haddam, remained Saybrook. In the mid nineteenth century, Chester, Westbrook, Essex and Old Saybrook were set off.

Old Saybrook encompassed the oldest part of town. Saybrook included the villages of Deep River and

Winthrop. But Old Saybrook was often called simply Saybrook, and Saybrook was called by the village name of Deep River, so to end confusion, the name was officially changed in 1947. The town was also once called Eight-Mile Meadow and Potopaug Quarter. (It's stories like this that confuse non-New Englanders!)

Phineas Pratt was making combs in 1809 and employed twenty workers. An outgrowth of this endeavor, the factory of the Pratt, Read Company, began making piano keys in 1866, importing the tusks of elephants from British East Africa. It was reputed that Deep River and Ivorytown imported half of Zanzibar's ivory output. Little did the inhabitants of this enterprising village suspect that the mighty elephant would be in danger of disappearing from the earth forever. George Read (1787–1859) was active in the Underground Railroad as well as influential in the ivory trade. Later, the company manufactured piano-action parts. The factory left in 1938.

Other businesses and industries prospered in the village. By the mid nineteenth century there were a total of eight quarries. Shipbuilding and the manufacture of buttonhooks, wire goods and crochet needles were also important.

Historic districts

Pratt, Read Company factory complex, Main Street between Bridge and Spring Streets and 5 Bridge Street.

Durham
Routes 17, 68, 77, 79, 157
Incorporated 1708

Native Americans
Wangunks

Historical notes
Coginchauge ("long swamp") was sold by the sachem Terramuggus to Richard and Samuel Wyllys in 1672–1673, though the 1662 Court had already granted the six hundred acres of upland and one hundred acres of meadow to the Wyllys family and two other men. Coginchaug was renamed Durham, after the English town, in 1704.

Nearly every male between the ages of sixteen and sixty participated in the Revolution. When the American Army was at Valley Forge, the people of Durham sent two oxen overland five hundred miles to feed George Washington and his officers. The General and his men thought it a fine meal.

Moses Austin, who was born in a house on the west side of Main Street, was a mining adventurer and businessman. He obtained permission to settle three hundred families in the Spanish province of Texas, where he planned to set up mines. He died before he could begin his colonization but his son, Stephen Austin, carried out his dreams, which is why the capitol of Texas bears the name of this Durham family.

Inventions, inventors and firsts

The Durham Book Company was organized in 1733 to purchase and circulate books, the first lending library in Connecticut.

In 1798 the Durham Aqueduct Company was formed to pump water from distant wells and springs and deliver it through a gravity-fed system of pipes. This was Connecticut's first water company.

Ghost stories and legends

The two churches in town were rivals. The parishioners of each wanted to have the highest steeple. The South Church won but alas, the steeple was so tall and so heavy it toppled one windy day in 1842. Lifted and spun by the gale, the spire fell like an arrow and impaled the roof. There it remained for days, upside down, a lesson to all of the folly of vanity.

Historic districts

Main Street Historic District, along Main Street, roughly bounded by Talcott Lane, Higganum Road and Maple Avenue.

East Haddam

Routes 82, 149, 151
Incorporated 1734

Native Americans

Several small clans belonging to the Wangunks or possibly the Mattabeseck. They believed that the spirit Hobbamock lived in the hill Machemoodus, "the place of noises" (now Mount Tom). The area was reputedly a center of many councils.

Historical notes

East Haddam was sectioned off from Haddam. It was purchased from the local Indians for thirty coats. The first settlers built their houses along Creek Row in 1685 (on the hill behind the Cove Burying Ground). Shipbuilding, trade with the West Indies, fishing, and the manufacture of hardware, cotton and muskets brought wealth and prosperity.

Venture Smith, born in Dukandara, Guinea, in 1728, and given the birth name of Broteeer, lived in Haddam Neck, in Haddam. His father was King Saungm Furro of Guinea. Unfortunately, his royalty had not saved him from capture. Sold into slavery, he belonged to a sea captain until, by his industry, he was able to earn enough money to purchase freedom for himself and his wife and children. Venture Smith was a large man, over six feet tall, and so wide that he had to turn sideways to fit through a doorway.

His strength was legendary, and it was said that he once cut four hundred cords of wood in a few weeks. People also said he could carry a barrel of molasses on each shoulder. But whether his reputed strength was true or the stuff of legend, it is his literary prowess that most impresses us today. His autobiography, which he dictated, sold briskly and went through several printings, the last as recently as in the late twentieth century (although it is currently out of print).

One of Venture Smith's sons served in the Revolutionary War. Another served in the War of 1812. Smith died in 1805 at the age of 77 and was buried in the First Church Cemetery on Route 151, in the Little Haddam section of East Haddam.

Geology

The Moodus noises (from Machemoodus) have been heard since before the arrival of the English. All sorts of explanations have been offered for the subterranean noises, including many colorful legends. Geologists tell us that Moodus is one of the most active earthquake zones in New England. They believe that the noises are caused by movements of the earth. Although they have identified many faults in the area they have not located the fault associated with the noises. We do know, however, that the earth has moved.

On May 16, 1791 a violent earthquake shook Moodus and the surrounding area. According to one local account, fish were thrown from the river as far as Killingworth, chimneys toppled, doors unlatched, stone walls collapsed and a fissure opened. Moderate to large earthquakes occurred again in the spring of 1917. Many tremors and micro-quakes have occurred over the years, five hundred in 1981 and 1982.

Ghost stories and legends

There are so many stories and legends about the Moodus noises that I will relate only one. There was, deep in the bowels of Mount Tom, a cave, and in the depths of the cave, a glowing carbuncle, a fiery red garnet, with great and magical powers.

Here, in the glowing light of the mysterious crystal, the evil witches of Devil's Hopyard confronted the good witches of Moodus, while the Devil himself looked on. Tired of the whole affair, the Devil extinguished the carbuncle, and the witches, suddenly cast into darkness, shrieked and wailed, and flew about, creating the most awful noises, which reverberated through the hills.

Notable buildings

Gillette Castle (c. 1919), 67 River Road, Route 9 Exit 6 or 7 (860-526-2336). Elaborate, castle-like hilltop mansion of fieldstone. Built by the actor William Gillette, famous for his portrayal of Sherlock Holmes. Now a state park. Gillette called the house "Seventh Sister."

Goodspeed Opera House (c. 1877), Route 82 (860-863-2336). Nathaniel Goodspeed was one of the earliest settlers of Goodspeed's Landing, where a ferry operated for years. His sons became successful shipbuilders and had a yard in East Haddam. One of the sons, William Goodspeed, built the Opera House to enhance the appeal of his Lower Landing and make it competitive with the Upper Landing, which boasted the Maplewood Music Seminary.

When the ornate six-story opera house opened, with much fanfare, it housed the theater, the family's store, a bar, the offices of the Hartford and New York Steamboat Company, and a freight and passenger station. It was an instant success. By 1943, however, it had become a state-owned storage facility for the Highway Department. In 1958, it was scheduled for demolition. After public hearings, a million-dollar restoration was undertaken and the theater reopened in 1963.

Nathan Hale Schoolhouse (c. 1750), Main Street/Route 149, rear of St. Stephen's Church (860-873-9547). Nathan Hale taught in this little red schoolhouse in the winter of 1773–1774.

Historic districts

East Haddam Historic District, Route 149, Broom, Norwich, Creamery, Lumberyard and Landing Hill Roads.

Hadlyme North Historic District, roughly bounded by Route 82, Town Street, Banning Road and Old Town Street.

Little Haddam Historic District, roughly bounded by East Haddam Road, Orchard Road and Town Street.

Millington Green Historic District, roughly bounded by Millington, Tater Hill, Hayardvile and Old Hopyard Roads.

Wickham Road Historic District, roughly the junction of Wickham and Geoffrey Roads.

East Hampton
Routes 16, 66, 151, 196
Incorporated 1767 as Chatham.

Native Americans
Wangunks and Mattabeseck, who were also probably Wangunks. The General Court stated in 1644 that "there was a parcel of land at Wonggum reserved for the posterity of Sowheage." Sowheage was the chief of the Wangunks. This reservation was in Indian Hill in Chatham and in part of Portland. Other Mattabeseck lived or frequented Pocotopaug (divided pond). The sachem Terramuggus owned the largest island in the lake.

Historical notes
Part of Middletown, the area was sectioned off and incorporated as Chatham, named after the Earl of Chatham. The village of Middle Haddam, along the eastern banks of the Connecticut River served the towns further east as a water gateway and as a center of shipbuilding and trade. The breakwater at Middle Haddam was made from brownstone quarried in Portland and is famous for the dinosaur footprints encased in the facings.

In 1808, William Barton came to Chatham and began to make hand bells and sleigh bells. He was joined by other bell shops and casting shops, and soon there were so many bellmakers in the village of East Hampton that it became known as "Bell Town."

Lake Pocotapaug was a popular recreational area. Before the Civil War, winter horse races were held on the ice. A thousand or more spectators would gather to watch and cheer their favorites. There were numerous hotels and cottages dotting the shores, offering accommodations and hospitality to the winter tourists.

In 1915, the town was named East Hampton after the primary village in town.

Geology

Cobalt, north of Middle Haddam, and further inland from the river, was the site of considerable mining and quarrying activity. According to tradition, Governor John Winthrop himself spent weeks in the woods assaying minerals. Cobalt was discovered in 1661, but was too impure for commercial use.

In 1762, the mines were reopened, and the cobalt used in making blue paint and shipped to China to color the popular blue and white export pottery. A little more than a half a mile from the old cobalt mines, furnaces were built in 1844 to smelt nickel. Numerous minerals were found in these hills, including garnets.

Ghost stories and legends

A legend from colonial times tells us that the local Indians were deeply upset with the number of drownings in Lake Pocotopaug. They appealed to the Great Spirit. The Great Spirit promised an end to the drownings, but demanded the Chief's daughter in exchange. The chief, torn between loyalties, was loathe to sacrifice his beloved daughter, but felt duty-bound to his tribe. Before he could make his wrenching decision, his daughter spared him and their people by plunging to her death in the deep, cold water. For years after, until modern times, no one drowned in the lake.

Notable buildings

Comstock Bridge, off Route 16. This beautiful covered bridge crosses the Salmon River to Colchester. Pedestrian traffic only!

Historic districts

Belltown Historic District, roughly bounded by West High and Main Streets, Bevin Court, Skinner, Crescent, Barton Hill and Maple Streets.

Middle Haddam Historic District, Moodus and Long Hill Roads.

Essex

Routes 153, 154
Incorporated 1852

Native Americans

Hammonasetts

Historical notes

Called Potopaug by the Indians. Daughter town of Saybrook, Essex was the main port of Saybrook until 1871. Shipbuilding and trade with the West Indies began in the seventeenth century. In 1656, the first wharf was constructed, at the site of the Steamboat Dock on Main Street.

A warehouse was built south of the wharf in 1773. Essex sea captains sailed the world and were gone for months at a time, returning with cargoes of molasses and ivory. With their accumulated wealth, they built themselves showy and spacious houses, many of which survive to this day. Numerous shipyards made Essex one of the most important shipbuilding centers in New England.

This was not unnoticed by the British. During the War of 1812, they burned seventy ships in the Essex coves two years after the war began. The townspeople managed to drive them away, but the loss was considered the worst disaster to befall the country during the war. The financial loss was put at $160,000, a very considerable sum in those days.

The manufacture of ivory piano keys and piano action parts dominated Ivoryton, the little village in the west of Essex. Ivory was imported from Africa by the ton, thus giving the town its name. In 1859, Ivoryton and nearby Centerbrook became part of Essex.

Notable buildings

Connecticut River Museum, 67 Main Street, Steamboat Dock (c. 1878) Route 9 Exit 3 (860- 767-8269). Exhibits. Steamboat Dock is the third landing place to be built on this site since 1656. It served the steamboat era which began in 1823. Smaller steamboats sailed between Hartford and Saybrook. Larger steamboats traveled from Hartford to New York. A replica of the Turtle, the 1775 submarine, is on exhibit.

Valley Railroad, Essex Steam Train and Riverboat Ride, 1 Railroad Avenue, Route 9 Exit 3 (860-767-0103). Experience a bygone era in Connecticut transportation. Train and riverboat rides.

Haddam
Routes 81, 154
Incorporated 1668

Native Americans

Wangunks. Cockaponsit (Ponsett, West Haddam) was frequented by the Wangunks. Over the years many artifacts have been found.

Historical notes

After several members of the Colony petitioned the General Court and asked to settle a plantation at Thirty Mile Island, agents for the Colony purchased the land. They paid two Wangunk women, Sepunnemoe and Towkishk, and several men, including Taramaugus and Unlaus, thirty coats. The year was 1662. Thirty Mile Island included East Haddam, which was set off in later years. Haddam Neck, however, remains part of Haddam, making it the only town in Connecticut to straddle the Connecticut River.

Most of Haddam's history takes place west of the river. The village of Higganum (Higganumpus, or "fishing place") was a center of shipbuilding and manufacturing. Hoes, gun barrels and chandeliers were produced. Cordwood was cut and shipped in vast quantities to New York City, where it was burned for heat. Shad fisheries flourished. For many years a ferry crossed from the landing. Tradition has it that at least two houses here were part of the underground railroad.

Outside the village, farmers gathered the brush of the witch-hazel tree for extra income. The sticks were chopped into tiny pieces and steamed and boiled in great kettles. The liquor from this process was then distilled and used as a mild astringent in the healing arts.

Haddam Center, the "Upper Plantation," was settled in the 1660s. In 1785, when Middlesex County was established, Haddam shared the position of county seat with Middletown. The responsibility resided in each town for half the year. Like so many towns and villages along the river, sea captains, seamen and their families resided here. Shipbuilding and sea trade lasted only thirty years, from about 1790 to 1810.

Geology

In the nineteenth century, granite quarries were active in Haddam. The granitic gneiss was shipped up and down the the east coast and used for curbs, foundation blocks and pavers. Mica and some feldspar were also quarried. The largest quarry was along Mill Creek. It is no longer active.

What is believed to be the largest freestanding boulder in New England is on the east side of Route 154, between Boulder Dell Road and Christian Road. A glacial erratic, it is known as Shopboard Rock because an early tailor is supposed to have cut out a suit for a customer on its flat top.

Notable buildings

The Thankful Arnold House (c. 1794), Hayden Hill and Walkley Hill

The Thankful Arnold House.

Roads. From Route 154 South, turn right onto Hayden Hill Road (860-345-2400). This three-story gambrel, with an unusual bell-shaped roof, is painted an unmistakable mustard yellow. Period furnishings, heirloom flowers and herbs, and a collection of nineteenth-century iron kitchen utensils are on display.

Historic districts

Haddam Center Historic District, roughly two and a half miles along Walkley Hill Road and Route 154/Saybrook Road. The stretch of Route 154 from the Chester/Haddam town line to the Haddam/Middletown town line, a little more than nine miles, has been designated a scenic highway. It runs parallel to the River and passes more than one hundred antique buildings.

A road for more than three hundred years, it was traveled by the Old Leatherman. No one knows for sure who he was, but there are many legends. He dressed in ragged old leather clothes and walked through parts of Connecticut and New York following the same route over and over. He never spoke. People would put out food for him, which he ate, but that was all he would accept. He slept outdoors, often in caves.

Killingworth
Routes 80, 81, 143
Incorporated 1667

Native Americans
Hammonassetts

Historical notes
Killingworth was named for the English town of Kenilworth. Misspelling and mispronunciation led to the corrupted form. Present-day Killingworth was the northern part of the original town until the southern portion was sectioned off as Clinton.

Abel Buell (1742–1822) engraved one of the first maps of the country after the Peace of 1783. When he was a mere lad of twenty, however, neighbors caught the young silver engraver altering five-pound notes. As punishment, he was imprisoned, his forehead was branded with an F for forger, and his ear was cropped.

Because he was so young, the F was placed high enough that he could let his hair cover it, and he was allowed to keep the bit of his ear warm on his tongue so that it might be put back.

While in jail he invented the first lapidary machine. With this, he produced a beautiful gem-studded ring which he gave to the King's attorney. The King then commuted his sentence and he was released from prison early. Buell went on to have a life of both

great accomplishment and more scrapes with the law.

When Longfellow visited (Ely House, c. 1782), he was aghast at the local farmers' custom of shooting birds, which they considered pests. This experience inspired the great poet to write "The Birds of Killingworth."

Middlefield
Routes 66, 147, 157
Incorporated 1866

Native Americans
Wangunks

Historical notes
Settled as part of Middletown in 1700. Numerous industries grew up along the Coginchaug River. A grist mill was first to take advantage of the abundant water power at the Falls. It was followed by a short-lived snuff mill in 1779, which was later turned into a button factory.

Jehoshaphat Stow is thought to be the first businessman to make cut nails in this country. He built his factory in 1798. Paper and powder were made along the Coginchaug. In 1860 Universal Clothes Wringers claimed a world market for the wringers produced in its washing machine plant in Baileyville.

Dinosaur tracks were found near the base of Powder Hill and were preserved as an exhibit at the Peabody Museum.

Notable buildings
David Lyman II House (c. 1785), 5 Lyman Road. Eight carpenters came from Cromwell to carve the paneling

inside this house. The task took them several months.

Middletown
Routes 3, 17, 66, 157, 217
Incorporated 1651, as a city in 1784.

Native Americans
Wangunks. The Wangunk lands stretched from south of Hartford to south of Middletown. Sowheag, their sachem, was first encountered by European settlers when he lived at Pyquag (Wethersfield). After quarreling with the settlers, he moved to Mattabessett (Middletown). His fort was on Indian Hill, where a cemetery now overlooks Wesleyan University.

Montowese, Sowheag's son, held a large area southwest of Mattabessett. Mattabessett is first mentioned in the Public Records in 1639. "The manifold insolences that haue been offered of late by the Indians ... it was concluded that 100 men be levyed and sent down to Mattabesecke, where severall guilty persons reside and haue beene harbored by Soheage."

Settlement was delayed until 1650. In 1662, eleven Wangunks, nine men and two women, sold a tract of land which extended six miles on each side of the Connecticut River down to Pattyquounck (Chester). They reserved thirty acres in Pattyquounck and Thirty Mile Island. Successive sales left the Wangunks with three reservations in Middletown and Chatham (Haddam). One of these reservations was in the Newfield portion of

Middletown where Wangunks lived as late as 1713.

One of the last Wangunk sachems was Doctor Robbins, who died sometime prior to 1757. His son, Richard Ranney, was brought up among Europeans. He learned to read and write English and mastered the trade of joiner. He became a professor of religion. By 1772, the Wangunks were gone from Connecticut. The last was Mary Cuschoy, an old woman who lived in Chatham.

Historical notes
Mattabessett was named Middletown because it was halfway between Saybrook and the River towns. Settled by Puritans from Hartford and Wethersfield, by 1750 Middletown was the wealthiest and largest city in the state, a distinction it held for fifty years.

Ships sailed for the West Indies and China. A booming export business was conducted in cattle and horses. Rum, sugar, molasses and salt were imported. Yankee peddlers fanned out across the countryside.

Even George Washington was impressed. He was in Middletown in October of 1789, and wrote glowingly in his diary, "Monday, nineteenth. At one we arrived at Middletown, on Connecticut River, being met two or three miles from it by the respectable Citizens of the place ... While dinner was getting ready I took a walk round the Town, from the heights of which the prospect is beautiful. Belonging to this place, I was informed that there were about 20 sea vessels … The country hereabouts is beautiful and the Lands good." He went on to exclaim at the crops and said there were 250–260 houses, and guessing that there would be eight persons to a house, he estimated the population at a minimum of two thousand.

Good clay was discovered in 1751 by Joseph Wright, who commenced brick-making on his Westfield property. He built himself a fine brick house on the west side of Main Street, near the intersection of Washington Street.

Wesleyan University was founded in 1831. Parents were scolded in the first catalog, "When will parents learn, that money in the pockets of inexperienced youth is a suicidal dagger that oftener than otherwise destroys scholarship, character, health and life." That first year there were forty-eight students, three professors, one tutor and two buildings. A student's annual expenses totaled $120.50.

Samuel Russell left his hometown and moved to Canton (China), where he established Russell & Company, a trading center. It was one of only four such American enterprises to succeed. Russell remained with his company in Canton for twenty-five years, living as a recluse.

When he returned to Middletown, he built himself a luxurious mansion, Russell House (c. 1828), on High Street, near the corner of Washington Street. He founded Russell Manufac-turing in 1841 to weave elastic webbing. At first using hand looms, he soon switched to machine-operated looms.

Samuel Russell was also the president of the local bank. During the panic of 1857, when the bank faced collapse, he advanced $75,000 of his own money.

Notable buildings

General Mansfield House (1810), 151 Main Street. Route 9 Exit 66 (860-346-0746). Federal-style brick house. Special collections and exhibits with an emphasis on photographs, military history and genealogy.

Benjamin Douglas House, 11 South Main Street. A stop on the Underground Railroad.

West Burying Ground (Washington Street Cemetery), Washington and Vine Streets. The graves of local African-Americans are towards the rear of this cemetery, including many who fought in the Civil War. Fanny Beman is buried here. She was the mother of Amos Beman, one of the best-known black civil-rights leaders of the nineteenth century.

Historic districts

Broad Street Historic District, roughly bounded by High, Washington, Broad, and Church Streets.

Highland Historic District, Atkins Street and Country Club Road.

Main Street Historic District, roughly Main Street between College and Hartford Avenues.

Metro South Historic District, Main and College Streets.

Middletown South Green Historic District, Union Park area on South Main, Crescent Pleasant and Church Streets.

Russell Company Upper Mill, 475 East Main Street, and Russell House, corner of Washington and High Streets.

Wadsworth Estate Historic District, 15, 30, 33, 59, 73, 89 Laurel Grove Road, Wadsworth Falls State Park, and 421 Wadsworth Street.

Washington Street Historic District, roughly bounded by Washington and Main Streets, Washington Terrace and Vine Street.

Wilcox, Crittenden Mill Historic District, 234–315 South Main Street, Pameacha and Highland Avenues. Founded in 1847, this plant manufactured marine hardware.

Old Saybrook

Routes 1, 154
Incorporated 1635

Native Americans

Western Nehantic. Also Pequot. From the time of the Dutch arrival, there was animus between the Europeans and the Native Americans in Pabeshauke (Old Saybrook). In the first years of English settlement, considerable destruction and bloodshed ensued, culminating in the violent Pequot War, in which the English were determined to exterminate the Pequots. During this war, Saybrook Colony lost nine men and

nearly all its cattle, buildings and corn. The Pequot losses were far more devastating.

Historical notes

Pabeshauke, Old Saybrook, is the oldest part of the original Say-Brooke, a vast tract of land which eventually was sectioned off into other towns.

In 1614, Adrian Block sailed from Manhattan, up the Connecticut River as far as the Enfield Rapids. His exploration was the basis for Dutch claims to Connecticut. In 1623, a company of "two families and six men" were sent by the Dutch of Manhattan to take possession of the lands at the mouth of the River, where Old Saybrook now lies.

Their arrival was not welcomed by the Indians, who frightened them away. Ten years later, another Dutch party landed and named the point Kievet's Hook because of the cries of the sandpipers. To signify their claim, they fastened the Dutch coat of arms to the crotch of a tree.

Alarmed at the Dutch presence, the English granted a patent to Lord Say and Sele (one man), and Lord Brooke, who in turn prevailed upon John Winthrop, Jr., to act as governor. Winthrop arrived, named the place Saye-Brooke (before Hartford, Windsor or Wethersfield were named). He tore down the Dutch coat of arms and placed a grinning face on the tree.

Lion Gardiner arrived a few months later, bringing with him "Iron worke for 2 drawbridges." The English had barely finished making a rudimentary fort when a Dutch ship sailed into the harbor. The English hoisted the Union Jack and manned their guns. The Dutch retreated.

The original idea was to make Saybrook a refuge for the aristocratic sympathizers of Oliver Cromwell, and perhaps for Cromwell himself. There were to be baronial estates. Only one aristocrat actually arrived, Colonel George Fenwick. His wife was known for the roses and daffodils which she brought with her and grew in profusion, and for the wildflowers that she cultivated. She died after only a few years.

Life was difficult. The winters were harsh and the settlers were at war with the Pequots. As soon as his contract was up, Gardiner removed himself to the island which now bears his name.

Saybrook was a colony until 1644, when it agreed to come under the jurisdiction of the Connecticut Colony.

The Collegiate School (Yale, see Branford) opened in Old Saybrook in 1701. After a smallpox outbreak and political pressure to move the college to either Hartford, New Haven or Wethersfield, with each town vying for the fledgling school, it was decided to move the college to New Haven. However, when delegates were sent to move the books, many of them donated by the English philanthropist Elihu Yale, Saybrook residents put up a fight.

They refused to part with the books or the college. When the Yale delegates finally managed to break past the town guards and the fortifications they had erected, they began to gather the books to remove them. Not about to give up, the citizens of Saybrook set the delegates' horses free, causing pandemonium. All of the carts were damaged. Returning with new carts, the delegates found that various smaller bridges had been removed, and planks had been taken from the larger bridges, thus blocking their way.

Eventually, the Yale delegates did manage to pack up most of the books, but 250 were missing and never found, though one can surmise that the coveted volumes likely remained in town, where they were secretly enjoyed. In the 1970s a mysterious box of antique books was reputedly found in the town library attic!

Old Saybrook has seen numerous visitors. In 1704, Madam Sarah Kemble Knight complained in her diary, "The Rodes all along this way are very bad, Incumbered wth Rocks and mountainos passages wch were very disagreeable to my tired carcas." George Washington came through twice, in 1756 and in 1776, and probably dined at a tavern in town during his second visit. The Hart family, who resided in a spacious gambrel-roofed house on Main Street, entertained many guests, including Washington Irving.

There were seven daughters in the Hart family. One sister married Isaac Hull, the commander of the *Constitu-*

tion. Another sister fell in love with the South American revolutionary Bolivar, who was a household guest. Her father forbade the marriage, and she pined for Bolivar the rest of her life. Charles Dickens vacationed in Old Saybrook, a sojourn he immortalized in "A Message From the Sea."

Notable buildings

James Pharmacy, 2 Pennywise Lane. This is the birthplace of Ann Petry (1808–1997), the Harlem Renaissance writer best known for her masterpiece, *The Street.* Her aunt, Anna Louise James (1886–1977), was the first African-American woman, and one of the first women, to become a pharmacist. She operated her pharmacy here from 1911 until 1967 when she retired. She was also one of the first women to register to vote when women's suffrage became law in 1920. Ann Petry was also a pharmacist. She immortalized the James Pharmacy in her book for young adults, *The Drugstore Cat.*

General William Hart House (c. 1767), 350 Main Street, I-95 Exit 67 or Route 9 Exit 2 (860-388-2622). Hart was a prosperous merchant and leader in the Revolutionary War.

Fort Saybrook Monument Park, Saybrook Point, Route 156, Route 9 Exit 2 (860-395-3123). The site of the Saybrook Fort and the Connecticut Valley Railroad Roundhouse and Turntable. There are storyboards depicting Old Saybrook history as well as panoramic views of the mouth of

the Connecticut River where so much of this history occurred.

Elisha Bushnell House (c. 1678–1679), 1445 Boston Post Road. At first a one-room central-chimney house, with rooms less than seven feet high, it was later rebuilt as a saltbox. The house has the old wattle and daub construction.

Historic districts

Fenwick Historic District, roughly along Agawam, Neponset and Pettipaug Avenues.

North Cove Historic District, roughly North Cove Road from Church Street to the Connecticut River and adjacent properties on Cromwell Place.

Old Saybrook South Green District, Old Boston Post Road, Pennywise Lane and Main Street. See the notes for the James Pharmacy above.

Old Saybrook has a rich collection of architectural styles. When touring the historic districts, you will see seventeenth-century saltboxes, "Georgian" center-chimney and double-chimney houses, houses built in the Federal and Greek Revival style, and great Victorians.

Portland

Routes 17, 17A, 66
Incorporated 1841

Native Americans

Wangunks. Wangunk means "bend in the river." There were Wangunk settlements on the north and west sides of Indian Hill. On the east side of the hill was a burial ground. There was also a hothouse (sweating place).

Historical notes

Until 1767, Portland was East Middletown. Until 1841, it was Chatham (part of East Hampton). Finally in 1841, it became the town of Portland.

Portland is known for its quarries. Brownstone was at first free to anyone for the taking and used for building. In 1665, the inhabitants voted that only they could have the stone and that they would pay for it. Once quarrying became a commercial venture, the brownstone was shipped to distant cities.

The famous brownstone houses of New York City are made from rock quarried in Portland. Dinosaur footprints were found in the rock—it was said that in one small office building, a fireplace was made entirely of stones bearing dinosaur tracks. By 1850, at the height of the quarrying activity, nearly nine hundred men were employed.

Shipbuilding and sea trade were also important, especially in the northern, Gildersleeve part of town where a shipyard flourished from 1741 until 1930. During the peak, in the mid nineteenth century, packets were launched here for the New York to Charleston Line.

Inventions, inventors and firsts

Meshomasic State Forest is the oldest state forest in New England. Lands were first purchased for it in 1903.

Geology

In addition to the brownstone quarries, Portland is famous for the Strickland quarries, where more minerals have been found than at any other site in Connecticut. Gem collectors have come from all over to search the dumps for minerals to add to their collections. Feldspar has been mined here for pottery. Also, white mica, spodumene, golden beryl crystals, pale blue cleavelandite, lepidolite, wollastonite, zircon and numerous other minerals have been found.

Job's Pond, Route 66, is a large kettle formed when isolated chunks of ice, buried in sand and gravel during the glacial period, melted. The level of Job's Pond, sometimes called Mystery Pond, rises and falls, as much as 15 feet, but neither rainfall nor other weather has any bearing on this fluctuation. It is the largest of a series of glacial kettles in the area.

Historic district

Main Street and Indian Hill Avenue to the Connecticut River. Many interesting old mansions remain in Portland.

Westbrook

Routes 1, 145, 153
Incorporated 1840

Native Americans

Nehantic and later, Pequots. Obed, a sachem, lived in Pochaug with his people until 1676.

Historical notes

Originally settled as part of Saybrook, present-day Westbrook included Pochaug, a parish of Saybrook and Manunkateset, the western side of town. It was known as Pochaug until 1810 when it was named Westbrook.

The first grist mill was built sometime between 1680 and 1690 at the head of the Pochaug River. By the turn of the century a smelting furnace and blacksmith shop were in operation in the Pond Meadow district. A salt works and oil works were on Salt Island as well as warehouses for the goods that trading ships brought. Ship building became an important industry.

Toby Hill, on the west side of Toby Hill Road, is named for a former slave who lived in seclusion here.

George Washington and Lafayette probably dined at taverns in Pochaug.

Inventions, inventors and firsts

David Bushnell (1742–1824), born in Westbrook, made the first submarine, The Turtle. He did much of his designing and dreaming in his uncle's red story-and-a-half cottage in the western part of town.

New Haven County

The county is 610 square miles and has 27 towns: Ansonia, Beacon Falls, Bethany, Branford, Cheshire, Derby, East Haven, Guilford, Hamden, Madison, Meriden, Middlebury, Milford, Naugatuck, New Haven, North Branford, North Haven, Orange, Oxford, Prospect, Seymour, Southbury, Wallingford, Waterbury, Wolcott and Woodbridge.

Primarily urban, most of New Haven County was settled by 1730. The shore towns are particularly rich with history, beginning with the summer feasts of the Indians, and continuing with the arrival of the Europeans and the development of shipbuilding and seafaring industries. If you are interested in either dinosaurs or early native American history, you will want to include the Peabody Museum in New Haven on your trip.

Interstates 95 and 91 and Connecticut Route 15 (Wilbur Cross Highway) serve New Haven county. If you like pretty countryside, old houses and the salt spray of the ocean, take Route 77 in Guilford from the Durham town line, and follow it south across Guilford to Route 146 West along the shore in Branford.

Ansonia

Routes 115, 243
Incorporated 1889, chartered as a city in 1893.

Native Americans

Paugussetts

Historical notes

Ansonia was the Little Neck area of Derby, called Uptown Derby. It was named for Anson Green Phelps. Frustrated in his attempts to build copper and brass mills in Derby, Anson Phelps bought the dam on the Naugatuck River, plus the adjoining lands, and built his industrial empire in peace. Other manufacturers followed, and Ansonia became an important center of industry.

Notable buildings

General David Humphreys House (c. 1698), 37 Elm Street, Route 8 Exit 15 (203-735-1908). Humphreys was a poet, a member of the Hartford Wits, an aide and secretary to Washington, an ambassador to Spain and Portugal. He imported merino sheep and set up one of the first woolen mills in the country in Humphreyville (Seymour).

Richard Mansfield House (c. 1748

), 35 Jewett Street. Built for Mansfield while he was in England for his ordination. He lived in it for seventy-two years.

Historic districts

Upper Main Street Historic District, 36–100, 85–117 Main Street.

Beacon Falls

Routes 42
Incorporated 1871

Native Americans

Beacon Hill Brook was the boundary between the hunting ground of the Paugasuck and Tunxis tribes.

Historical notes

Settled by colonists from Derby, Beacon Falls was created from sections of Naugatuck, Oxford, Seymour and Bethany, the towns that now surround it. Woolen capes were made here before they went out of fashion after the Civil War. They were replaced by the macintosh.

The production of high-grade rubber footware by Top Notch brought prosperity to the village. There was a company band, company store, company theater, even a company hotel until U. S. Rubber bought the business and moved it to Naugatuck.

Toby, an Indian, was the slave of Captain Ebenezer Johnson of Derby for twelve years, then gained his freedom in 1688. In 1693 he paid some Paugasucks ten pounds and a barrel of cider for a large tract of mountainous land in the northwestern corner of Beacon Falls. It became known as Toby's Rock Mountain.

Inventions, inventors and firsts

Thomas Sanford likely invented and did make the first sulphur matches around 1835. His matches were a boon to households everywhere, and quickly made the tedious process of striking flint to steel obsolete. To satisfy the demand, he packed his matches in little barrels that were sold for ten cents by Yankee peddlers.

Sanford saved his money to build himself a huge factory. He bought land on Bladen Brook in Woodbridge and built his factory and a huge wheel for power. Unfortunately, the wheel was too big for the stream. He was reduced to selling his secret recipe for sulphur match heads for a mere ten dollars. This was the recipe that the Diamond Match Company later purchased and which brought them—from then to this day—great success.

Bethany

Routes 63, 69
Incorporated 1832

Native Americans

Quinnipiacs

Historical notes

Part of the land purchases made by the towns of New Haven and Milford, Bethany included present-day Woodbridge and Bethany. Woodbidge and Bethany were separated into two towns in 1832, but in 1844, the Straitsville area was taken for Naugatuck, and in 1871, the western part of Bethany became part of Beacon Falls. Bethany, the Hebrew word for "House of Dates," is the name of the Biblical village at the foot of Mount of Olives.

For some now-forgotten reason, the people of Bethany developed the custom of giving each other nicknames, usually related to their occupation. Barber lists some of the nicknames in his *Connecticut Historical Collections:* "Teachum, Hiccups, Toadmounter, Satan's kingdom, &c were names by which some of the most respectable inhabitants of Bethany were designated. Teachum was the schoolmaster of the place." According to Robert Brinton, the town historian, the custom of giving nicknames continues to this day.

Ghost stories and legends

The infamous Dayton Robbery took place in Bethany in 1780, during the Revolution. While Captain Ebenezer Dayton was away in Boston on business, a gang of seven young Tories (one a deserter from Washington's Army), broke into his house in the middle of the night. They tied up Phoebe Dayton, Ebenezer's wife, and their two little children. After smashing china and furniture for two hours, causing £5,000 worth of damage, they made off with bags of gold.

While the robber Tories were making their escape through the forest, they met Chauncey Judd, a young man on his way home from taking his girlfriend to a quilting bee. They kidnaped him so that he would not identify them, or tell of their whereabouts.

Meanwhile, Ebenezer Dayton returned from Boston to find that his family had been terrorized and his home ransacked. He gathered a band of Patriots together, and they set out to find the culprits.

The Tories hid for a time in an old fruit cellar. They then made their way to the tavern of a Tory sympathizer, but were unexpectedly turned in by one of the slaves who had been mistreated by his master. On the run again, the robbers fled by boat across the sound to Long Island, where they were eventually caught by the Patriots. The leader of the gang was hanged, and the rest were sent to Newgate Prison, from whence they escaped to Nova Scotia.

Chauncey Judd was known after that as the Stolen Boy of the Revolution. Detailed accounts of this story were the stuff of Connecticut gossip. The story has been written about in numerous newspapers and books over the years. It is included in both Glenn E. White's *Folk Tales of Connecticut* and David Philips' *Legendary Connecticut.*

Notable buildings

The self-taught, highly respected builder-architect, David Hoadley (1784–1839), of Waterbury, was responsible for some of the splendid churches and houses of the pre-incorporation period. The Wheeler-Beecher House (c. 1870), 562 Amity Road, is attributed to him. This center-chimney house boasts ten fireplaces and a ballroom.

Old Town Hall (c. 1914), 512 Amity Road (203-393-1832—the phone number cleverly celebrates the date of incorporation), now the headquarters of the Bethany Historical Society. On the same street, near the Episcopal Church, is the only remaining church horse shed in Connecticut. Because services lasted for the better part of the day, all early churches had sheds to shelter the horses while their masters worshiped. Also in the area, on the school grounds, is the restored 1834 School House, which is still used by students on occasion.

Branford

Highways 1, 146
Incorporated 1653

Native Americans

Quinnipiac

Historical notes

A few days after the New Haven colonists purchased Quinnipiac (New Haven) from Momaugin, the sachem of the Quinnipiacs, they gave Mantowese, son of the sachem of the Mattabeseck, and Sausounck "eleven coats of trucking cloth and one coat of English cloth made in the English fashion" as payment for Totoket (Branford). This was in 1638.

In 1644, settlers came from Wethersfield and Long Island. It is believed that ancient Branford was enclosed by a palisade five miles long. The settlers feared both the Indians and the Dutch. In fact, the English had trouble with the Dutch throughout their first decade at Totoket, during which time the Dutch maintained a trading post (Dutch House Wharf).

Shipbuilding and coastal trade were important activities in Branford's harbors. In 1655 Connecticut's first iron furnace was set up at Furnace Pond (called Lonotononket, meaning "tear of the great spirit,"), now Lake Saltonstall (see East Haven), giving manufacturing a boost.

Yale College got its beginning when ten ministers gathered at the home of Rev. Russell to donate books for the new school. The railroad arrived in 1852, followed by more industry. In time, a summer colony grew up along Branford's waterfront.

Ghost stories and legends

Governor Gurdon Saltonstall acquired the Rosewell estate when he married Elizabeth Rosewell. He built a huge house on it, along the eastern shore of Furnace Pond, which straddled Branford and East Haven.

He was deeply interested in bog iron and was responsible for the furnace that was built there. He was also a bit of an insufferable dandy, and despite his eminence, the folks of Branford found him to be a disagreeable old man.

When geese settled on the lawns of his estate and despite his strenuous efforts would not leave, Saltonstall was immeasurably upset. His neighbors thought the situation amusing.

One day, particularly well-dressed for a trip to New Haven, he needed a ferry ride across Stoney River. The ferry was operated by Deborah Chidsey, who was married to the miller. Saltonstall bargained with Dame Chidsey in a most unpleasant and arrogant manner. She felt put upon, and so in midstream she let her little craft run aground on a sandbar.

The governor was beside himself and demanded to know what she was going to do. She chuckled and flapped her arms like the geese that plagued him, and, her skirts hoisted to her knees, waded ashore. Saltonstall would do no such thing himself, and so he sat, in the burning sun, until the tides rose and the ferry was released.

Historic districts

Branford Center Historic District, roughly bounded by Route 1 and Branford River on the east, and on the south by Monroe and Kirkham Streets.

Branford Point Historic District, roughly along Harbor Street, north from Curve Street to Branford Point, also Maple Street east from Reynolds Street to Harbor Street.

Route 146 Historic District (also in Guilford), Route 146 between Flat Rock and West River Bridge.

Stony Creek/Thimble Islands Historic District, roughly Thimble Islands Road between Route 146 and Long Island Sound and the Thimble Islands.

Cheshire
Routes 10, 42, 70
Incorporated 1780

Native Americans
Quinnipiacs

Historical notes

Settled as West Farms of Waterbury in 1695, Cheshire was recognized as the village of New Cheshire in 1723, before becoming the town of Cheshire. Prospect was sectioned off in 1827.

Mining was the most important early industry. Large transparent crystals were taken from the two barite mines, each actually called Barite Mine. The specimens often ended up in museums and collections. Copper was discovered around 1711 or 1712, two miles east of Cheshire village, near the Wallingford line. It was mined as the Copper Valley Mine. Once the Canal reached Cheshire from New Haven in 1825, the ore and minerals could be easily shipped. The mines flourished until, in comparison with the great mines out west, they became unprofitable.

Agriculture was also important and the land was intensively farmed. A button factory in West Cheshire supplied hooks and eyes for Yankee peddlers.

The Episcopal Academy of Connecticut was founded in 1794. Funds to build the school, plus the land, were donated by the people of Cheshire. Masonic rites were conducted when the cornerstone was laid. An early faculty member was Bronson Alcott. J. Pierpont Morgan was a student. The Episcopal Academy was later moved to Hartford, where it became Trinity College. In Cheshire, the school continued as the nonsectarian Cheshire Academy.

Notable buildings

Farmington Canal Lock, runs south, roughly parallel to Route 10, from the northern town line to Mt. Sanford Road.

First Congregational Church of Cheshire (c. 1827), 111 Church Drive. Designed by the famous David Hoadley, it is one of a series of nearly identical churches with tall spires and freestanding Ionic columns that Hoadley designed for several Connecticut towns.

Historic districts

Cheshire Historic District, roughly bounded by Main Street, Highland Avenue, Wallingford Road, South Main Street, Cornwall and Spring Streets.

Marion Historic District (also in Southington), along Marion Avenue and Meriden-Waterbury Turnpike.

Derby

Route 34

Incorporated 1675, chartered as a city in 1893.

Native Americans

Paugussetts. Molly Hatchett (1738–1829), a Paugusett, lived on Turkey Hill. She was the widowed mother of four children. Molly was known throughout western Connecticut because whenever a child was born, she would visit and present the baby with a tiny basket rattle. In each rattle were six dried kernels of corn. If the baby was a seventh child, she would put seven kernels inside the rattle, and if the eighth she put eight, and so on. When she became old, many of the mothers she had visited remembered her kindness, and offered her assistance.

Historical notes

A trading post was established in 1642. Originally called Paugasuck (Paugussett) for the Indians who lived here, the town was named for Derby, England. In the eighteenth century Derby was a busy and prosperous seaport, serving merchants trading with the West Indies and the northern Mediterranean. When the turnpike from Bridgeport, through Newtown, opened in 1801, Derby was bypassed and its fortunes as a sea-trading city dwindled. In the nineteenth century, extensive manufacturing developed, much of it based on copper and iron.

Commodore Isaac Hull, who commanded the U.S.S. *Constitution* (Old Ironsides) against the British in the War of 1812, was born in Derby. His uncle, General William Hull, served honorably during the Revolutionary War. During the War of 1812, while Governor of Michigan, he surrendered the fort at Detroit. He was sentenced to be shot, but was subsequently pardoned by President Madison.

Inventions, inventors and firsts

The first hoop skirt was made in Derby in 1830.

Notable buildings

John I. Howe House, 213 Caroline Street. Howe invented the first pin-making machine.

East Haven

Routes 1, 142, 337
Incorporated 1785

Native Americans

Quinnipiac

Historical notes

East Farms, as East Haven was known, was included in the purchase made from the sachems Momaugin and Mantowese by New Haven Colony. It was part of New Haven until its incorporation in 1785. In 1881, the western part of East Haven (Fair Haven, Grannis Cove and Morris Cove) was ceded back to New Haven.

The earliest settlement was probably at Solitary Cove (Morris Cove), made in 1639 by Thomas Grigson. However, it was around Lonotononket (later Furnace Pond, and now Lake Saltonstall) that settlement began in earnest and the town gained fame. The lake is in East Haven and Branford. Governor Saltsonstall (see Branford), discovered bog iron here.

Bog iron was at first skimmed from the surface of the lake. Later, it was brought up from the bottom. The bog iron was placed in a great furnace with lime made from clam and oyster shells and melted into pig iron. This was the first iron works in Connecticut and the third in New England. East Haven became known as Iron Works Village.

East Haven was invaded by the British during the Revolution and suffered heavy losses. Property, cattle and crops were burned or confiscated, and the men were taken prisoner or killed.

Historic districts

Branford Electric Railway Historic District (also in Branford), 17 River Street to Court Street, features the Shore Line Trolley Museum, I-95 Exit 51N/52S (203-467-6927). One hundred classic trolleys are exhibited, including a rare parlor car, the oldest rapid transit car, and the first electric freight locomotive. Perhaps best of all, you can take a three-mile trolley ride on the oldest operating suburban line. Restoration work is continuing.

Guilford

Routes 1, 146
Incorporated 1639

Native Americans

Quinnipiac

Shaumpishuh, sister of Momaugin and sachem of the Indians of Guilford, sold Menunketuck (Guilford), the land from the Aigicomock (East River) to Kuttanoo (East Haven), to the Reverend Henry Whitefield.

She and her people were paid twelve coats, twelve fathoms of wampum, twelve looking-glasses, twelve pairs of shoes, twelve pairs of stockings, twelve hatchets, four kettles, twelve knives, twelve hats, twelve porringers, twelve spoons and two English coats.

After the sale, she moved with some of her people to Kuttanoo to live near her brother. Others of the tribe moved to Branford. This was in 1639. By 1774, there were twenty-three Quinnipiacs left in Guilford (including Madison) but within a few years, there were none.

There is a tradition that Uncas, the Mohegan sachem who was allied with the Colonists and fought with them in the Pequot War, shot a fleeing Pequot sachem swimming across the harbor. He placed the Pequot's head in the fork of an oak tree, where it was found two years later by the Reverend Whitefield. Whitefield named the point of land Sachem's Head, a name it bears today. On the east side of the bay was a rock shelter used by the Indians.

Historical notes

Guilford was settled in 1639 by Puritans from Kent and Surrey under the leadership of Reverend Whitefield. He enlisted the help of local Indians to carry stone for his fort/house and persuaded carpenters and masons to come from New Haven and Old Saybrook to help. The Puritans probably slept in nearby wigwams during their first weeks, perhaps for several months.

Guilford was one of the few shore towns which escaped attack by the British. The town was ardently Patriot,

however. In May of 1777, the residents organized a successful raid on the British provision stores at Sag Harbor.

When the regicides, Edward Whalley and his son-in-law William Goffe (see New Haven), left the cave at West Rock where they had hidden from the British soldiers, they slipped through the woods to Guilford. This was in June of 1661. Governor William Leete concealed them in his Guilford cellar for three days, before they went on to Milford.

Granite was quarried on Leete's Island, the low-lying land in the southwestern part of Guilford, beginning in 1837. Stone from the quarries was used in the foundation of the statue of liberty, for breakwaters at Block Island, for the foundation of the Brooklyn Bridge, the lighthouse at Lighthouse Point in New Haven and many other places.

Oyster culture also flourished. Later industries included the manufacture of birch extract, and schoolroom furniture. At the beginning of the twentieth century, tomatoes canned in Guilford were used by households all over the East.

Ghost stories and legends

Jared Leete, who built his house in 1781 on Broad Street, had the reputation of being a heavy drinker. He was also quick to compose ribald rhymes. One day, feeling hot and thirsty after hunting on Moose Hill, he stopped at a farmhouse and asked for a drink of cider. The woman of the house demurred, knowing his reputation for intoxication, but then, thinking better of it, she said she would give him a drink if he would write an epitaph for her. He immediately wrote: "Margaret, who died of late Ascended up to heaven's gate." whereupon she gave him his cider. Taking the drink, he added, "But Gabriel met her with a club And drove her down to BEELZEBUB."

Notable buildings

Henry Whitefield State Museum (c. 1639), 248 Old Whitfield Street, I-95 Exit 58 (203-453-2457 or the Connecticut Historical Commission at 860-566-3005). Connecticut's oldest extant house and New England's oldest stone building. Also known as The Old Stone House. It was built by the Rev. Whitefield as a town fort and meeting place as well as a home for his family. Stones for the walls were dragged an exhausting distance.

Hyland House (c. 1660), 84 Boston Street, I-95 Exit 59 (203-453-9477). Classic saltbox with leaded, diamond-pane windows. Ebenezer Parmelee lived here. He built one of the first town clocks in America. It was in-stalled in the First Congregational Church on the green, and in two subsequent edifices. Herb garden.

Thomas Griswold House (1774), 171 Boston Street, I-95 Exit 59 (203-453-3176). Saltbox, blacksmith shop, colonial garden.

Acadian House (c. 1670), Union Street. A simple saltbox with few windows, the house served as a sanctuary for exiled Acadians who were put ashore by the British in 1755.

Ezra Griswold House (c. 1777), Boston Road. Saltbox. One of the most photographed houses in Connecticut.

Historic districts

Dudleytown Historic District, roughly Clapboard Hill Road from Tanner Marsh Road to Murray Lane, East River Road southeast to Trailwood Drive and Duck Hole Road.

Guilford Historic Town Center District, bounded by West River, I-95, East Creek and Long Island Sound.

Meeting House Hill Historic District, roughly bounded by Long Hill, Great Hill and Ledge Hill Roads.

Route 146 Historic District (also in Branford), Route 146 between Flat Rock Road and West River Bridge.

Hamden
Route 10
Incorporated 1786

Native Americans
Quinnipiac

The Old Stone House, Whitfield.

Historical notes

Hamden was part of the original land purchase by New Haven Colony. The first settler was most likely the sheep farmer Matthew Gilbert, who arrived in 1664, though serious settlement didn't begin in central Hamden until Jonathan Ives arrived seventy years later.

Soon other settlers built homes and they dotted the countryside with mills, taking advantage of the abundant water power. The Farmington Canal and later the railroad ensured success for Hamden's industries. The town was named for John Hampden, an English statesman.

Inventions, inventors and firsts

The first truss bridge in the United States was erected in Whitneyville in 1823. It was from a design patented by Ithiel Town. After the Whitneyville dam was constructed, Eli Whitney moved the bridge to protect it.

Eli Whitney pioneered the concepts of interchangeable parts and assembly-line construction in 1798, at the foot of Lake Whitney. Discouraged by the litigation involved in protecting his patents for the invention of the cotton gin, he sought a government contract to produce 10,000 muskets.

Geology

Mount Carmel, called the Sleeping Giant because of its profile, lies within Hamden. Beautiful green stone was taken from the Giant and used for building. Extensive traprock mining has been conducted and the mountain is not as high as it once was.

Tree stumps occasionally emerged from the pit of the Davis brickyard, at the foot of Benton Street. In the midst of the pit was a deposit of tidal marsh peat, formed from organic material when the sea level rose after the ice sheet melted. It gives one pause to think of ancient, preglacial tree stumps emerging so many thousands of years after they died.

Notable buildings

Farmington Canal Lock 13, runs roughly south through town from Mount Sanford Road to Cherry Ann Street and Brooksvale Avenue. The canal once ran the length of town. In 1838 passengers made an excursion to Northampton in a line of gay packets. The trip took a bit more than a full day.

Eli Whitney Museum, 915–940 Whitney Avenue, I-91 Exit 6 (203-777-1833). The site of Eli Whitney's factory. Also the site of New Haven's first grist mill.

The Jonathan Dickerman House (c. 1792), 105 Mount Carmel Avenue (Hamden Historical Society, P. O. Box 5512, Hamden, 06518). This beautiful but modest eighteenth-century

The Jonathan Dickerman House.

farmhouse has never had central heating or plumbing. Moved to its present site in 1961, the gardens display commonly used herbs of the late eighteenth and early nineteenth centuries.

Madison
Routes 1, 79, 80
Incorporated 1826

Native Americans
Hammonassets

Historical notes
Madison was originally East Guilford. It was named for ex President Madison when it became a separate town.

Early industries were the burning of charcoal, fishing, and from 1825 to 1890, shipbuilding and a considerable sea trade. A porpoise fishery operated briefly from 1792 -1793 on the west side of town. The fishery tanned porpoise skins and extracted oil for lighting. In 1799, whetfish were first used as fertilizer for rye, potatoes, corn and grass on Madison farms.

Though Connecticut legislated against slavery in 1774 ("No Indian, Negro or Mulatto Slave, shall, at any Time hereafter be bought or imported into this Colony by Sea or Land, from any Place or Places whatsoever to be disposed of, left, or sold within this colony"), sea traders from the shore towns managed to circumvent the law and thereby profit.

They would leave the Connecticut coast loaded with staves, lumber, and other goods and sail to legitimate trading destinations across the Atlantic. But unknown to the folks at home, after completing this business, they would then dip south to the slave market on the African coast, where they would pick up a cargo of recently captured slaves. They would then trade the slaves in the West Indies for molasses, rum, salt and sugar, which they would bring back to Connecticut. It was a lucrative though wretched business.

In the 1750s a four-year-old African boy was captured while tending crops with his brother. Bought by a Connecticut slaver, he was brought to New Haven, where Linius Bishop of East Guilford (Madison) purchased him. Bishop named the boy Gad Asher. Asher enlisted in the Continental Army, and won his freedom, but he was blinded in battle and sent back to Madison, where he lived to be an old man of eighty.

Jeremiah Asher, his grandson, grew up listening to his grandfather's stories, and those of two old veteran friends in Guilford, and understanding that they fought for the country's freedom, Jeremiah refused to be subservient to the whites he encountered. In 1862 he published his autobiography.

By the middle of the nineteenth century, Connecticut's economy had switched from agrarian to industrial. Unlike farmers, workers enjoyed a day off each week. This new leisure, plus the growth of the railroads, made the shore towns popular playgrounds.

Hotels sprung up. The wealthy built Victorian cottages. And the working classes came to picnic and bathe. In 1919, the state purchased Hammonassett Beach, now the largest of the shore-line parks. Less than twenty years after the beach was opened to the public, it was serving more than a million and a half visitors a year.

Notable buildings

Allis-Bushnell House and Museum (c. 1785, sometimes given as 1739), 853 Boston Post Road/Route 1, I-95 Exit 61 (203-245-4567).

Deacon John Grave House (c. 1685), 581 Boston Post Road, Tunxis Farm, I-95 Exit 61. Considered the best preserved seventeenth-century house in Connecticut, this home was inhabited by the same family for three hundred years. Deacon Grave, who was a magistrate, held court in a room known as the Judgement Chamber. Over the centuries the house was used as a school, infirmary, weapons depot, tavern and inn.

Historic districts

Madison Green Historic District, 446–589 Boston Post Road, and the buildings surrounding the green. Many eighteenth- and nineteenth-century houses have been preserved, and give a good sense of the architectural history of the shore.

Meriden

Routes 5, 70, 71. Incorporated as a town 1806, as a city 1867. Town and city were consolidated in 1922.

Native Americans

Quinnipiacs

Historical notes

Jonathan Gilbert, a fur trader and innkeeper, was granted three hundred and fifty acres at "Cold Spring" in 1661. He was also given permission to keep an Ordinary at his house. Apparently he had built his house before he was granted any of these permissions. He called his farm Meriden, and quickly hired Edward Higbee to run the inn for him.

For awhile, Wethersfield, Wallingford, Farmington and Middletown all claimed the northern part of Meriden, but in 1670 it was decided that most of present-day Meriden would be part of Wallingford. It continued as part of Wallingford until 1806.

The regicides (see New Haven) made their way to the wilderness near Hanover Lake in Meriden after giving the slip to the King's men in Milford. They hid in the swamps and traveled only at night. Pilgrims' Harbor Brook, the main stream that flows through Meriden, was named for them and the refuge they sought in the forest and fields nearby. It is believed they walked to the Connecticut River Valley, then followed the River as far as Massachusetts, where they lived safely and anonymously in Hadley.

Manufacturing gained early importance. In 1835, the historian John Barber described Meriden as "one of the most flourishing and enterprising manufacturing towns in the State." In

1854, several small companies joined to form the Meriden Britannia Company, which merged with still others to become the International Silver Company. This gave Meriden the nickname the "Silver City of the World."

Inventions, inventors and firsts

Orchardist W. W. Lyman invented the first airtight canning jars with a spring-fastened top, and was granted a patent in 1858.

Geology

Meriden is flanked on the west and east by traprock ranges. The Hanging Hills, rimming the west of Meriden, were formed by two successive lava flows. West Peak is particularly interesting. Polished by glacial action, you can see the pillow effect of the more recent layer of lava laid down upon the earlier layer. You can also see veins of quartz.

Also of interest is Castle Craig, a stone tower (c. 1900), on the central peak of the Hanging Hills. There are

Solomon Goffe House.

several parks serving visitors to the traprock ranges, including Hubbard Park. On the east are Mount Lamentation, Mt. Beseck and Mount Higby. Most of the eastern traprock mountains are in the town of Middlefield. North of the city is an old, abandoned quarry. Underlying the city itself is red sandstone.

Notable buildings

Solomon Goffee House (c. 1711), 677 North Colony Street, I-691 Broad Street Exit (203-237-6629). This is the oldest house in Meriden. It was built with unusually large chimneys and floor beams.

Moses Andrews House (c. 1760), 424 West Main Street. A center-chimney salt box maintained by the Meriden Historical Society. The Society also maintains the Bernice C. Moorhouse Research Center at 540 West Main Street.

Historic districts

Colony Street/West Main Street Historic District. 1–62 Colony, 55 Grove, 1–119 and 82–110 West Main Streets.

Moses Andrews Homestead.

Middlebury

Routes 63, 64, 188
Incorporated 1807

Native Americans
Paugussetts

Historical notes
Middlebury got its name from its Meeting House being in the middle of Southbury, Woodbury and Waterbury. Noted for its ponds and rugged terrain, Middlebury was early a farming town, though many small industries were carried on at these farms, such as blacksmithing.

Until 1840 there were several sawmills and small factories. In the eastern part of town, called Bradleyville, Enos Bradley had a clothing works and saw mill. He also made knives. Later dairying and the raising of saddle horses became important.

Ghost stories and legends
Chauncy Judd was the son of Isaac Judd, a well-to-do Middlebury farmer. He was taking a short cut home to Middlebury when he happened upon a party of Tory thieves (see Bethany for the rest of the story).

Notable buildings
Nathaniel Richardson House (c. pre 1750), Kelly Road. Kept as a tavern on the old road from Waterbury to Woodbury.

Josiah Bronson House, Breakneck Road. Rochambeau was entertained here while the French army encamped at the foot of Breakneck Hill.

Historic district
Middlebury Center Historic District, roughly bounded by Library Road, North and South Streets and Whittemore Road.

Milford

Routes 1, 162
Incorporated 1639

Native Americans
Paugussetts
For centuries, Native Americans came to Wepawaug (Milford) to feast on the abundant shellfish. As evidence, they left a shell heap covering twenty-four acres on both sides of Gulf Street, north of New Haven Avenue. Ansantaway, the sachem, had a wigwam on Poquahaug (Charles Island).

Ansantaway and his council were given "6 coats, 10 blankets, 1 kettle, 12 hatchets, 12 hoes, 2 dozen knives, and a dozen small glasses (mirrors)" in exchange for Wepawaug (Milford).

Though there are no records of any of the settlers being killed by the Indians, relations were tense. In 1645, the Indians set fire to the surrounding country. As it was their habit to burn the underbrush in the forests, which gave the woods the park-like appearance at which the Europeans marveled, the Milford fire was probably not an act of aggression. However, the English perceived it as such and fortified their houses.

About 1648, the Mohawks came up along the coast from the west. The

Milford Indians attacked them in a swamp and kept them at bay. Then, some young boys of the town set fire to the Milford Indians' fort in 1671, completely destroying it. This further increased tensions.

Historical notes

Fifty-four planters, led by the Reverend Peter, and guided by Captain Thomas Tibbals, settled on the banks of the Wepawaug in the autumn of 1639. They named their new home Milford, and began at once to build a village.

They were an independent lot who caused a stir in the Colony when it was discovered that they had "taken in as free burgesse, six planters, who are nott in church fellowship." It was agreed that though the six could vote in town affairs, they could not hold office.

Despite their relaxed attitude toward the unbelievers in their midst, the inhabitants of Milford were a righteous sort, a people of their time. In 1640 they passed the following resolutions:

Voted: That the earth is the Lord's, and the fullness thereof.

Voted: That the earth is given to the Saints.

Voted: That we are the Saints.

During the first years, the English deeply feared an attack by the Indians, and so lived inside a square-mile palisade. It was on both sides of the Wepawaug River and made of stakes, set close together, ten to twelve feet high.

Pillory. Colonial punishment was harsh and public.

Early industry focused on harvesting the oyster and clam beds as well as fishing and farming. There were grist mills and sawmills to meet the needs of the community. Quarrying began in 1800. Eleven years later a Yale student discovered Verde antique marble, which was used for four chimney pieces at the Capitol in Washington. Shipbuilding and trade began almost from the start and lasted until the 1820s. The shipyard and docks were on the northeast side of the head of the harbor.

The regicides, Edward Whalley and his son-in-law William Goffe (see New Haven), hid in the cellar of Micah Tomkins' house for three years. They had stolen through the woods in the dark of night from Guilford. Towards the end of their three years of safe hiding in Tomkins' cellar, special royal English soldiers in determined pursuit of the regicides arrived and began to search the area.

Whalley and Goffe knew they had to move to a safer place. The King's men, however, quickly suspected Micah Tomkins of harboring the regicides and kept a 24-hour watch on the house. One chilly night, however, the King's men, bored with the watch and freezing cold, decided to warm themselves for a few minutes in a local tavern. The regicides seized the moment and escaped on foot, going first to the swamps of the Quinnipiac, then heading north, traveling always at night.

George Washington passed through Milford five times and seemed to be impressed. His diary entry for October 17, 1789 states, "In this place (Milford) there is but one steeple—but there are Grist and Saw mills, and a handsome Cascade over the Tumbling dam ..."

Notable buildings

Eells-Stow House, 34 High Street (203-874-2664). The home of Captain Stephen Stow, who on New Year's Eve in 1777 volunteered to nurse forty-six ill Revolutionary War prisoners who had been put ashore by a British prison ship.

They were cared for in various homes the first night. The next morning the Meeting House was turned into a hospital, and Stow took care of the sick men by himself. It turned out they had smallpox, and he and they all died. The victims and Stow were buried in a common grave.

Stow's house was built, and remodeled, over a period of years. It appears that the first remodeling and an enlargement took place in 1720. There are unusual "dog-legged" stairs which double back on the handrail.

Historic districts

River Park Historic District, roughly bounded by Boston Post Road, Governors Avenue, AMTRAK right of way and High Street.

Naugatuck
Routes 63, 68
Incorporated 1844, as a borough in 1893.

Native Americans
Paugussetts

Historical notes

Naugatuck is one of only two towns in Connecticut to have an Algonquin name. It means "tree." However, it was settled in 1702 as the Society of Salem Bridge. It was incorporated from Bethany, Oxford and Waterbury.

Though surrounded by steep, rocky hills, the valley became a busy industrial borough. Woolen mills and metal factories were followed by the rubber industry.

Amasa Goodyear, Charles Goodyear's father, was a successful New Haven merchant involved in the West Indies trade. Like many merchants, his business floundered during the embargo of 1812. He decided to become a manufacturer, and moved to Naugatuck to produce pearl buttons. Soon he was also making patented steel pitchforks for the government and he sent his son, Charles, to Philadelphia to learn the hardware trade. Charles became a partner in his father's business. They extended too much credit to their customers and the business failed. Charles found himself in debtors' prison.

It was in prison that he determined to become an inventor, and his long obsession with rubber began. After ten difficult years of work, he stumbled on the technique for vulcanizing rubber, when a gum and sulphur mixture accidentally, but fortuitously, touched a hot stove.

Charles himself was without personal resources, but his brother and his brother-in-law helped fund the Goodyear Metallic Rubber Company, founded in Naugatuck in 1843. The first product was rubber shoes. Charles' brother-in-law also founded the Naugatuck India Rubber Company. By 1845, both companies were thriving, and Naugatuck had become the rubber capital of the world.

In 1892, U. S. Rubber was founded by a rubber importer. Eventually, U. S. Rubber merged with fifteen other rubber companies, including the company that made pneumatic tires for Pope's bicycles in Hartford, and formed Uniroyal. Once the automobile came on the scene, the demand for rubber tires surged.

Notable buildings

Salem School (c. 1894), 124 Meadow Street. Designed by the prominent New York architectural firm of McKim, Mead & White. Also designed by this prestigious firm was the Whittemore Memorial Library (c. 1894), Congregational Church (c. 1903), and Hillside School (c. 1904), formerly Naugatuck High School. These buildings, as well as the Hop Brook School (c. 1916), designed by Theodate Pope Riddle, were donated to the town by the wealthy Whittemore family.

New Haven
Routes 1, 10, 63, 122
Incorporated 1638, as a city in 1784

Native Americans

Quinnipiac

The Quinnipiac territory stretched from the Wepawaugs, on the west, to the Hammonassetts on the east. This was present-day New Haven, East Haven, Branford and Guilford. Momaugin was their chief. His sister was the sachem of Guilford.

Historical notes

The Dutchman Adrian Block named New Haven Rodeberg, meaning Red Mount Place, when he made his historic exploratory trip along the coast of Connecticut and up the Connecticut River in 1614. Twenty-four years later, the Reverend John Davenport, a Puritan, and the prominent merchant Theophilus Eaton arrived with a band of English merchants, and set about building a town.

They had arrived in Boston the previous year, seeking a place to freely practice their beliefs and conduct business. It was soon apparent that Boston was not the most receptive town for their ideas. Hearing reports from returning veterans of the Pequot War of an excellent harbor at the Quinnipiac hunting grounds, they were intrigued. Eaton went to investigate and found the reports to be true, and the following April, the group moved to Quinnipiac. They planned to build a great commercial port governed by a theocracy.

As a group, they had more wealth than any others that had settled towns in New England. Nevertheless, their first homes were primitive dugouts or sod and log huts on the banks of West Creek. One settler, Reverend Michael Wigglesworth, wrote in his autobiography, "Winter approaching we dwelt in a cellar partly under ground covered with earth the first winter. But I remember that one great rain broke in upon us & drencht me so in my bed being asleep that I fell sick …"

Davenport and Eaton purchased a tract of land from the Quinnipiacs that includes present-day New Haven, East Haven, North Haven, Hamden, Cheshire, Wallingford, Branford, North Branford, Woodbridge and Orange. In exchange they gave the sachem Momaugin and his forty-seven men "by way of … thankful retribution … twelve coates of English trucking cloath, twelve alcumy spoones, twelve hatchetts, twelve hoes, two dozen of knives, twelve porengers

John Davenport. According to legend, the Rev. Davenport preached to the first English settlers of New Haven under the spreading branches of an oak tree. Along with Theophilus Eaton and a few other "gentlemen," Davenport negotiated with the sachem Momaugin for peace as well as land.

& foure cases of French knives and sizers." To Mantowese and his ten men they gave "eleven coates made of trucking cloth and one coate for himself of English cloth, made up in the English manner." Planting grounds and hunting privileges were reserved for the Indians.

The Puritans now set about creating a theocracy based on their tenets of faith, which they called "Seven Pillars." Their Capital Laws (blue laws), strictly governed all aspects of life and left little room for differing ideas. Quakers were branded, whipped and expelled from the Colony. Fines were imposed on those who owned a Quaker book or consorted with Quakers.

Meanwhile, Puritans gained strength in England when Oliver Cromwell

The Judges Cave, West Rock, New Haven, where the Regicides hid. From a 1930s postcard.

came to power. The deposed King Charles I went before a panel of 135 judges. They ordered his execution, and fifty-nine judges signed the death warrant. Two years later, King Charles II was in power and, as can be imagined, he was not happy with the regicides, or judges, who had condemned his father to death.

Three of the regicides, Whalley, Goffe and Dixwell (for whom the streets are named), fled to Boston. The year was 1660. They had not only signed the death warrant, but they had been supporters of Cromwell. For awhile they lived openly in Boston and Cambridge. Davenport invited them to New Haven.

Soon, King Charles II ordered all of the judges to appear in his court, and then ordered Dixwell, Whalley and Goffe brought to him, dead or alive. Dixwell lived in New Haven under an assumed name and identity, and

revealed himself only when he was near death many years later. Whalley and Goffe, however, began an odyssey of flight and hiding.

At first they lived with the Reverend Davenport, but then word came that British soldiers were looking for them. The next day, Davenport preached, "Hide the outcasts; betray not him that wandereth; let mine outcasts dwell with thee ..." His congregation understood.

Whalley and Goffe, who were father and son-in-law, escaped and climbed to the pinnacle of West Rock where they hid in a cave, now called Judges Cave. Food was brought to them at night. But West Rock was a different land than it is now, populated with wildcats, and the men were frightened by the howls and the yellow eyes that peered at them. They snuck back to New Haven and then to Guilford.

Eventually, and with difficulty, they

managed to get to Hadley, Massachusetts, where they lived with the Reverend John Russell. Whalley died sometime between 1774 and 1776 and his body was hidden in the cellar. His bones were discovered in 1795. Goffe lived under assumed names and secretly wrote to his wife, though he never returned to England. (See also Guilford and Milford.)

In 1660, representatives of the Connecticut Colony met in Hartford, and after declaring their allegiance to the King, decided to seek more autonomy. Governor Leete of New Haven Colony did not dare ask for similar favors, as the King knew he had harbored the regicides. He asked Governor John Winthrop, Jr., of Connecticut to speak for both colonies, a mission Winthrop gladly accepted.

Winthrop successfully negotiated the most liberal charter of any of the colonies. However, to the consternation of New Haven, the two colonies were now one. Reluctantly, Leete agreed that it was better to be part of the Connecticut Colony than New York, and from then on, Connecticut was one colony. It was this liberal charter that was hidden in the Charter Oak (see Hartford).

New Haven became a center of culture and commerce. Beans, peas, wheat and corn were grown. Wharves, warehouses and ships were built. Opium, olive oil, silk, Spanish wine, tobacco, coffee, tea, sugar, rum, molasses, indentured Irish servants and some slaves were imported. Clockmakers and engravers plied their trades.

Yale College was begun in 1701 when a group of ministers gathered in Branford and donated books for its founding. In 1714–15, the English benefactor Elihu Yale and Sir Isaac Newton donated books. Instruction was held in several different towns at various times. In 1716 it was decided that the college should be located in New Haven.

Sleeping Giant as seen from New Haven. From a 1930s postcard.

During the Revolution, the British invaded and attempted to burn the city. Despite their greater numbers, they were repelled by the Patriots. Washington visited New Haven five times, dined and sometimes stayed for a few nights. Martha Washington visited once.

In 1839, a Mendi captive from the Sierra Leone named Sengbe Pieh (whom the Spanish called Joseph Cinque) and fifty-two other kidnapped Africans seized control of the Spanish slave ship *Amistad,* bound for Havana, where they would have been sold into slavery.

The Africans killed all but a few of the Spanish seamen and ordered the survivors to sail the ship back to Africa. The Spaniards, however, secretly headed the ship northwards at night, hoping to land in the port of a southern slave state. They landed instead in Long Island Sound, where the ship was taken into custody.

Cinque and his fellow Africans were jailed in New Haven while their fates were decided. At issue was whether they were slaves or free; whether they had the right to go home, or were property to be returned to the Spanish. Eventually, after arduous legal wrangling and much public discussion, the case was heard by the Supreme Court in 1841. Former President John Quincy Adams successfully argued the African's case and the court declared them free (see also Farmington and Hartford).

Notable buildings

Black Rock Fort and Fort Nathan Hale, Woodward Avenue, I-95 Exit 50N/51S (203-946-8790). Black Rock is from the Revolutionary War, Nathan Hale from the Civil War.

East Rock Park, East Rock Road, I-91 Exit 6 (203-946-6086). Spectacular views of Long Island Sound.

New Haven Colony Historical Society, 114 Whitney Avenue, I-91 Exit 3 (203-562-4183). Research library, exhibits of New Haven from 1638.

Pardee-Morris House (c. 1780), 325 Lighthouse Road, I-95 Exit 50 (203-562-4183). The original Morris House (c. 1671) on the highway to Solitary Cove (Morris Cove) was not totally destroyed when the British set it on fire on July 5, 1779, because the ends were built of stone. One wall, the foundation, one of the chimneys, and the kitchen wing survived. The house was rebuilt in 1780, and a ballroom was added in 1800.

Peabody Museum of Natural History, 170 Whitney Avenue, I-91 Exit 3 (203-432-5050). This museum contains exhibits of Connecticut Native American History, dinosaurs and minerals from Connecticut and elsewhere, and exhibits of Meso-American, ancient Egyptian, neolithic and Pacific cultures.

The Beinecke Rare Book Library, 121 Wall Street, I-91 Exit 3 (203-432-2977), has original Audubon prints and a Gutenberg Bible.

The first building for Yale college was built on the corner of College and Chapel Streets.

Yale University Art Museum, 149 Elm Street, I-95 Exit 47 (203-432-2300), is the oldest university art museum in North America.

Yale University Visitor Information Center, 149 Elm Street, I-95 Exit 47 (203-432-2300). The University offers guided tours of its historic campus. You can see Connecticut Hall where Nathan Hale and Noah Webster studied.

Historic districts

Beaver Hills Historic District, roughly bounded by Crescent Street, Goffe Terrace and Boulevard.

Chapel Street Historic District, roughly bounded by Park, Chapel, Temple, George and Crown Streets.

Dwight Street Historic District, roughly bounded by Park, North Frontage, Scranton, Sherman and Elm Streets.

Edgewood Park Historic District, roughly bounded by Boulevard, Derby, Sherman, West Park, Whalley and Yale Avenues and Elm Street.

Hillhouse Avenue Historic District, bounded by Sachem, Temple, Trumbull and Prospect Streets, Whitney and Hillhouse Avenues and the railroad tracks.

Howard Avenue Historic District consists of properties along Howard Avenue, between I-95 and Cassius Street.

New Haven Green Historic District, bounded by Chapel, College, Elm and Church Streets. The first settlers created a plan for the village in 1638. It consisted of nine squares, with the central square designated a central marketplace or common. The Green is the original central square.

At first the common was a tangle of felled trees and brush, and was crisscrossed with ruts from carts. At the end of the seventeenth century it was cleared, and in subsequent decades, commemorative elms were planted, including one when Benjamin Franklin died. The three churches represent Gothic, Federalist and Georgian design.

Ninth Square Historic District, roughly bounded by Church, State, George and Court Streets.

Orange Street Historic District, roughly bounded by Whitney Avenue, State, Eagle and Trumbull Streets.

Oyster Point Historic District, roughly bounded by I-95, South Water Street, Howard Avenue, Sea Street and Greenwich Avenue.

Prospect Hill Historic District, off Route 10.

Quinnipiac River Historic District, roughly bounded by Quinnipiac Avenue, Lexington, Chapel, Ferry, Pine, Front and Lombard Streets.

River Street Historic District, roughly bounded by Chapel Street, Blatchley Avenue, New Haven Harbor and James Street.

Trowbridge Square Historic District, roughly bounded by Columbus and Howard Avenues, Loop Road, Liberty Street and the railroad tracks.

Upper State Street Historic District, roughly State Street from Bradley Street to Mill River Street.

Whitney Avenue Historic District, roughly bounded by Burns, Livingston, Cold Spring, Orange, Bradley Streets and Whitney Avenue.

Winchester Repeating Arms Company Historic District, roughly bounded by Sherman Parkway, Ivy, Mansfield, Admiral and Sachem Streets.

North Branford
Routes 28, 80, 139
Incorporated 1831

Native Americans
Quinnipiac

Historical notes
North Branford, part of Totoket, was opened for settlement as the Third Division of the Town of Branford in the last decade of the seventeenth century. A mill and farm town, it produced milk, wheat and silk in the eighteenth century. The nineteenth century saw the development of industry. Common pins, horseshoe nails, tin, greeting cards, and desiccated coconut were all produced. Many of the early industries centered on the Farm River.

Inventions, inventors and firsts
One family, the Fowlers, was particularly inventive and industrious in the mid nineteenth century. Maltby Fowler invented one of the first machines to make pins. It was purchased in 1842 by some Waterbury men and merged with their American Pin Company. In 1840, Horace Fowler invented a machine for embossing silk. Frederick Fowler made a machine for rolling brass lamps. And Thadeus Fowler invented another pin machine.

Geology
In 1914 a trap rock quarry was opened.

North Haven
Routes 5, 17, 103
Incorporated 1786

Native Americans
Quinnipiacs

Historical notes
Part of the original New Haven purchase, North Haven was first settled by William Bradley in 1650. He had been an officer in Cromwell's army and was sent by Theophilus Eaton, who owned a large tract on the west bank of the Quinnipiac River. It was ten years before anyone else arrived.

Benjamin Trumbull wrote of the early town, "some of the first planters attended public worship, and buried their dead in New Haven. The women usually went on foot to New Haven, on the Lord's day, attended two long exercises, and returned. In some instances they did this with a child in their arms." Though the towns are close, a modern-day mother would not think of walking from one to the other carrying a child.

Benjamin Trumbull built a house in North Branford in 1761 with timber "out of the Society's lot." An early historian of the colony, he wrote *History of Connecticut* while he lived in this house. Another early historian was born in North Branford. Ezra Stiles (1727–1795) wrote *History of Three of the Judges of King Charles I,* which was an account of the regicides (see New Haven), plus *Itineraries* and *Literary Diaries.* The last book recorded early Connecticut and early Yale history.

Beginning as an agricultural town, North Haven developed both manufacturing and truck gardening. One of the first industries was the mining of bog iron in 1656 near Pool Road. A shipbuilding center flourished along the Quinnipiac. It focused on coastal trade, particularly with Boston.

Clay beds ten to thirty feet thick led to an early brickmaking industry. The clays, of alternating colors and layers, were deposited in an old glacial lake. The 1937 WPA tour guide describes the brickmaking:

"Beside the railroad station, a side road leads south a short distance to a Clay Pit which for generations has furnished material for brickmaking, one of the town's chief industries.

"When the bricks are being cured here, there is an appearance of a major conflagration in the brick sheds— clouds of wood smoke roll out from beneath the eaves and through the siding, and an acrid odor fills the air for miles around."

What was being described, of course, was not curing but firing—or burning as it was sometimes called—of the clay to make bricks. Many of the local houses are made from North Haven brick.

Notable buildings
Rising Sun Tavern (c. 1732), first called Todd's Half Mile House, Old Tavern Lane. An old toll gate was located at this tavern.

Historic districts
Pine Bridge Historic District, 3–17 Bishop Street, 70–99 Old Broadway, 2–10 Philip Place, 9–56 State Street.

Orange
Routes 1, 34, 114, 121, 152, 162
Incorporated 1822

Native Americans
Paugusetts. This was the northern part of Wepawaug.

Historical notes
Orange was purchased by the Reverend Peter Pruden's Milford Colony in 1643 but it wasn't until after 1700 that it was settled as Bryan's Farms, a part of Milford. Orange was sectioned off from Milford in 1822, and almost one hundred years later, West Haven was sectioned off from Orange. The town was named for William of Orange III, who restored the Royal Charter.

Farming, particularly seed corn, has dominated Orange's economy over the centuries.

Notable buildings
Fieldview Farm, Route 34 (203-795-5415). This farm has been in the same

family for three hundred and fifty years, perhaps the oldest continuously operating farm in the state.

Stone-Otis House (c. 1830), corner of Orange Center and Tyler City Roads, on the Green (203-795-3106). Carefully restored farmhouse, includes a general store as well as living quarters. A fully equipped blacksmith shop is housed in a shed behind the house.

The Academy (c. 1878), a building on the north side of the library (203-795-3106), served first as a meeting place and high school and later as a town hall and courthouse. An earlier almost identical building was built on the same site in 1812, but was moved.

Historic districts

Orange Center Historic District, roughly Orange Center road from Orange Cemetery to Nan Drive.

Oxford

Routes 42, 67
Incorporated 1798

Native Americans

Paugussett and Pootatuck. Toby's Rocks, on the south side of High Rock, were named for a freed Indian slave. An early eighteenth-century deed reads, "These may certifi whom it may consarn that tobee a Ingan that lived with me I had of a mogeg Indian at new london 30 7 years agoo he lived with me 12 years and is now and has bin a free man ever senc october the 6 1713, Ebenezer Johnson."

Historical notes

Oxford was part of Derby, and was named for Oxford, England. Despite the rugged landscape, farming was an early endeavor. Coastal trade was carried on with the West Indies via Derby and New Haven, though this ended with the embargo of 1807.

Grist mills and the raising of sheep for wool remained viable enterprises after they had vanished from other towns. The railroad bypassed Oxford, thus isolating it and changing its future. Poultry and dairy farming then became the primary endeavors as the population dwindled.

Historic districts

Quaker Farms Historic District, 467–511 Quaker Farms Road.

Prospect

Routes 68, 69
Incorporated 1827

Native Americans

Quinnipiacs

Historical notes

Prospect was settled in 1712, near the Waterbury and Cheshire boundaries. In 1797 it was established as Columbia Parish and was governed by the Columbia Company. When the town was incorporated, it was named for its fine view. The town has an elevation of 800 feet.

In addition to farming (particularly apple orchards), hoes, pins, needles, matches, Britannia ware, umbrella trimmings and buttons were manufactured. There were grist mills and lumbering operations. Prospect was, for a time, larger than Waterbury.

Notable buildings

Center Schoolhouse on the Green (c. 1867). A one-room school for 69 years, later serving as town hall, telephone center during World War II, and emergency headquarters during the flood of 1955. Exhibits of local history.

David Hotchkiss House (c. 1815–19), Waterbury Road. Though a private residence, the upstairs rooms were used as classrooms. Later, these rooms were used to board Irish immigrants.

Seymour

Routes 115, 313
Incorporated 1850

Native Americans

Paugusetts
Included the native American village Nawcatock. Also Amaugsuck, "the fishing place where waters fall down." In the mid eighteenth century, Sachem Chuse, a scout in the French and Indian war, and his people coexisted here with the Europeans. Once a year, Chuse's tribe went to what we now call Milford, and participated in a two-week seaside feast of clams and oysters.

Historical notes

In 1803 General David Humphreys (see Ansonia) purchased the land, then called Rimmon Falls, and two years

later, renamed it Humphreyville. Humphrey imported merino sheep to produce wool for his mills. To find workers to care for these sheep, and to work in his newly established mill, he visited asylums and brought back orphan boys, whom he trained and educated. The town was later named Seymour after the Connecticut governor.

Inventions, inventors and firsts

Seymour was the first planned factory town in the U. S. Established by General David Humphreys, who in 1806 built the first large and successful woolen mill in the U. S.

Notable buildings

Matthies House, 59 West Street (203-888-7471). Opulent twenty-one room home of philanthropist Katharine Matthies, now the headquarters of the Seymour Historical Society.

Historic districts

Downtown Seymour Historic District, roughly bounded by the Naugatuck River, Main, Wakely and DeForest Streets.

Southbury

Routes 6, 67, 172, 188
Incorporated 1787

Native Americans

Paugussetts

Historical notes

Southbury was the South Purchase of Woodbury. In 1673 when the first settlers arrived, there were several hundred Paugussett Indians in residence. Early industries included sawmills, three taverns, shoe making shops, and a paper mill. The village of South Britain, along the Pomperaug River, was a center for carpet and hat making.

Samuel G. Goodrich, who wrote 116 popular books for children under the name of Peter Parley, lived in Southbury. Millions of copies of his books were sold. Better known today, Wallace Nutting lived in Southbury and photographed the countryside for his book *Connecticut Beautiful,* forever immortalizing this picturesque town. His photographs show quiet lanes, flowering trees, old gates and fences, and meandering streams. Many were taken in the South Britain area.

Notable buildings

Bullet Hill School (c. 1778) Main Street, Seymour Road. This schoolhouse was built from bricks made on the premises.

Historic districts

Hurley Road Historic District, 6 and 17 Hurley Road.

Russian Village Historic District, roughly bounded by Kiev Drive and Russian Village Road between U. S. 6 and the Pomperaug River. Count Ilya Tolstoi founded Churaevka here, a colony for Russian refugees.

Sanford Road Historic District, 480 and 487 Sanford Road.

South Britain Historic District, East Flat Hill, Hawkins, Library and Middle Roads and 497–864 South Britain Road.

Southbury Historic District Number 1, Main Street from Woodbury Town Line to Old Waterbury Road.

Wallingford
Routes 5, 68, 150
Incorporated 1673, borough in 1853

Native Americans
Quinnipiacs

Historical notes

Part of the tract purchased by New Haven Colony from Montowese in 1638, Wallingford was settled in 1670 by planters from New Haven and Stratford. The town included present-day Cheshire, Meriden and the eastern part of Prospect. It was named after Wallingford in England. The first village was along the south part of Main Street.

When Benjamin Franklin's son, William Franklin, Governor of New Jersey, was found to be a "virulent enemy of the colonies," he was sent to Governor Trumbull of Connecticut. This was on July 4, 1776. Trumbull sent him to be confined at a house in Wallingford. Two weeks later Franklin's prodigal son was sent to Middletown.

Washington visited three times and dined twice. He remarked on the white mulberry trees that were raised in town for silk worms.

Agriculture played an important early role. Bushels of peaches, pears, apples, pickles, cherries and grapes were produced for market. In 1835, Robert Wallace started his Britannia ware factory, and made Wallingford synonymous with silverware. In 1838, native son Moses Yale Beach became the sole owner of the *New York Sun.* He came up with the concept of speed in securing news, and used everything from pigeons to special trains to horse express to get a scoop.

The Wallingford Disaster struck on August 9, 1874. A devastating tornado coupled with torrential rains ravaged the town. Thirty-four died, one hundred were injured, and thirty houses were destroyed.

Notable buildings

Samuel Parsons House (c. 1770), 180 South Main Street (203-294-1996). This house contains period furnishings and old documents. It is owned by the Wallingford Historical Society.

Historic districts

Wallingford Center Historic District, roughly Main Street from Ward Street to Church Street. This was the commercial hub of town in the nineteenth century. There are good examples of eighteenth-, nineteenth- and twentieth-century architecture, including the William Wallace block (c. 1857), a four-story commercial building in the Renaissance Revival Style.

Wallingford Railroad Station (c. 1871), 51 Quinnipiac Street. Second Empire style, two-story brick, this station is still in use.

Waterbury

Routes 8, 69, 73, 322
Incorporated 1686

Native Americans

Paugussetts

Historical notes

Mattatuck ("thickly wooded region") included parts or all of Waterbury, Watertown, Plymouth, Wolcott, Prospect, Naugatuck, Thomston and Middlebury. It was named Waterbury because there were so many streams flowing into the Naugatuck River. The first settlers, planters from Farmington, built dugouts or huts at Sled Hall in 1677.

The following year they brought their families and built houses in what is the contemporary center of town. The terrain, deep valleys between the Naugatuck and Mud Rivers, was considered suitable to support only thirty families. In fact, the first settlement numbered only one hundred fifty people, and did not grow in number for thirty-five years.

As early as 1750 brass buttons and buckles were being made by John Allen. Forty years later, Henry Grilley was manufacturing pewter buttons in his home. Then, in 1802, Grilley joined Levi and Abel Porter and together they bought old kettles, ship sheathing, and other scrap copper and produced their own brass.

They sent the brass to an iron forge in Litchfield, where it was rolled, and then transported it back to Waterbury where they manufactured brass but-

"Climax Table Lamp" made by The Plume & Atwood Manufacturing Company in Waterbury.

tons from the sheets. Waterbury's love affair with the brass industry had begun in earnest.

Others took up the business. Aaron Benedict, who had been making ivory buttons, smuggled heavy machinery out of England, hauled it by wagon from the coast, and set himself up in the brass button making business. Soon there were brass kettle factories, and hook and eye factories, and brass clock makers, and brass pin makers, and manufacturers of plumbing supplies. Yankee peddlers' carts were loaded with Waterbury brasswares, which were in high demand wherever they traveled.

In 1837, Connecticut passed legislation permitting the sale of stocks. This brought an influx of capital to the brassworks. By 1899, the companies began to merge.

Inventions, inventors and firsts

The American Brass Association formed in February of 1853 was the first trade association in America.

Historic districts

Bank Street Historic District, 207–231 Bank Street.

Downtown Waterbury Historic District, roughly bounded by Main, Meadow, and Elm Streets.

Hillside Historic District, roughly bounded by Woodlawn Terrace and West Main and Willow Streets.

Overlook Historic District, roughly bounded by Helca Street, Farmington and Columbia Boulevards, Cables Avenue, Clowes Terrace, Lincoln and Fiske Streets.

Waterbury Municipal Center Complex District, 195, 235, 236 Grant Street, 7, 35, 43 Field Street.

West Haven

Routes 1, 162

Incorporated 1921

Native Americans

Quinnipiac

Historical notes

Although West Haven was settled in 1648 as West Farms of New Haven Colony, it was the last town in Connecticut to be incorporated. In 1822, the societies of West Haven and North Milford merged to form Orange. When the residential area of West Haven was later split from the more rural parts of Orange, the new town of West Haven became Connecticut's youngest town.

In the early morning hours of July 5, 1779, British General Tryon anchored forty-eight British vessels off West Haven. Thomas Painter sounded the alarm. Painter had joined the Continental Army when he was fifteen, left to privateer, then rejoined and was the guard on duty when the British Fleet appeared.

Fifteen hundred British troops disembarked at Old Field Shore (Savin Rock), and stormed the town. They marched along Savin Rock Road, entering and raiding houses along the way, even demanding breakfast at one tavern! They continued to the Meeting House where they destroyed documents. They stayed at the Green for two hours. The Patriots fired upon them as they marched up Milford Hill.

One hundred Yale students formed a company, and under the leadership of several Patriots, marched across the bridge where the Patriots of New Haven had hastily thrown up an earthen barrier. The boys successfully dispersed the British advance guard, but then found themselves surrounded. The British were finally driven off after much skirmishing. In September of 1781, another British fleet anchored in the West Haven harbor. This time two thousand Patriots gathered, and the fleet set sail.

After the Revolution, Allen's Tavern at Savin Rock became a popular hangout for veterans. The Tavern was first opened in 1771 with ten rooms which rented for fifteen cents a night and offered the free use of cooking ovens.

Over the ensuing years, other taverns flourished, hotels were built, the trolleys came.

By the end of the nineteenth century, there were bandstands, eateries, and other amusements at Savin Rock. Rides were added, including a state of the art roller coaster, and Savin Rock was billed as the "Coney Island of Connecticut." Savin took its name from the red cedar that grew in the vicinity. Today, all evidence of the past is gone, and the Rock itself is smaller than when the British invaded.

Wolcott
Routes 69, 322
Incorporated 1796

Native Americans
Tunxis

Historical notes
Hilly Wolcott was originally part of Waterbury and Southington. When the General Assembly voted on whether or not a separate town should be incorporated, Governor Wolcott cast the deciding vote. In gratitude, the town was named for him.

Amos Bronson Alcott (1799–1888), Louisa May Alcott's father, was born on his father's farm on Spindle Hill, Wolcott. He changed the family name from Alcox to Alcott. Too poor to attend Yale, he was largely self-taught. He became a Yankee peddler, and went to Virginia with a tin trunk on his back.

The life of a wandering merchant disagreed with him, and he sold his trunk and his wares for five dollars.

He returned to Connecticut where he taught school (see Bristol) before moving to Concord, Massachusetts.

Alcott's radical educational views held that gymnastics and play were important to learning. Both his school and his Utopian community floundered and his family lived in dire poverty until daughter Louisa's pen changed their fortunes.

Clockmaker Seth Thomas (1785–1859) was also born in Wolcott. Because there wasn't a road to Cheshire, he moved out of Wolcott to Plymouth.

Woodbridge

Routes 63, 67, 69, 114, 243, 312
Incorporated 1784

Native Americans
Quinnipiacs

Historical notes
As early as 1737, Woodbridge was known as the Parish of Amity. When it was later incorporated from New Haven and Milford, the town was named for its first minister.

Initially dependent upon agriculture, Woodbridge later turned to small industry. A tanbark crusher was brought from North Branford in 1700. This was a large, notched stone wheel turned by oxen around a circular stone track.

Corkscrews, melodeon, cement, candlesticks, clocks and spinning wheels, and friction matches were early products. The friction match industry was started by Thomas Sanford in his home (see Beacon Falls). Later, in 1835, William Clark set up a friction match factory employing fifteen men. He also employed seventy-five women, who made boxes for the matches in their homes.

The last Negro Governor was installed in Woodbridge. This was a custom begun in the days of slavery and continued until 1820. The governor was permitted to wear a high hat, something blacks were not otherwise allowed to do. During the "inauguration" ceremonies, the governor led a gay procession astride a horse. In addition to his high hat, he wore a sash over his left shoulder and a rosette on his breast.

After 1900, Woodbridge became largely a residential town.

Notable buildings
Thomas Darling House and Tavern (c. 1765), East of Woodbridge at 1907 Litchfield Turnpike (203-387-2823). Teamsters drove ox-carts laden with cargoes from the interior parts of the state to the docks and warehouses in New Haven. While enroute, they would often spend the night and eat at this tavern. Darling was friends with Benjamin Franklin, Ezra Stiles, Roger Sherman and Benedict Arnold.

New London County

The county is 669 square miles, and has 21 towns: Bozrah, Colchester, East Lyme, Franklin, Griswold, Groton, Lebanon, Ledyard, Lisbon, Lyme, Montville, New London, North Stonington, Norwich, Old Lyme, Preston, Salem, Sprague, Stonington, Voluntown and Waterford.

In 1860, New London County claimed three of the largest cities in the state: Norwich, New London and Stonington. Today, these cities have been eclipsed in size by others outside New London county. Nevertheless, the old mill towns along the rivers, and the seaports along the Sound, possess considerable charm and have much to attract the amateur historian. New London County is also home to Connecticut's two most active tribal nations, the Mashentucket Pequots and the Mohegans.

Interstates 395 and 95, plus State Routes 11 and 2, serve New London County. Route 49, from North Stonington north through Voluntown, provides a tour of one of the most rural areas of the state. Route 32 from the Windham border in Franklin, south through Norwich and on through Montville, will give you a good drive-by of the local history, including the site of the Mohegan Fort and Uncasville. Also of scenic and historic interest is Route 164, particularly through Griswold.

Bozrah

Route 163
Incorporated 1786

Native Americans
Mohegans

Historical notes
Originally part of the "Nine Miles Square" of the town of Norwich, the first settlers called the town New Concord. The name was changed to Bozrah, Hebrew for "sheep fold," at its incorporation.

Fitchville, in the northeastern corner of town, was the site of Asa Fitch, Sr.'s ironworks and Huntington Iron Works. Asa Fitch, Jr., who lived abroad much of his life due to ill health, returned to the U. S. in 1828, and built grist and cotton mills in Fitchville, a church, and a large house for himself. Nearby, in Bozrahville, cotton and wool mills operated.

Colchester

Routes 2, 16, 85
Incorporated 1698

Native Americans

Mohegans

Historical notes

The Governor's Highway—so-called because Governor Gurdon Saltonstall (1708–1725), often traveled this way between his New London mansion and his offices in Hartford—runs southwest out of Colchester on present-day Route 85. It enters town from Hartford on old Route 2. In 1800, the road became a turnpike and heavily traveled stagecoach route.

Saltonstall was the first man of the cloth to become governor in Connecticut, and was known for his fancy dress.

Nathaniel Hayword established The Hayword Rubber Company in 1847. It was one of the earliest rubber shoe factories. Hayword worked with

Governor Gurdon Saltonstall. He was known for his energy and commanding presence.

Charles Goodyear to develop the process to vulcanize rubber. He sold the plant to the United States Rubber Company in 1893, but it burned down in 1908 and was not rebuilt.

During the height of manufacturing in town, large numbers of Irish immigrated to work in the factories. Because of the influx of industry and an increase in population, Colchester was chartered as a borough in 1824. After the decline of manufacturing, Jewish immigrants settled on the old farms, followed by Poles and eastern Europeans.

In 1803, Pierpont Bacon founded Bacon Academy, a preparatory school which attracted students from all over the world. It rivaled New Hampshire's Phillips Exeter in reputation. Later, the school became the town's public high school. A well-kept brick building, painted yellow, with deep brown trim, and an imposing cupola, Bacon Academy is located in the center of town, on Route 85, on the southwestern corner of the Green. North of Bacon Academy is the site of the Encampment of Rochambeau's Army in 1781.

Inventions, inventors and firsts

The first Masonic Order of the Knights Templar in the United States was organized in a former stagecoach tavern, the Deming House (built in 1771). The hip-roofed house still stands at the north end of the green.

The first school for blacks in Connecticut was conducted in Colchester from around 1805 to the 1840s. The school was housed in a building which stood next to the Congregational Church.

Notable buildings

Comstock Bridge, one of the few remaining covered bridges in the state, is located off Route 16. It was built in the early 1870s and spans the Salmon River. No longer in use except as a pedestrian bridge, it is popular with photographers and fishermen.

Historic districts

Colchester Village Historic District, roughly along Broadway, Hayward, Linwood, and Norwich Avenues, Cragin Court, Pierce Lane, Stebbins Road, Main and South Main Streets. Route 85 runs along Main Street.

The center of Colchester (Route 85 and Route 16), is unusual in that not only do many of the magnificent early houses still encircle the spacious green, but there are shops, churches, the high school, eateries, and a B&B, all within walking distance.

At the south end of the green is the tiny, gambrel-roofed Nathaniel Foote House. The house was built in 1702 at the north end of town by the settlement's leader. To preserve it, the DAR (Daughters of the American Revolution) dismantled it and reconstructed it in its present position.

Another notable gambrel-roofed house is the imposing two-story Hayword House, built in 1776.

East Lyme

Routes 1, 156, 161
Incorporated 1839

Native Americans

Nehantic, who fished and hunted along the shore in present-day Niantic.

Historical notes

Originally part of Lyme and New London, East Lyme was later incorporated from Lyme and Waterford.

During the settlement's first winter of 1646, a Saybrook couple planned to wed. A great snowstorm blanketed the region, preventing the magistrate from going to Saybrook to perform the ceremony. Determined to tie the knot, the couple appealed to Governor Winthrop of New London, who was nearer. But the Governor did not have jurisdiction over Saybrook. The solution? Winthrop stood on the New London bank of Sunkipaug brook, which marked the boundary, and the couple stood on the east bank. Sunkipaug afterwards became known as Bride's Brook.

Later, when a boundary dispute erupted between Saybrook and New London, Winthrop settled the dispute, and declared the brook to be the boundary, citing the validity of the wedding as proof. Apparently, this was satisfactory, as Winthrop concluded, "Soe drinking a dram together, wih some seeming friendship, every man departed to his home."

A plaque on Route 156 marks the spot of the wedding.

Notable buildings

Thomas Lee House (c. 1664), Route 156. This house began as one room, facing south, with a stone chimney on the west. In 1690, a second room was added on the other side of the chimney by the second Thomas Lee, who had fifteen children. When the road changed in 1713 to where the present Route 156 lies, the house faced backwards. So, a lean-to was built across the old front on the south, making the back the front and the front the back. This kind of change is typical of early houses.

Thomas Avery House (Smith-Harris House, c. 1840), Society Road.

Franklin

Routes 32, 87, 207
Incorporated 1786

Native Americans

Mohegans. In the summer, the Nipmucs followed a path across present-day Franklin on their way to the shore to feast on the abundant seafood.

Historical notes

Settled as West Farms of Norwich in 1663, the town was named for Benjamin Franklin when it was incorporated. By the end of the seventeenth century, Franklin was well served by roads leading to Windham, Lebanon, Norwich and Hartford.

The town was sometimes known as the "Place of Seven Hills," because there were indeed seven notable hills: Portipaug Hill, Pleasure and Hearthstone Hills, Center or Middle (Great) Hill, which had a large cavern called Dragon's Hole, Meeting House Hill, Blue Hill and Little Lebanon Hill.

Franklin has been an agrarian town since its settlement in the seventeenth century, with some farmlands remaining in the same families for three centuries.

Ghost stories and legends

One spring evening in 1693, an itinerant peddler stopped at the green. The women of town gathered around him and admired the trinkets and tinware in his bags. The arrival of a peddler was always cause for excitement and an occasion to gossip. The next morning, however, the peddler had disappeared. At first everyone thought he had moved on, but later that day, his body was found at the foot of an apple tree in the orchard of Micah Rood. The peddler's head was split open and his pack of wares was empty.

Everyone suspected Micah Rood. He was a taciturn man who kept to himself and had nothing to say about why the body was found on his farm. After the murder, he seemed even more solitary.

The following autumn, when the apples ripened in the orchard, there was a strangeness about the fruit on the "murder tree." Each apple was stained as if with a drop of blood. Folks in the village said that the peddler had cast a curse on Rood just before he died.

Ever after, the blossoms of the apple tree have born a red stain, and the fruit has been marked as with blood. Micah Rood never confessed to the crime, and went to his own death, years later, without ever saying a word about the whole mystery.

Griswold

Routes 12, 138, 164, 165, 201
Incorporated 1815

Native Americans

Pauchaug. There was still a community of Pauchaug living here when Griswold was incorporated.

Historical notes

Pauchaug (Griswold) was part of Preston, and was named for Governor Griswold. Early settlers began arriving from Stonington and the south of Preston around 1690. One of the first settlers, Samuel Leonard, built a home on the Pauchaug River. His son was a captive of the Indians on the Merrimac River for two years, but escaped and made his way back to Pauchaug, an exploit which caused the neighbors to marvel.

Others followed Leonard's lead and staked their futures on Pauchaug. By 1711, there were corn mills and saw-mills near the falls in Hopeville. An ironworks was founded at Glasgo on the "island" in the Pauchaug. Hammers, anvils, shovels and tongs were produced. Dr. Elisha Perkins invented a tractor made of knitting needles to massage sore muscles and began offering relief to his hardworking patients.

In 1771 Eliezer Jewett arrived from Norwich, set up his farm and opened a tavern, later known as the Fenner House, near the Lisbon town line.

Shortly afterwards, Jewett built saw, grist and fulling mills on the Pauchaug River and opened a clothiers' shop. As if that wasn't enough, he built the first irrigation plant, parallel to the river. The town was starting to hum.

John Schofield came from England in 1804 and built a small mill with his son. For ten years he had been attempting to make a carding machine, and now that he had succeeded he was ready to go into business. A flaxseed mill opened along the river in 1804. Other mills followed. Soon, the village of Pauchaugville was called Jewett City in honor of Eliezer.

When the Marquis de Lafayette visited the U. S. in 1824, he arrived in Jewett City at midnight late in August. All the houses had candles of welcome in the windows, some as many as two rows. One of the old veterans who came out to meet him was Simeon Simons, Washington's Indian body-guard, and another was Enoch Baker, who had taken the news to the Continental Congress of Burgoyne's surrender.

Notable buildings

Edward Cogswell House (c. 1790), 1429 Hopeville Road, off Route 138. Cogswell owned a share of an ironworks in Glasgo.

Enoch Baker House (c. 1790), 62 East Main Street, Jewett City. Baker was a veteran of the Revolutionary War. He served at Bunker Hill and was one of the men to carry the news of Burgoyne's surrender.

John Wilson House (c. 1782), 11 Ashland Street. A gem!

Groton
Routes 1, 12, 117, 184, 215, 349
Incorporated 1705

Native Americans

Pequots. Sassacus, chief sachem of the Pequots, lived on the top of Fort Hill in Poquonick. A smaller fort was on the east side of present-day Mitchell Street in Groton Bank.

The history of Native Americans in Groton is inextricably intertwined with the Pequot War and the Mystic Massacre. It is a complicated and horrifying story, and though at the time, preachers such as the renowned Cotton Mather exclaimed that God was on their side, it wasn't long before even the most conservative nineteenth-century historian questioned the morality of the whole affair. You can still go to the place where all this happened. A monument, albeit to John Mason, is near the site of the Pequot fort.

The Mystic Massacre

(see also Fairfield, Saybrook and Wethersfield) By 1637 the situation had grown so dire that neither Sassacus and his Pequots nor the colonials thought coexistence possible. The General Court at Hartford decided to take an aggressive stance, and declared war on the Pequots. They raised a levy of ninety men from Hartford, Windsor and Wethersfield under the command of John Mason. Mason's

Uncas, the leader of the Mohegan Pequots, arguing his case before the English court.

plan was to attack Sassacus' strongholds in Groton and (West) Mystic. He received an unexpected offer of help from the Mohegan, Uncas, who had himself been at war with the Pequots.

At first distrustful of Uncas, Mason finally accepted him as an ally and the ninety English plus the Mohegans set out for the Pequot fort. They arrived at the fort well before dawn on Friday, June 5, the English in the lead, the Mohegans in the rear. The English split into two groups and silently approached from the south and the west. When they were close, a dog barked and a Pequot yelled, "Owanux! Owanux!" (Englishmen! Englishmen!) The English stormed the fort, where they found the inhabitants—estimates range from four hundred to eight hundred—somewhat confused, as they were startled from sleep.

Fierce fighting ensued. Mason decided to set fire to the fort and shouted, "We must burn them!" He ran into a wigwam, grabbed a torch and ignited the fort. A northeast wind hastened the spread of the fire, and within moments, the fort was a raging inferno. As the Pequots tried to escape, including women, children and old men, the English killed them, until they lay about in heaps, "all dead by a horrible and agonizing death."

About three hundred Pequots now came from the other, smaller fort, and seeing the carnage, they tore their hair in grief and rage, and then rushed down the hill after the English, but they were no match for the English muskets. The surviving Pequots fled, eventually making their way to the Great Swamp in Fairfield.

Historical notes

Groton was settled by John Winthrop the younger and a band of Puritans from Massachusetts. It was part of the New London plantation. Groton was the site of two bloody massacres, the massacre of the Pequots described above, and the massacre of American troops by Benedict Arnold and his men. No other Connecticut town has suffered so much spilled blood on its soil.

The siege and subsequent massacre of the Patriot forces at Groton began when a British fleet was discovered in the harbor in the early morning of September 6, 1781. The Groton guards fired two guns, the signal that the British were at hand, but the British, knowing the code, fired a third gun. Three shots was the signal for "good news."

The Patriots were deceived and did not answer the alarm. By eight in the morning, eight hundred British, commanded by Benedict Arnold, had landed. There were about one hundred and fifty men in the fort, most of them untrained and recently enlisted from local farms. They were commanded by Colonel William Ledyard.

Arnold was stationed on a hill in New London where he could watch the proceedings through his spyglass. He demanded surrender. Ledyard replied, "We shall not surrender, let the consequences be what they may."

Ledyard expected reinforcements to arrive shortly, and indeed a few did. They advised Ledyard and his men to come out of the fort and fight on open ground. Ledyard demurred, and the fort was soon overrun by the large British regiment.

Ledyard knew they hadn't a chance, so when a British officer cried out, "Who commands this fort?" Ledyard answered, in surrender, "I did sir, but you do now!" and offered his sword. The British officer took the sword, but rather than taking Ledyard and his men prisoner, as they expected, he plunged the sword into Ledyard repeatedly, killing him.

The British then proceeded to slaughter everyone inside the fort. When they were done killing, they set fire to the fort. Some families lost every male member. Nearly every family lost at least one, a few lost as many as nine. Within a few hours, Groton had become a town of widows and bereft mothers, daughters and sisters. The British went on to burn several houses before returning to their ships.

In 1792, the General Assembly offered a half-million acres in the Western Reserves (Ohio) to those families who had lost loved ones in the Fort Griswold Massacre. In 1842, the fort became property of the U. S. government and a stone marker was placed at the spot where Ledyard fell, commemorating his heroism. Oddly, a memorial was also placed in honor of the British Major Montgomery, who was killed with a pike by Gordon Freeman, Ledyard's black servant.

Groton developed various industries, including shipbuilding, sea trade, fishing as far away as the coast of Cuba and the West Indies, and salvaging operations. Groton seafarers also engaged in whaling, and sometimes found themselves at the mercy of pirates.

Though it has been centuries since a battle was fought on Groton land, the town has long been engaged in supplying ships and submarines to the military. Groton was threatened during the War of 1812, but not attacked.

Ghost stories and legends

This is the story of Mother Bailey's petticoat. Mother Bailey (Anna Warner Bailey) lived in a two and a half story house on Thames Street. She was in her house minding her business in June 1813, when a messenger from the fort raced through town. This was during the War of 1812. Commodore Stephen Decatur, whose fleet was pursued by the British, had taken refuge in New London harbor.

It had been not so many years since the massacre of 1781, and Groton residents feared the worst. They hastily bundled their most important possessions into carts and headed inland. The messenger came from the fort in search of rags for gun wadding, but everyone was so busy fleeing, he was unsuccessful in finding one scrap.

When he got to Mother Bailey, she yanked off her red flannel petticoat, and said, "There are plenty more where that came from!" The messenger brought the petticoat back to the fort, where the men flew it from a pikestaff and called it "The Martial Petticoat." The British did not invade the town. After the war, President Jackson visited Mother Bailey and gave her an iron fence for her house as a gift.

John Ledyard (1751–1789), a nephew of Colonel William Ledyard, was a freshman at Dartmouth in 1772, when he was struck with wanderlust. He made himself a fifty-foot canoe from a pine tree, and sailed down the Connecticut River to Hartford. Here he "shipped to mast" and voyaged to Gibraltar, the Barbary Coast and the West Indies. He then sailed with Captain Cook from London and was with him when he discovered the Sandwich Islands (Hawaii). They also sailed to China, Siberia and the Arctic.

When the young Ledyard returned to America, he published a journal of his travels. His wanderlust unabated, his travels continued. He was in Stockholm when he learned of Thomas Jefferson's plan to explore the Pacific Northwest via Siberia. Nothing would do but he must go, and he walked an astonishing 1,400 miles in the next seven weeks to St. Petersburg, Russia. At Irkutsk, he was stopped and ordered to leave the country.

Ledyard died at the age of thirty-seven while he was in London preparing to go to Cairo to explore Africa.

Notable buildings

Fort Griswold Battlefield State Park, Monument Street and Park Avenue (860-446-9257). Site of 1781 massacre of American troops. See historic notes above.

Ebenezer Avery House (c. 1750). This house was used as a hospital for the wounded in the massacre. There is a corner cupboard with a carved rose, and wonderful battened doors.

Historic districts

Eastern Point Historic District, roughly bounded by Beach Pond Avenue, Tyler Point Drive, Shore Avenue, Hillside Avenue and Eastern Point Road.

Groton Bank Historic District (Groton Bank, Groton Heights), roughly bounded by Monument, School, Thames and Broad Streets.

Mystic River Historic District, west side of Mystic River. Most of the pre-1900 houses have been researched and placqued.

At 20 High Street is the house where Daniel and Carrie Packer began making "Lightening Soap" in 1869. Now called Packer's Tar Soap, it was reputed

to cure everything from baldness to acne.

The Portersville Academy (c. 1839), 74 High Street. Upstairs is a recreated 1840s schoolroom. Also headquarters of the Mystic River Historic Society (860-536-4779). The Society offers a wonderful booklet, *Curbstones, Clapboards and Cupolas,* for $3.00.

Noank Historic District, Noank Peninsula.

Lebanon

Routes 16, 87, 207, 289
Incorporated 1700

Native Americans

Mohegans

Historical notes

Poqucchaneeg was ceded by Owenco, son of Uncas, in six tracts. The first tract went to John Mason (see Groton). The early years were marked by litigation and boundary disputes. Settlement began in 1695, and five years later the town was named for the Biblical town of Lebanon.

Lebanon and the Trumbull family name are almost synonymous, and for Revolutionary War buffs, a visit to the town is a must. The Trumbulls were a wealthy merchant family with extensive trade in the West Indies and branch offices in Norwich, Wethersfield and East Haddam. Jonathan Trumbull was the only governor in the Colonies to support the Revolution.

Because Lebanon was on the crossroads of routes from Norwich to Hartford to New York, it was a

Revolutionary War strategy was planned in this buccolic Lebanon setting.

convenient place to conduct meetings. Trumbull and his family directed efforts to keep the Continental Army in provisions and earned Connecticut the title of the "Supply State."

Ghost stories and legends

In the winter of 1780 the French Hussars camped on the town green, and were known to forage on the neighboring farms. The townsfolk complained of this nuisance and so a regulation was enacted forbidding the Hussars from leaving their camp between sundown and sunset. Anyone absent from the camp during those hours would be considered a deserter and shot. But whatever the time period, when it comes to love between a young man and a young woman, rules are meaningless.

And so, perhaps inevitably, one young Frenchman, rumored to be a nobleman serving as a private, snuck out to visit a young Englishwoman, Prudence Strong, for a romantic tryst. The Hussar was caught returning to camp, tried as a deserter, and condemned to death. As soon as Prudence got word of this, she rushed to Lauzun, her lover's commander, and begged for mercy. Lauzun sent a messenger with a reprieve, but it was too late. The young Frenchman was executed in front of his entire legion. He was buried in a field beside Colchester Road with a pile of stones as a marker. The cairn came to be known as "The French Deserter's Grave."

Captain S. L. Gray, the skipper of a whaling ship, was killed at sea when he was struck by a shell from the Confederate warship *Shenandoah*. His wife, who was aboard, pickled his body in a cask of spirits and brought it home to Lebanon. He is buried in the cask in Liberty Hill Cemetery on Route 87.

Notable buildings

Dr. William Beaumont House (1760), 169 West Town Street, on the Green, Route 87 (860-642-7247). Dr. Beaumont gained worldwide fame when he reported on his patient, Alexis St. Martin, who was left with a hole in his abdomen after recovering from a gunshot wound. The hole enabled Dr. Beaumont to study the digestive processes. The house contains exhibits of surgical instruments.

Revolutionary War Office (c. 1727), West Town Street (860-642-7558). This was originally built as the Trumbull Family Store, but during the Revolution, served as Trumbull's office where he held conferences with Washington, Lafayette, Rochambeau, de Lauzun, Adams, Jay and Franklin. The War Office was also used by the Council of Connecticut Safety for more than twelve hundred meetings. And Benjamin Franklin's Tory son, William, was held prisoner in this building for awhile.

Governor Jonathan Trumbull House (c. 1735), West Town Street, on the Green (860-642-7558). Also the Wadsworth Stable where George Washington's horse slept. The Governor's house was moved to its present location in 1825. During the Revolutionary War, there was a tunnel from the house to the War Office.

Jonathan Trumbull, Jr., House (c. 1769), Route 87 (860-642-6100). Isaac Fitch built this eight-room Georgian-style house for the Governor's son, who like his father, was an active

patriot. Especially intriguing are the eight intricately carved corner fireplaces.

William Williams House (c. 1712), Route 87 and Route 207. Squire Williams entertained Washington and Lafayette in his home. William Williams drafted a declaration of rights and liberties six years before the Declaration of Independence was written.

Historic districts

Lebanon Green Historic District, Routes 87, 207, and 289, West Town Street and Kolar Drive. The Green is a mile long. Two hundred French Hussars camped on the Green during the winter of 1780–81. Later that same winter, Rochambeau arrived with five regiments, who also camped on the Green. A tablet was placed on the Green to mark the spot where the French had their bake oven. The Congregational Church on the Green was designed by John Trumbull the artist, and its architecture is a particular point of pride with many Lebanon residents.

Ledyard
Routes 2, 214, 117
Incorporated 1836

Native Americans

Pequots. After the Pequot War, the Pequot population was less than half of the four thousand prewar population. Captured survivors were sold into slavery or killed. Those who managed to escape dispersed into other tribes. Gradually there came to be two groups, one which lived in Misquamicut under the control of the Narragansett and Eastern Niantic tribes. These Pawcatuck Pequots were granted a 250-acre reservation in Stonington in 1683.

The other group, the Nameag or Noank Pequots, was granted a reservation in Nameag in New London by Governor Jonathan Winthrop, Jr., in 1638. They refused, however, to submit to Uncas. Their leader, Robin Cassacinamon, negotiated with Governor Winthrop for a reservation along the Mystic River at Mashantucket (Mashantuxet) in present-day Ledyard.

Through Cassacinamon's political skills, the Mashantucket Pequots managed to regain their homeland in 1650, and by 1666 most of them had moved to Mashantucket from Noank. Their numbers were small, and the tract of land was meager, but they were back on their ancestral soil, a position they have successfully maintained to this day. Driving along Route 2 in Ledyard, when you see Foxwoods Casino looming before you, you are seeing a monument to the Mashantucket Pequots' resilience.

Historical notes

After the conquest of the Pequots, Uncas gave a tract of land to Jonathan Brewster. He already owned adjoining land where he had established a trading post. This tract, Brewster's Neck, became successively part of New London, of Norwich, of Preston, and of North Groton. Farms, called the Pocketannock grants, were laid out in 1653. In 1836 these lands became part of the new town of Ledyard, which was named for Colonel William Ledyard, killed at Fort Griswold (see Groton).

Gales Ferry became the principal village of Ledyard. Here, Roger Gale built a shipyard. There were likely a few other yards. Ships were built for the East India trade. The last large schooner was built in 1888–89.

Silas Deane (1737–1789) was born in what became Ledyard. Deane, who moved to Wethersfield, was instrumental in obtaining secret supplies from France during the Revolution. However, he was called back when his transactions came under suspicion. Unable to clear his name, he returned to France and later moved to London, where he lived in poverty. On his return trip home, he died aboard ship. In 1842, he was exonerated by Congress and his heirs were paid $37,000. A highway (Route 99) is named for him.

Ghost stories and legends

Ledyard has had its share of, shall we say, unusual religions. The Rogerine Quakers established themselves in the southeastern part of Ledyard. They were followers of John Rogers, who had organized a church in New London in 1674. They strongly disagreed with the Congregationalists, and by the Eighteenth century their zeal was unbounded, leading them frequently to disrupt Congregational services. The men would crouch down outside the church windows during service and make loud, heckling noises. The women carried their spinning wheels into church and set to work, an affront to those who held to the sanctity of the Sabbath.

Even more curious is the story of the eccentric Jemima Wilkinson, who reputedly died sometime between 1770 and 1790. Although no one much cared for her, when she died, neighbors dutifully gathered about her casket to pay their last respects. A friend lifted the coffin lid so that the mourners could look one last time upon her. Suddenly, the diminutive Jemima popped out of the coffin and announced that she would do the preaching. She declared she had been sent back from heaven as a Redeemer.

Continuing with a fiery sermon, she told her astonished neighbors that her redemption marked the regeneration of the world. News spread quickly, and folks came from all over to see the woman risen from the dead. She gathered a congregation about herself and moved to Tioga County, Pennsylvania, where she attracted additional enthusiastic "Jemimakins." From there, she and her followers moved to Yates County in New York state, and founded Penn Yan (from Pennsylvania and Yankees), a name the town bears to this day.

Notable buildings

Ledyard Water-Powered Up-Down Sawmill, Iron Street, Route 214, east of the center of town (860-462-888,

860-433-4050). Once these sawmills were in every town and village. Lumber was not only a necessity for house building, but was one of the colony's important exports.

An Up-Down was essentially a six-foot-tall blade set vertically within a wooden square, housed in a shed and powered by water.

Mashantucket Pequot Museum & Research Center, (800-411-9671), I-95, Exit 92, or I-395, Exit 79A. Located off Route 2, on the Mashantucket Reservation. Permanent exhibits include a recreation of a 16th century Pequot village. Extensive library and research center.

Avery Homestead (c. 1700–1725), 20 Avery Hill. The rear roof line of this old saltbox is unusually high and accommodates a row of tiny, second-story windows. This is the oldest house in Ledyard.

Historic districts

Gales Ferry Historic District No. 1, junction of Hurlbutt Road and Riverside Place. East of Gales Ferry, early settlers cut ship's masts from the towering trees of the Gungywamp Hills.

Lisbon

Routes 169, 12, 138
Incorporated 1786

Native Americans

Mohegan

Historical notes

Oweneco conveyed the tract of land "in the crotch of the rivers Showtucket and Queengauge" to John Fitch, a land speculator, in 1687. Around the same time, a Norwich man, Josiah Reed, was probably already living there. Shortly after, the Perkins brothers arrived. The newly formed society was called Newent. Nevertheless, Oweneco and his descendants did not give the English a quitclaim deed for the "crotch" until 1756. The settlement was incorporated from Norwich and named for Lisbon, Portugal.

Inventions, inventors and firsts

The first railroad tunnel built in America was built in Lisbon by the Norwich & Worcester Railroad in 1837. The tunnel had to be blasted under Bundy Hill where the line came in from Taftville. The Norwich & Worcester Railroad was a rail and boat line. Steamships met the rail in Norwich and continued the journey down the Thames and on to New York City.

Lyme

Routes 156, 82
Incorporated 1667

Native Americans

Pequots, then Mohegans.

Historical notes

Lyme is in the northwestern corner of what was a larger town, which included East Lyme, sectioned off in 1839, and Old Lyme, sectioned off in 1855. The larger town was the result of an even earlier sectioning when the "Loving Parting" between Saybrook and East Saybrook was signed in 1665.

William Lord purchased a tract of land from the sachem Chapeto which included the entire valley of the Eight Mile River in April of 1669 and settled in the present Old Lyme section. By 1667 there were thirty families living in East Saybrook. The name was changed to Lyme, for Lyme Regis in England.

However, complications arose when Joshua (Attawanhood, the third son of Uncas), the sachem of the western Nehantics, also claimed land in Lyme, citing his inheritance from his uncle and namesake, Attawanhood. A committee was appointed by the Court in 1671 to look into the matter. The committee advised the town of Lyme to allow him the lands.

Joshua lived there until his death in the spring of 1676. The area was called Joshuatown. His will left the lands he claimed to his three children, but litigation quickly ensued over their rights to it. The land was sold to Richard Ely that same year. At the turn of the century, around 1700, Joshua's land became Sterling City and Pleasant Valley.

Shipbuilding villages grew up along the Connecticut River. Hadlyme (within the bounds of Lyme) to the north and Hamburg (also within the bounds of Lyme) further south, trafficked in lumber. Oxen would line up, sometimes a hundred yoke in winter, their carts laden with ties and other forest products. As many as eighty schooners a year left Hamburg loaded with lumber. Ferries brought passengers and cargo back and forth across the River. When the era of schooners passed, artists flocked to the river villages of Lyme, attracted by the picturesque scenery.

Ghost stories and legends

Lyme had its own "tea party" during the time leading up to the Revolution. William Lamson, a peddler from Martha's Vineyard, arrived one day, and as with the arrival of any peddler in town, people gathered around him to see what he was selling. Tea! It was truly a luxury, but the citizens of Lyme suspected that it was the some of the hated tea which had lately landed on Cape Cod.

They examined the leaves and declared the tea to be exactly as they suspected. Then, according to the Connecticut Journal of March 25th, 1774, "a number of the sons of liberty assembled in the evening, kindled a fire, and committed [the tea] to the flames, where it was all consumed and the ashes buried on the spot, in testimony of their utter abhorrence of all tea subject to a duty for the purpose of raising a revenue in America."

Historic districts

Hadlyme Ferry Historic District, 150, 151,158, 162 Ferry Road, and ferry slip. Second oldest continuously operating ferry in the state (860-566-7635).

Hamburg Bridge Historic District, Joshuatown Road and Old Hamburg Road.

Montville

Routes 32, 82, 163
Incorporated 1786

Native Americans

Mohegans. Montville was the seat of power for Uncas and remains home to Connecticut's Mohegans. Uncas took up leadership of a splinter group of the Pequots when he failed to become sachem of the Pequot tribe. His tribe became known as the Mohegan Pequots, or Mohegans, though it was his dream to reunite the two tribes.

The Narragansetts besieged Uncas and his people. Unable to leave their fort, they were near starvation when Thomas Leffingwell came to Uncas' rescue, bringing food. This began a mostly friendly relationship between Uncas and the English. Uncas joined with the English in the Pequot War, against the Pequots, and in King Philip's War, against the the loose confederation the Wampanoag sachem Metacom, whom the English called Philip, had put together in an effort to remove or contain the English.

Uncas was a complicated, politically astute and resourceful man, depicted somewhat romantically, and inaccurately, in James Fennimore Cooper's novel, *Last of the Mohicans*. Anthropologist Eric Johnson points out that, "By the end of King Philip's War, the Mohegans were one of very few Native communities in the region that had avoided invasion by English troops and had retained their guns, much of their land, their religion, and their political autonomy. By these measures, the Mohegans, through their sachem Uncas, resisted the forces of colonialism."

Historical notes

There were early sawmills and forges in Montville. John Winthrop owned a sawmill on the Oxoboro River as early as 1653. It was later converted to a puddling forge (also called a bloomery), where iron was melted into puddles or lumps. Afterwards, the lumps were hammered into wrought iron. There were cattle and sheep, and later carding mills. Cotton and woolen fabrics were manufactured in Uncasville.

Madam Knight, the celebrated solo female traveler, later moved to Montville to be near her married daughter in New London. Madam Knight had extensive real estate interests in Connecticut, including a farm in New London, land on the Norwich Town green and a tavern.

The history of Mohegan/Montville is inextricably bound up with the Mohegans, who continue to live on their ancestral lands today. In the second half of the twentieth century the Tantaquidgeons, anthropologists Gladys and her brother John, devoted themselves to research about and preservation of not only the Mohegan/Pequot cultures, but eastern woodland Indians in general. A few years ago, the tribe opened a gambling casino, the Mohegan Sun, which attracts large numbers of visitors.

Samson Occom.

Inventions, inventors and firsts

Samson Occom (1723–1792), a Mohegan, was the first Native American in Connecticut to be ordained a minister. After converting to Christianity in 1741, he studied with the Reverend Wheelock in Columbia and was the inspiration for Wheelock's Indian Charity School (see Columbia). He was a missionary to the Oneida, and then went to England, where he raised substantial sums of money that became the nucleus of the Dartmouth College endowment. Occom organized some Mohegan, Pequot, Narragansett and Tunxis into the Brotherton Indians and moved to land given them by the Oneida. They later moved to Wisconsin.

Geology

Cochegan Rock is believed to be the largest glacial erratic in New England, estimated to weigh 6,000 tons. Uncas and his councillors held secret meetings at this rock. It is named for Caleb

Cochegan, who reputedly lived in the shelter of this massive boulder. Off Raymond Hill Road, which extends east of Route 163.

Notable buildings

Tantaquidgeon Indian Museum, Route 32 (860-848-9145). This is the famous museum and collection of the Tantaquidegons, including displays of wigwams and crafts. The emphasis is on eastern Woodland Indians.

Mohegan Congregational Church (c. 1831), Route 32.

Fort Shantok, home of Uncas (860-204-6100), near the village of Mohegan, contains the remains of a Mohegan fort.

New London

Routes 1, 213
Incorporated 1647

Native Americans

Pequots

Historical notes

New London harbor, a "drowned valley" at the mouth of the Thames, is one of the deepest harbors on the Atlantic coast. The area was called Nameaug by the Indians, but Pequot by the colonists. In 1641, five hundred acres of "Pequot Country" were granted to John Mason after the Pequot War, and another five hundred to "such souldears as joyned wth him in the searvice when they conquered the Indeans there."

The disposition of another "10,000 acres of grownd in Pequoyt Country,"

was authorized by the Court in 1642. The first permanent houses were built in 1646 when John Winthrop, Jr., and others arrived, numbering forty families within two years. Believing that their settlement would become a great commercial center, they named it New London, after London, England.

Shipbuilding, sea trade, fishing and whaling developed into lucrative businesses. Wealth was accumulated. Taverns were built. A bank was created. The harbor did not quite rival its namesake, but it thrived.

During the Revolution, many privateers sailed from the harbor. One vessel sailed to Long Island, where the crew disembarked and hauled the ship overland on wheels to the opposite shore! They set sail from Southampton and captured five British ships.

Washington visited New London several times, as it was the Naval Headquarters. The townspeople expected British attack, and moved the town records to Waterford for safekeeping, a good idea, because Benedict Arnold set fire to the city in 1781 (see Groton).

In addition to ships, New London has produced bedding, sewing and embroidery silks, paper boxes, silk fabrics, hats, caps, clothing and many other goods. It is home to the Coast Guard Academy and Connecticut College.

Inventions, inventors and firsts

In 1760 or thereabouts, the first lighthouse on the Connecticut shore was built at the entrance to New

London harbor. It was funded by a lottery. A second lighthouse was built on the same site in 1801.

Thomas Short (1682–1712) was the first printer in Connecticut. In 1708 the General Assembly appointed him to "print all the publick acts of this Colony (and the election sermon if desired)." Until his appointment, printing was done in Boston. His first book, and the first book published in Connecticut, was *Saybrook Platform or The Confession of Faith,* printed in 1710. Short was born in Maine where he, his brother and his sisters were captured by Indians and held in captivity in Canada. They were redeemed, probably by Cotton Mather.

Notable buildings

Connecticut College Arboretum, Williams Street, I-85 Exit 83S/84N (860-439-5020). 425 acres and a fine collection of trees.

Hempstead Houses, 11 Hempstead Street, I-95 Exit 83N/84S (860-247-8996). The Joshua Hempsted House (c. 1678) was built in stages, and traces

The ancient and beautiful Hempstead House of New London in its earlier days.

the evolution of the Connecticut salt-box. The house began as a single room with an end chimney and a single "summer" beam (second-floor support beam) running front to back. A second room with two summer beams was added on the other side of the chimney, and later a lean-to room was added.

The house is insulated with seaweed. It was one of the few to escape ruination when Benedict Arnold burned New London. The Hempsted family were early Abolitionists and their house was a stop on the Underground Railroad. Joshua Hempstead published his journals as *Hempstead Diary.*

The neighboring stone house, the Huguenot House (c. 1758), was built by Nathaniel Hempstead for Huguenot refugees.

Shaw Mansion (c. 1765), 11 Blinman Street, I-95 Exit 83N/84S (860-443-1209). The granite for this imposing house was quarried by thirty-five Acadian refugees. Shaw's son Nathaniel was in charge of Naval operations during the Revolution and the house became the Naval Headquarters.

When New London was burned in 1781, the family used vinegar stored in casks in the attic to extinguish the flames, a quick-thinking deed that saved their home.

The Mansion was used as a hospital during the war. Lucretia Shaw, who was married to Nathaniel, caught gaol fever from one of the young soldiers and died. George Washington, Nathan

Hale and many others dined or met at the Shaw Mansion.

Monte Cristo Cottage, 325 Pequot Avenue (860-442-0051). This was the boyhood summer home of Eugene O'Neill, the Nobel-Prize-winning playwright. Two of his plays, "Long Day's Journey into Night" and "Ah! Wilderness," were set in this house. O'Neill's father was an actor. He named the house for his most famous role, as the Count of Monte Cristo.

New London Custom House (New London Maritime 1833 Robert Mills Custom House Museum), 150 Bank Street, on the Thames River, I-95 Exit 75N/84S (860-447-2501). The doors are made from planks taken from the U.S.S. *Constitution* (Old Ironsides).

Nathan Hale School, near the railroad station, on the Thames (moved from its original site). Nathan Hale was teaching school in New London when he heeded the Lexington Alarm and joined Knowlton's Rangers (see Ashford).

Lyman Allyn Art Museum, 625 Williams Street, I-95 Exit 83 (860-443-2545). American impressionist art, decorative arts, dolls and dollhouses.

Historic districts

Civic Institutions Historic District, 156–158, 171, 173–175 Garfield Avenue, 179 Coleman Street, 32 Walden Avenue.

Coit Street Historic District, roughly bounded by Coit, Washington Tilley, Bank and Washington Streets.

Downtown New London Historic District, roughly bounded by Captain's Walk, Bank, Tilley and Washington Streets. Also, along Huntington, Washington and Jay Streets, the southwest corner of Meriden and Governor Winthrop Boulevard, and along Bank and Sparyard Streets. You will want to walk rather than drive—there are sidewalks and the buildings are all close together.

Hempstead Historic District, roughly bounded by Franklin and Jay Streets and Mountain Avenue, with the Hempstead Houses in the center. This district includes houses purchased by free African-Americans during the 1840s. The Hempsteads were ardent Abolitionists. Descendants of the family sold these properties to Savillion Haley, who believed that African-Americans were entitled to housing that was equal in quality to the houses of whites. African-Americans have lived in New London since the Revolution.

Montauk Avenue Historic District, roughly bounded by Ocean, Willets, and Riverview Avenues and Faire Harbor.

Pequot Colony Historic District, roughly bounded by Gardner, Pequot, Glenwood and Montauk Avenues. Pequot parallels the Thames and boasts many old estates.

Post Hill Historic District, roughly bounded by Bulkeley Place, Huntington, Federal and Hempstead Streets.

United States Housing Corporation Historic District, roughly bounded by

Colman, Fuller, and West Pleasant Streets and Jefferson Avenue.

Whale Oil Row District, 105–109 Huntington Street. This was the heart of New London's whaling industry.

Whaling is first referred to in the public record of 1647. Whales were then plentiful along the Connecticut coast. By 1750, whaling was a flourishing industry. The first ship sailed on May 20, 1784, and from that time, whaling ships left the harbor and sailed great distances in pursuit of this enormous sea mammal, returning with barrels of oil and tons of bone.

When ships returned from Brazil with more than three hundred barrels of whale oil, the *New London Gazette* excitedly exhorted everyone to "all strike out." Whaling was a high-profit endeavor, and even ships sailing to the Arctic and Antarctic could yield a fortune. The industry was the main employer of area men and attracted African-Americans and Native Americans as well as Europeans. The last ship sailed in 1909, after the coming of electricity had eliminated most of the demand for whale-oil lamps.

Williams Memorial Park Historic District, roughly bounded by Hempstead and Broad Streets, Williams Memorial Parkway and Mercer Street.

North Stonington

Routes 2, 49, 184, 201, 216
Incorporated 1804

Native Americans

Pequots. Sassacus had a lookout on the quartz mountain, Lantern Hill. This became a Pequot reservation in 1683 and continues as such to the present.

Historical notes

First settled in 1680. North Stonington was sectioned off from Stonington at incorporation. During the eighteenth century, agriculture and small mills—fulling, saw, and grist—occupied the inhabitants. A silex (silica) mine was opened near Lantern Hill.

The eighteenth century brought increased population and increased commercial activity. There were now tanneries, cabinetmaking shops, dye houses, iron works, drygoods and grocery stores. North Stonington became a busy mercantile center.

In 1814, when watchmen spotted British ships, they ignited hogsheads of tar and effectively turned the summit of Tar Barrel Hill into a warning beacon for the folks living below. The flames roared brightly throughout the night.

By the turn of the century, North Stonington had once again become agricultural. As shops closed up, dairying took over.

Notable buildings

Deacon Gershom Palmer House/ Colonel William Randall House/John Randall House (c. 1680–1720), Route

2 near the Stonington town line, now Randall's Ordinary (860-599-4540), an inn and restaurant. (An "ordinary" is so called because it is licensed by town ordinance to operate as a business.) This unusual two-story house once had an elm-lined garden. There are double summer beams in some of the rooms, "tombstone" panels, and reputedly, a former slave-dungeon in the basement.

The murder of the Narragansett Miantinomo.

Historic district

North Stonington Historic Village District, vicinity of Route 2.

Norwich

Routes 2, 12, 32, 97, 169
Incorporated 1659

Native Americans

Norwich and its environs saw terrible Indian conflict, particularly between the Narragansetts, led by Miantinomo, and the Mohegan Pequots, led by Uncas. There is a tradition that after the battle of Great Plain between the Narragansetts and Mohegans, some of the Narragansetts were driven over the Yantic Falls. This is where the Yantic River drops into the Thames valley, on Route 32 in Norwich. Uncas captured Miantinomo on the plain and brought him to Hartford, where he was granted permission to execute him.

Historical notes

Jonathan Brewster operated a trading post in present-day Norwich. Even though the General Court of 1650 judged his actions to be "the thinge very disorderly," since he had no right

to be settled in the area, it decided to allow him to continue. Less than a decade later, Uncas deeded the lands including all of Norwich, Franklin, Bozrah, Lisbon, Sprague and the western parts of Preston and Griswold to John Mason and James Fitch.

For the first sixty years, the present downtown of Norwich was used for sheep, and the center of activity was in Norwich Town. Later, following New London's lead, Norwich turned to seafaring. Trade was entertained with coastal cities and with distant ports.

By 1760, there were seven ships making regular voyages to the West Indies. Ships left with cargoes of cordwood, barrel staves, horses and produce. Many took up whaling. Some engaged in the slave trade. The town prospered and many grew rich.

In addition to the sea trade, blacksmith shops, gristmills, tanneries and sawmills operated in Norwich. Combs and clocks were manufactured and cotton was spun. Potteries produced crocks, jugs and other domestic ware.

Dr. Daniel Lathrop (1712–1782) opened an apothecary shop at present-day 377 Washington Street, the first in Connecticut, and the only one between New York and Boston. Customers came from across the state. Daniel and his brother built a lucrative trade importing drugs.

Lathrop and his wife, Jerusha Talcott, lived at 380 Washington Street. They surrounded their home with lavish gardens, famous for the flowers, herbs, vegetables and fruits they produced. The poet Lydia Huntley Sigourney lived on the property while her father served as the Lathrop's gardener. Sigourney Street in Hartford is named for her.

Benedict Arnold (1741–1801), the infamous Revolutionary War traitor, was a Norwich native who apprenticed with Daniel Lathrop and learned pharmacy. When he was twenty-one he opened a combination bookstore and drugstore in New Haven.

Worse for Arnold's family and friends in southeastern Connecticut even than his better-known traitorous actions, he was also responsible for burning New London and for the Groton massacre, although he was offshore at the time of the actual killings (see New London and Groton).

During the Revolution, two thousand barrels of flour were stored in Norwich for Washington's army. Volunteers left daily after the Lexington Alarm. And Washington visited several times.

The Worcester & Norwich line connected to Boston at Worcester. In Norwich, the line connected with modern steamships, outfitted with electric lights and dining rooms, which sailed to New York City.

Noah Webster was booked to sail from Norwich on one of these steamships, but decided to postpone his trip because the stormy weather made him uneasy. His caution saved his life: the ship sank, drowning all its passengers (sailors on the rescue ship said the ship's bell tolled until all the bodies were recovered).

But most journeys were without mishap, and Norwich continued to blossom. New houses were built in the Victorian style, and gardens were planted. Waves of immigrants came to the prosperous city, while other waves of Norwich citizens left to begin life elsewhere.

In 1755, Acadians came down in large numbers from Nova Scotia. One irate skipper rounded two hundred and forty of them up in 1767 and brought them back to Quebec, where he dumped them.

Ironically, a number of Norwich citizens migrated to Nova Scotia where they founded Dublin, Horon, Falmouth and Amherst. Settlers left for New York, New Hampshire and the Midwest. Nevertheless, by 1860 Norwich was one of the largest cities in the state, and along with New London, the largest city east of the Connecticut River.

Inventions, inventors and firsts

The first typewriter was patented by Charles Thurber of Norwich in 1843.

The first toll gate in New England, and the second in the country, was on the Mohegan Road from Norwich to New London.

The Mohegan Road was first laid out in 1670, and followed the Indian path that paralleled the west bank of the Thames. The road was a narrow and muddy affair. One could not make the trip to New London and back in a single day.

In 1789, improvements were authorized and a lottery was conducted to pay for them. Once the improvements were completed, the trip to New London and back could be made in a remarkable four hours, and the Mohegan became a busy thoroughfare.

In order to keep the road in good repair, a toll gate was authorized in 1792, and the fees used for maintenance. Then, in 1849, the New London, Willimantic and Palmer Railroad laid its bed alongside the Mohegan Road, and revenues from the toll gates declined sharply. The gate was closed three years later, signifying the end of an era.

The Montville Street Railway connecting Norwich and New London opened in 1900. It more or less followed the old Mohegan Road.

Ghost stories and legends

In the earliest days, there were many (some said far too many) rattlesnakes in Norwich. At one time, property was considered so worthless because of the snake infestation that the Reverend Gurdon Saltonstall was given a grant of land simply for preaching an election sermon. Reportedly, a violinist came through town, playing his fiddle, a sort of Pied Piper of Norwich. Not only were rattlers drawn to his plaintive tune, but other snakes as well, and mice and rats and various troublesome varmints, and even goats.

Still, rattlers were a problem. Goats seemed to be the only livestock that could co-exist with the troublesome serpents. An added benefit was they could live in good health on the thin and rocky pastureland. Soon, one local farmer after another took up raising goats, until the town was nearly overrun with them.

In 1722, a flock of fifty-four rambunctious goats strayed into town and wreaked havoc. There was an outcry from the urban citizenry, and the offending animals were eventually caught and impounded. The farmer was fined for his carelessness.

In March of 1842, the waters of the Thames suddenly rose. The freshet washed away the Methodist Chapel. The astonishing thing was that the church lights stayed lit, and the Chapel bobbed down the Thames, upright and illuminated, all the way out into the Sound. Bystanders talked about it for years—no one more than Aaron Cleveland, great-great grandfather of Grover Cleveland.

Notable buildings and locales

Christopher Leffingwell House/ Leffingwell Inn (c. 1675), 348 Washington Street (860-889-9440).

The oldest part of this house was built by Stephen Backus. Thomas Leffingwell purchased it in 1701. It was Thomas Leffingwell who, while he lived at Saybrook, brought provisions to the besieged Uncas. Thomas was granted permission to keep a "publique house," and consequently made additions and refinements to the structure.

George Washington dined in a room in the northeast corner. There is a tradition that slaves were auctioned off at the north door. Christopher Leffingwell (1734–1810) later lived here. He was active in the Revolution. He was also amazingly enterprising. He established a fulling mill, dyehouse, gristmill, chocolate mill, pottery and paper mill, often in partnership with his brother Elisha.

Bradford Huntington House (c. 1660), 16 Huntington Lane. This was originally a one-room house built by John Bradford, son of the Plymouth Governor. The huge stone chimney and framing may be all that remain from his tenure. In 1691, Simon Huntington bought the property. His son, Captain Joshua, added the gambrel roof and made other additions. Later his son, General Jabez Huntington, a wealthy West India trader, came into possession of the house and added many other refinements. During the Revolution, lead sash weights were removed from the windows and melted to make bullets.

Governor Samuel Huntington House (c. 1769), 34 East Town Street.

Samuel Huntington was President of the Continental Congress, a signer of the Declaration of Independence, Governor of Connecticut, and State Supreme Court Chief Justice. The face of Uncas decorates the chimney!

Jebediah and Ebenezer Huntington House (c. 1765), 23 East Town Street. Home to Jebediah Huntington (son of General Jabez) and Faith Trumbull (daughter of Governor Jonathan Trumbull) until Jebediah was appointed Collector of Customs at New London and the couple moved. Jebediah's brother Ebenezer moved into the house in 1789.

Colonel Joshua Huntington House (c. 1711), 11 Huntington Lane. Note the 12 over 12 windows. This is a fine Georgian house, built by the third son of General Jabez Huntington.

Thomas Danforth House (c. 1746), 25 Scotland Road. Danforth made plates, bowls and tankards of pewter. Some of his work is exhibited in the Metropolitan Museum of Art and in the Leffingwell House.

Reverend Joseph Strong House (c. 1778), 30 Huntington Lane. There is a stepping stone near the street. This was used by the women of the house to step down from their carriages.

Christopher Huntington House (c. 1720), 410 Washington Street. Note the 12 over 8 windows on the upper level and the 12 over 12s on the ground floor.

Daniel Lathrop School (c. 1783), 69 East Town Street. Brick, with a gambrel roof and wooden belfry.

Joseph Carpenter's Silversmith Shop (c. 1772), 73 East Town Street. Believed to be the only surviving frame silvermith shop in New England. Joseph Carpenter made clocks, jewelry, engravings and some pewter. He shared the building with his brother Gardiner, who kept a mercantile shop.

Jesse Brown Tavern (c. 1790), 77 East Town Street. President John Adams dined here. The tavern was licensed in 1790 and was famous for its fine food.

Daniel Lathrop Coit House (c. 1785), 387 Washington Street. Georgian/Federal style.

Thomas Lathrop House (c. 1783), 385 Washington Street. Georgian-style mansion.

East District School (c. 1789), 365 Washington Street. Boys and girls were taught all subjects together in this progressive (for its time) school.

Thomas Williams House (c. 1759), 363 Washington Street. This was the home and shop of the tailor Thomas Williams.

Norwich, South View, 1834.

Samuel Manning House (c. 1750), 85 Town Street. Dieh Manning, who inherited this house from his father Samuel, was the bell ringer for Norwichtown.

Lord's Tavern (c. 1760), 86 Town Street. Eleazor Lord's tavern was popular with lawyers. It was called the "Compass House" because it faced due north.

Lathrop House (c. 1764), 14 Elms Street. Colonial with Victorian additions.

Knight-Peck Tavern (c. 1717), 8 Elms Street. Sarah Kemble Knight operated a tavern here for several years. She got into trouble with the law for selling alchohol to the local Indians.

Simon Huntington House (c. 1690), 2 Elms Street. One of the oldest houses in Norwich.

Indian Burial Grounds, Sachem Street, off Route 32. Uncas is buried here.

Historic districts

Bean Hill Historic District, Huntington Avenue, Sylvia Lane, Vergason

Avenue and West Town Street. In 1772 the Bean Hill blacksmith Edmund Darrow made cut nails from barrel hooping and launched Norwich on its industrial future.

Chelsea Parade Historic District, roughly bounded by Crescent, Broad, Grove, McKinley, Perkins, Slater, Buckingham, Maple, Grove, Washington and Lincoln Streets.

A stroll or drive down Broadway and Union Streets (both in and out of the historic distict) will reward the visitor with a look at many eighteenth and nineteenth-century houses in many architectural styles: Late Georgian, Federal, Gothic Revival, Italinate, and Richardsonian Romanesque, Victorian Gothic, Greek revival, and French Second Empire. Broadway was home to many of Norwich's wealthy entreprenuers and mill owners.

Downtown Norwich Historic District, roughly bounded by Union Square, Park, Main and Shetland Streets and Washington Square.

Jail Hill Section, Fountain and Cedar Streets. From about 1830, when the jail was built, until the turn of the century, this was an African-American community, active in the Underground Railroad. Daughters of several families attended Prudence Crandall's school in Canterbury. James L. Smith, an escaped slave, wrote his autobiography while residing here. Two of his daughters attended Norwich Free Academy.

Little Plain Historic District, both sides of Union Street and Broadway and Huntington Place in an irregular pattern, 120–156 Broadway, and 10–88 Broadway.

Norwichtown Historic District, East Town Street, Elm Avenue, Huntington Lane, Mediterranean Lane and Washington Street. It is believed that Mediterranean Lane was named by a skipper during Norwich's shipping days.

Yantic Falls Historic District, Yantic Street.

Old Lyme
Routes 1, 156
Incorporated 1855

Native Americans
Nehantics

Historical notes
Farmers from Saybrook cleared and planted land on the east side of the Connecticut River as early as the 1640s. In 1649, Matthew Griswold built a long, log building here and left his African-American servant (or slave) to look after it while he sailed to Lyme Regis in England.

Soon a small wave of settlers arrived, and called the settlement on the east side of the river Black Hall, in honor of Matthew Griswold's ancestral home. In 1665, there was a "loving parting" between Black Hall and Saybrook. Two years later, Black Hall was named Lyme. Old Lyme is the oldest part of the original town. The area was subject to numerous and rancorous border disputes, including one which was settled by a wrestling match.

Old Lyme was a center of fishing, shipping and shipbuilding. It held a salt monopoly. It was said there was a sea captain in every house. We know there were at least sixty. Clipper ships sailed to China, the Far East and the West Indies. Packets plied the route between New York, Liverpool, London and Havre. Many Old Lyme residents began their seafaring careers as cabin boys or they shipped to mast. To be a ship's officer, one needed an education in navigation, naval astronomy, mathematics, French and maritime law.

Mills, furniture shops, a nail manufactory, iron mines and other industries also flourished in Old Lyme. Silks, Paisley shawls, teakwood chests, tapestries and other trade goods adorned the interiors of the houses.

By the nineteenth century, Old Lyme had evolved into a summer artists' colony. The Lyme School of Art, the Lyme Art Association, and the Lyme Academy of Fine Arts became the centerpieces of the town. Florence Griswold hosted many of the artists in her home, now a museum.

Notable buildings
Florence Griswold Museum (c. 1817), 96 Old Lyme Street, I-95 Exit 70 (860-434-5542). Florence Griswold took artists into her home, many of whom painted panels in the house itself. The house is a treasure trove of impressionistic art surrounded by six picturesque (and oft-painted)

acres. The site includes perennial gardens and William Chadwick's studio.

Historic district
Old Lyme Historic District, Lyme Street from Shore Road to Sill Lane to Rose Lane. The Peck Tavern, (c. 1675), at 1 Sill Lane, housed the only store on the Boston Post Road between New London and Guilford. The store was operated by John McCurdy, who traded with Ireland, Holland and the West Indies. He entertained George Washington at his home, at the corner of Lyme Street and Shore Road, in 1776, and Lafayette in 1778. The projecting closed porch on the Peck Tavern and other houses in the District is characteristic of Old Lyme architecture and is also found in Massachusetts.

Preston
Routes 2, 2A, 12, 117, 164, 165
Incorporated 1687

Native Americans
Pequots. Amos Lake (Route 164) was called Anchemesnoconnuc, "left-hand water." Avery's Pond (Route 164) was called Anchemaunnackaunack, "little left-hand water." Near here (on land now owned by the Mohegans), the local Indians built fish weirs, stone dams topped with boughs. In the vicinity of Route 2, just over the Norwich town line, Jonathan Brewster established an Indian Trading Post. (He and his wife Lucretia [see Norwich] are buried in Brewster's Neck Cemetery.)

Historical notes

The first settlers arrived in 1673. In 1686, they petitioned the Court, saying they were "remote," and after a confirmatory deed was obtained from Oweneco, son of Uncas, the town was incorporated and named for Preston, England. Preston originally included Griswold, which was sectioned off in 1815. In 1901, part of Preston was annexed to Norwich.

Historic districts

Hallville Mill Historic District, Halls Mill Road, Route 2A on Hallville Pond. The Halls brothers manufactured woolens in their mills.

Poquetanuck Village Historic District, roughly along Main Street between Route 117 and Middle Road, and along School House and Cider Mill Road. This village was part of Long Society in Norwich. It was annexed by Preston in 1786.

Preston City Historic District, Amos, Old Shetucket and North West Corner Road and Route 164. The land grants of the earliest settlers came together here, leading to the development of the town.

Salem

Routes 82, 85 (Governor's Highway), 354
Incorporated 1819

Native Americans

Mohegans

Historical notes

The Salem area, which was created from parts of the towns of Colchester,

Lyme and Montville, was called Paugwonk by the Indians who lived near Fairy Lake. The northern (Colchester) part was purchased from Oweneco by a Wethersfield man. The southern portion was deeded by Chapeto, a relative of Uncas in 1669.

Actual settlement began around the turn of the century. The parish was known by its Indian name, Paugwonk, for the first twenty-five years, at which point it was named by Colonel Samuel Browne, one of the first settlers, for Salem, Massachusetts.

Colonel Browne (1669–1731) made extensive land purchases, amassing thousands of acres. He had a house built for his family in present-day Salem along the Governor's Highway. He brought with him sixty families of slaves. At his death, he left bequests to Harvard and his Connecticut lands to his son, Samuel the second.

William Browne, son of the second Samuel, attended Harvard, where he graduated with Jonathan Trumbull, destined to become the second of the two Governor John Trumbulls of Connecticut. William was next to take possession of the huge acreage. In 1774, as the Revolution stirred, he left Salem and sought protection in Boston. When the British evacuated two years later, he went with his son to England, where he died.

Two years after William Browne went to England, the selectmen of Lyme complained that Browne "went over to join and screen himself under the protection of the King … [and]

he hath aided … sd Enemies in their Hostile Measures." They recommended confiscating his property.

The Court agreed and took Browne's estate, totaling 9,526 acres in what was then Lyme, New London, and Colchester, plus "9 slaves." The lands were parceled out and sold. Later, President John Adams said he did not believe that Browne was really a Tory. In any event, the confiscated Browne holdings included much of present-day Salem.

Salem enjoyed its moment of fame when Oramel Whittlesey (1801–1876) established his Music Vale Seminary there in 1835. The son of a minister, he worked in his father's ivory factory before going to New York with his brother to seek his fortune. In the city, the brothers took a piano apart, copied it, and built their own, superior version, which they carried back to Salem. Once home, they opened a piano factory, where they produced some of the world's finest pianos.

Oramel dreamed of even more glorious undertakings, and founded the Music Vale Seminary for the training of musicians and singers. The seminary was the first of its kind authorized to confer degrees. It attracted students from all over the country. Performances created a whirl of excitement in Salem Village. Musicales and operas were performed in the Seminary Hall, which with its frescoes, elaborate boxes, and glittering appointments, far surpassed the halls in Norwich or New London.

Unfortunately, Salem then, as now, was not near a transportation hub. Whittlesey solved this by ordering Concord coaches, painted blue, and transported audiences to the performances himself. The Seminary burned in 1869, was rebuilt, and burned again in 1890, leaving only cellar holes on Route 85.

Ghost stories and legends

Lover's Leap, the cliff along Route 85 overlooking Mountain Lake, is said to be where a native American woman and her English lover leaped to their deaths on a white horse, as her disapproving father pursued them. Some say that on a moonlit night, you can get a glimpse of the silvery horse's mane, the same glimpse the saddened chieftain had when he last saw his beloved daughter as she disappeared over the cliff's edge.

Historic district

Salem Historic District, Route 85.

Sprague
Routes 97, 138, 169
Incorporated 1861

Native Americans
Mohegans

Historical notes

Sprague was settled sometime before 1700. It lay along the Shetucket River and included parts of Franklin and Lisbon. The manufacturing villages of Baltic (formerly Lord's Bridge), Versailles (formerly Eagleville), and Hanover were combined to form a town and named for Governor Sprague of Rhode Island, who had invested in the mills.

Like most Connecticut towns, Sprague had an agricultural beginning. Gristmills and sawmills harnessed the abundant water power, followed by cotton and woolen mills, papermills, and looms for grey worsteds and seamless cotton bagging.

Ghost stories and legends
Salt Rock Road (off Route 87 in the village of Hanover) is named for a large boulder said to taste like salt.

Notable buildings
Ashlawn (Joshua Perkins House, c. late eighteenth century), 1 Potash Hill Road.

Historic district
Baltic Historic District, roughly bounded by Fifth Avenue, River, High, Main, and West Main Streets and the Shetucket River. When the cotton mill was built in 1856, it was the largest in the continent and employed nine hundred hands. Six thirty-foot waterwheels powered 1,800 looms. Later, even more workers were employed.

Stonington
Routes 1, 2, 184, 201, 234
Incorporated 1649

Native Americans
Pequots, under Sassacus. They called the points of land Pawcatuck and Mistick. The Mystic River was Siccanmor, meaning "river of the great sachem." (See also Groton for the Mystic Massacre, which took place on Pequot Hill).

During King Philip's War, Canochet, the son of Miantinomo, was captured on the Pawcatuck River and sentenced to die. In response, he said, "I like it well that I should die before my heart is softened and I say things unworthy of myself."

Historical notes
William Cheseborough and a group of Colonists came to Stonington from Plymouth in 1649. The town was named for the stony terrain. Both Connecticut and Massachusetts claimed the town, and disputes raged for several years. To Massachusetts it was Souther Towne. Finally, in 1662, the dispute was settled and it was agreed that Stonington was indeed part of Connecticut.

Stonington developed two shipping and shipbuilding centers: Mystic and Stonington. Mystic was known for its clippers, Stonington for its whaling and sealing fleets. Ships from this "Nursery for Seamen" voyaged the Seven Seas. The shipyards produced the world's fastest clippers. Numerous privateers operated from Stonington waters.

Both centers became hives of commerce, their streets crowded with merchants and traders. Wealthy sea captains built comfortable houses, many with a widow's walk on the roof, where a waiting wife could watch for returning ships. Cargoes from all over the world filled the wharves and warehouses.

The town was attacked by the British twice. During the Revolution, a British foraging party landed, but was quickly chased away by the local militia. The second attack, in 1814, lasted four days. Five British ships bombarded the village, firing 140 cannons. Many of the cannonballs fell harmlessly in fields. The Americans managed to drive the British away and the cannonballs became souvenirs.

Economic growth continued, even after the great clipper ships became obsolete. Steamboats and trains ushered in a whole new period of prosperity. As many as seventeen train tracks converged in Stonington at the height of rail and steamboat travel. Trains would whistle down from Boston with passengers and goods bound for New York and other coastal cities. From Stonington, the journey would be continued by steamboat.

A few words about all the Mystics would probably be appropriate here. This is the kind of Yankeeism that can drive someone from outside the northeast, where a town is a town, and boundaries and streets are straight, to distraction, but here goes:

First of all, there is no town named Mystic. The village of Mystic is on the east and west sides of the Mystic River and is in both the towns of Stonington and Groton. Old Mystic, to the north, is in Stonington. West Mystic, is in Groton. Mystic Seaport, which is a museum, is in the town of Stonington. Ditto the Mystic Aquarium.

Notable buildings

Captain Nathaniel B. Palmer House (c. 1852), North Water and Palmer Streets. I-95 Exit 91, south on 234, left on North Main, right on Route 1 to North Water Street (860-535-8445). A magnificent sixteen-room Victorian mansion with an octagonal observation cupola, built by two seafaring brothers, Captains Nathaniel and Alexander Palmer. Nathaniel Palmer discovered Antarctica when he was only twenty-one.

Old Lighthouse Museum, 7 Water Street, I-95 Exit 91 (860-535-1440). This stone lighthouse was built in 1823 and moved to higher ground in 1840.

Carousel Museum of New England, 193 Greenmanville Avenue, I-95 Exit 90 (860-536-7862). Antique carousels, miniatures and a carving shop.

Denison Homestead (c. 1717), Pequotsepos Road, I-95 Exit 90 (860-536-9248). This house contains period heirlooms from 1717 to 1941, representing eleven generations of one family.

The Indian & Colonial Research Center, Main Street/Route 27 (Old Mystic). Originally the Mystic National Bank (c. 1856). Old maps, manuscripts, photographs, rare American schoolbooks, Indian artifacts (860-536-9771).

Mystic Seaport, 75 Greenmanville Avenue, I-95 Exit 90 (860-572-5315). World-famous recreation of a nineteenth-century seacoast village.

Historic districts

Mechanic Street Historic District, roughly bounded by West Broad Street, Pawcatuck River, Cedar Street and Courlant Street. Most visitors focus on Mystic Seaport Museum, but a wander through the streets of Stonington is rewarding too.

Mystic Bridge Historic District, Routes 1 and 27.

Stonington Borough Historic District. This was the first borough incorporated in the state.

Voluntown

Routes 49, 138, 165
Incorporated 1721

Native Americans

Narragansetts. Mohegans. Recent archaeological work in the Pauchaug State Forest has uncovered an ancient native American smoke house and shelter. The relics, a necklace, clay pipe, pottery shards, and chips of flint and green slate, indicate that the inhabitants, probably Narragansetts, were not only hunter-gatherers, but led a somewhat settled life. Complete study of the site will take four or five years.

Historical notes

Voluntown was given to the volunteers in King Philip's War (Narragansett War) after Thomas Leffingwell of Norwich and John Frink of Stonington petitioned the court in 1696. The Court granted them "a tract of land six miles square for a plantation, to be taken out of some of the conquered land." However, because some of the lands were already claimed and various complicated boundary disputes ensued, it was twenty-five years before Volunteers Town was formed. By then some of the volunteers had sold their interest.

The Pauchaug River offered excellent water power. Cotton goods, silk and braid were manufactured. In 1794, Sterling was sectioned off. The new town line went straight through the middle of the Meeting House. When a wedding couple stood in front of the pulpit, the bride would be in one town and the groom in the other, making marriages illegal!

Pauchaug State forest covers much of Voluntown. Land purchases were begun in 1928. The forest includes 24,000 acres. Dense with hemlock, white pine and cedar, the Pauchaug was once cleared for subsistence farms. Cellar holes, stone walls, and old mill sites can be found throughout the woods.

Waterford

Routes 1, 213
Incorporated 1802

Native Americans

The Nehantics had their summer camping grounds at Oswegatchie, meaning "clams," at Sandy Point on the west banks of the Niantic River.

Historical notes

Colonists began farming in Mamacoke (Waterford) as early as 1645. Governor Jonathan Winthrop was an early landowner. He gave his land around Millstone Point to his daughter when she married.

For many years the granite taken from the quarries at Millstone Point was used solely for millstones. It was first quarried in 1737. Later, as the demand for millstones declined, the finely grained granite was used for monuments and building materials.

A number of taverns and several ferries served the early settlers. The manufacture of paper, bleaching and dying were later industries. Pleasure beaches and summer colonies followed.

Historic districts

Jordan Village Historic District, Junction of North Road and Avery Lane with Rope Ferry Road. This area was first settled in 1663.

Jordan Green, Route 156, junction of Avery Lane and Rope Ferry Road (860-442-2701). A replica colonial village that includes the Beebe-Phillips farmhouse (c. 1840), a blacksmith shop, farm implements, and the Jordan Schoolhouse (c. 1737).

Harkness Memorial State Park, 275 Great Neck Road, Route 213 (860-443-5725). Mansion, park and partially restored formal gardens.

Tolland County

The county is 412 square miles and has thirteen towns: Andover, Bolton, Columbia, Coventry, Ellington, Hebron, Mansfield, Somers, Stafford, Tolland, Union, Vernon and Willington.

Tolland County includes old mills, abandoned farmland, quaint hamlets and villages, rugged and wooded terrain in the higher elevations, and expanding suburbs. It is presently experiencing more growth than the other counties in Connecticut. History buffs will especially enjoy driving through the centers of Tolland and Ellington.

Interstate 84 bisects Tolland County. A drive along Route 74 from Rockville, east to Tolland and Willington will afford a look at once thriving textile mills, stagecoach routes, old inns, houses, town greens and a jail. Take Route 44 west across the county and you will follow the route George Washington took. Take Route 190 west from Union (the least populated town in Connecticut), to Stafford Springs, and then follow Route 140 to Ellington. This journey will include the CCC camp in Union, the glorious fountain in Stafford Springs, and Ellington's marvelous town green and Indian grinding stone. Route 195 will take you from the heart of the University of Connecticut north to the Tolland Green.

Andover
Routes 6, 87
Incorporated 1848

Native Americans
Mohegans

Historical notes
Captain John Mason was given part of the present Andover for his services in the Pequot War, though he never lived here. The southeastern part of Andover was first settled in 1713. The Ecclesiastical Society of Andover was formed from portions of Lebanon, Hebron and Coventry and recognized in 1747, though it would be a century before Andover was incorporated.

The clockmaker Daniel Burnap was born in 1759 in Andover (in a section that at that time was Coventry, so both towns claim him). He learned his trade from Thomas Harland of Norwich and then opened his famous clock shop in East Windsor. Eli Terry was one of his apprentices.

Burnap, a fine craftsman, made

moon phase clocks, musical clocks and brass eight-day clocks. He engraved brass and silvered dials. About 1800 he moved back to Andover where he bought a farm and built a sawmill and shop. He repaired watches and made buckles, jewelry and silverware. He made the "glimpse" (flash) mechanism for the Point Judith Light in his Andover (Coventry) workshop. It was transported by oxen to the coast.

During the Revolution, Rochambeau's army of six thousand men marched through town in 1781. On the return trip, the army camped for three days near the Congregational Church. The officers were entertained at the neighboring house of Mr. Kingsbury.

The railroad came in 1848. Andover had two hotels, the W. Dorrance, near the Church, and G. W. Webster's opposite the station. Businesses that were clustered in the center of town near the station included two sawmills, a toy manufacturer, a wagon and sleigh manufacturer, an attorney, a dealer in drygoods and groceries, and a manufacturer of "warps, batts, twine and wicking." In outlying areas of town, there were more wagon manufacturers, another toy shop, and a twine and batting manufacturer.

A house listed as belonging to Miss E. Hendee (c. 1760), on old maps is reputed to have been on the Underground Railroad. There are "mysterious secret closets and a tunnel from the cellar to a thicket, 100 feet from the house," according to

research done in the 1930s. Proving participation in the Underground Railroad is, of course, difficult since it was necessarily carried on in secrecy. Nevertheless, it seems likely, as the researchers supposed, that this house was a stop on the way to Canada and freedom. The house now, sadly, backs up to Route 6 and not to a thicket.

Off Route 6, on Boston Hill Road (1.7 miles from the junction of Route 6 with State Route 14), are two stone markers. Tradition has it that Captain Simon Smith of New London was at the front in the French and Indian War when he contracted the dreaded smallpox. Immediately released from the campaign, he attempted to make his way home to New London. He died in Andover. Fearing contagion, the local residents buried both Smith and his horse. The stone is inscribed, "Loved, yet unattended. All alone. Sweetly repose beneath this humble stone ye last remains." We don't know what age Simon Smith was, but he was likely young.

The federal government purchased failing agricultural lands in Andover and "retired" them, creating part of the Nathan Hale State Forest. The railroad long ago stopped hurtling along the Hop River, the hotels closed up, and no one needs a wagon anymore. By the mid twentieth century, Andover had become primarily a residential town.

Notable buildings

White's Tavern, 131 Hutchinson Road, Route 6. Rochambeau dined here.

Old Town Hall, Monument Road, off Route 6 (742-5473). Museum operated by the Andover Historical Society. Exhibits and artifacts.

Bolton

Routes 6, 44, 85
Incorporated 1720

Native Americans

Mohegans. At the Notch, Sagumsketuck, or "place of the hard rock," is where the Podunk hunting grounds bordered Mohegan lands. The top of the mountain, visible from the highway, was Wiahquagmumsuck ("on top of the rock"), There is evidence that native Americans were in the Bolton highlands as early as ten to fourteen thousand years ago. There is also evidence that, near the present middle Bolton Lake, there was a workshop where stone implements or projectiles were made.

Several important paths crossed Bolton. One, the Connecticut Path, came down from Boston and ended at Hockonum in East Hartford. It was the path taken by Wahinicut, Jack Straw, and John Sagamore when they called on Governor Winthrop (the elder) in Massachusetts and invited the English to come to Connecticut.

Historical notes

Bolton was called the Hartford Mountains, and sometimes Hanover. Settlers arrived from Hartford, Windsor and Wethersfield in 1716, legatees of the sachem Joshua. The General Assembly stepped in two years later and paid these first settlers for "so much as the land was made better for their improvement." With the less desirable settlers out of the way, the plantation could now proceed, and the town was incorporated in just two more years. The town of Vernon was divided from Bolton in 1808.

George Washington's expense account records two stops in Bolton. His trip took him through Bolton Notch. Rochambeau also was in Bolton twice, but he was on the other side of town, near the center (Route 85). One of his aides wrote of the trip, "We have reached Bolton the 22d with the greatest difficulty. All the roads were frightful."

Taverns, sawmills, five cider brandy stills, grist mills, a cigar shop, hat shop and farming occupied the people of Bolton. The center of town, where the meeting house was erected, boasted taverns, a post office, houses and a few enterprises such as cigar making, but was commercially eclipsed by Quarryville in the southwest corner of town.

In 1815, operations began at the soon to be famous Bolton Quarries at Bolton Notch. The micaceous slate, shimmering, and sometimes embedded with garnets, was greatly valued for sidewalks, laboratory tables and doors. Until the railroad came, in 1848, the heavy slate was hauled by oxen. After the Hartford, Fishkill and Providence Railroad Company blasted a cut through the Notch, and built a station near the quarries, trains trans-

Bolton Notch. Stone from the quarries were used for sidewalks in cities throughout the east.

ported the flagstones to distant cities.

Quarryville was a bustling village with houses, taverns, a station, a shop and a warehouse. It was the site of late-night dances and midnight laughter, and once when the circus train came through, it stopped to let the elephants out to have a drink of water.

Inventions, inventors and firsts

The first camp meeting held in New England took place in Bolton on June 3, 1805. A great crowd gathered near the Andover Bolton line to hear Lorenzo Dow (see Coventry), the fiery traveling preacher.

Geology

A fault plane to the sandstone of the Connecticut River valley lies below the hills, west of the Notch. The hills, once volcanoes, contain a micaceous rock that is particularly impermeable to stains or water leakage. Known as Bolton schist, it was heavily quarried (see above).

Ghost stories and legends

If you drive through Bolton Notch when the leaves are off the trees, you will be able to see Wuneetah's cave, a slit in the mountain that looms over the north side of the road. Wunnetah was a Podunk who lived with the remaining members of her people in a village on Toby Hill, in Manchester. She fell in love with a Dutchman, Peter Hager.

Romance between whites and Indians was not countenanced by the whites in Bolton or in Manchester. The couple was harassed and had to move about. They stayed at the springs in Manchester for a time, and they were sometimes seen in the pine grove in Manchester, on a road now called Love Lane. When this story takes place they were living in the cave at the Notch that locals call Squaw's Cave.

One day when Wunnetah was picking blueberries near Wiahquagmumsuck she heard a shot. She scrambled down the hillside. There was a trail of blood leading to the cave. Standing outside the cave was a group of white men, armed and dangerous looking. They had shot Peter, who had gone into the cave. They knew if they followed Peter in, and he was still alive, he would shoot back. They offered Wuneetah a jug of rum if she would go in, thinking that Peter would mistake her for them and shoot her, and then they would be rid her too. Wunnetah took the jug and shouted to her lover as she dashed into the cave.

Peter was badly wounded and died in her arms. She remained with him in the cave until the vigilantes left. In the night she slipped away to her people and a few of them came back and helped her to bury him. She lived with a family in Windsor afterwards, and is buried there. Her grave is marked "One Hager."

Notable buildings

Jared Cone House (1800) 25 Hebron Road. Georgian colonial. Bolton does not have an official historic district, but the center of town, where the Cone house is located, has a pretty green and several other good examples of early Connecticut architecture.

Columbia
Routes 66, 87
Incorporated 1804

Native Americans
Mohegans

Historical notes
Columbia was a part of Lebanon known as Crank, or the Lebanon Crank, because of the shape. Abimeleck, sachem of the western Nehantics, gave a deed for some of the Crank to Deacon Josiah Dewey and William Clark in 1699. The following year, Oweneco, the son of the Mohegan sachem Uncas, gave a confirmatory deed. Settlers began to arrive, and in 1716 Crank became a separate parish. When Crank was incorporated from Lebanon, it was given the patriotic name of Columbia.

A small Indian school in Columbia gave rise to Dartmouth College. Eleazar Wheelock became a pastor in Lebanon Crank in 1735. He was a leader in the Great Awakening and believed that missionary work to the Indians was of great importance. After Samson Occum (see Montville), asked to study with him, he became convinced that the best missionaries to Indians would be other Indians.

In 1754, Wheelock began a school in his house. Two Delaware Indians enrolled. Then, Joshua Moor of Mansfield gave Wheelock a house and shop in Crank to use for his school. Here he opened Moor's Charity

School. Within a few years, he had more than twenty pupils from three tribes. Samson Occum, by now Wheelock's star pupil, went on a fund-raising tour to England and caused a sensation. He raised thousands of dollars, a large portion of it from the Earl of Dartmouth.

There is a tradition that the people of Columbia urged Wheelock to take his school elsewhere, not caring to have an Indian school in their midst. Another tradition holds that they thought the Indian boys would steal their apples, as boys were wont to do. Whether or not either is true, Wheelock was offered land on the Connecticut River in Hanover, New Hampshire, and with the money that Occum raised as a nucleus for funds, he accepted the New Hampshire land and moved his school north. It became Dartmouth College, in honor of the Earl who was so taken with Occum's requests for donations.

Cider making was an early industry in Columbia. A mill was built along the Hop River. The Columbia Turnpike, authorized in 1808, connected with turnpikes from Providence to Middle Haddam, Hartford and New London. Another turnpike from Bolton Notch to Willimantic skirted the town. Stagecoaches rumbled over these bumpy and, depending upon the season, dusty or muddy roads, and patronized the inns and taverns.

In 1865, the Willimantic Linen Company created a 375-acre lake as a reservoir. A thriving summer colony grew up along the shores of the lake, which was later taken over by the town.

Historic districts
Columbia Green Historic District, along Route 87 at the junction with Route 66. Dr. Eleazar Wheelock's house, where he first taught Occum Samson, overlooks the green.

Coventry
Routes 31, 32, 44, 275
Incorporated 1712

Native Americans
Mohegans

Historical notes
Known as Wamgumbaug (meaning "crooked pond") by the Indians, Coventry was set off in 1706 from the tract east of the Connecticut River that Joshua (Attawanhood) bequeathed to "gentlemen in Hartford." It was divided up by the deed holders and settlement began in 1706.

In the eighteenth century, farmers raised livestock for the West India trade, including dressed beef and pork. Later, in the first half of the nineteenth century, they raised horses and mules. A pacing horse was developed and bred to make the trip to Boston and back in a day. The horse was noted for its stamina.

There were paper, grist, saw, carding and fulling mills along the streams. Gun cartridges, satinets, gloves, paper boxes, silk goods, wagons, enameled fishing lines, bookbindings and leather boards were manufactured over the years.

Nathan Hale grew up in Coventry. His father owned extensive acreage and raised beef cows and pigs for trade. Hale attended Yale and taught school in East Haddam and New London. He was teaching in New London when he decided to join the Continental Army. He served under Colonel Knowlton in Knowlton's Rangers (see Ashford).

While behind British lines in New York, posing as a Dutch schoolteacher in order to gather intelligence, he was captured and hanged as a spy. According to legend his last words were, "I regret that I have but one life to give for my country."

Hale's father erected a monument to Nathan and to his brother Richard, who died in the West Indies where he had been sent to regain his health. It is in the cemetery on the hill above the village of South Coventry. Later, in 1846, an imposing granite shaft was erected in the same cemetery in Hale's honor. Hale, however, was actually buried in some unknown and unmarked spot by the British in present-day New York City.

North Coventry was on the heavily traveled Boston Turnpike and became a busy center. Stages frequented the taverns. Peddlers brought news along with bags of goods. The later Windham Turnpike (Route 31), was built from Canterbury to Windham in order to connect with the Boston Turnpike. It was Main Street in South Coventry. Trolleys later ran over this route from Willimantic to South Coventry village.

Lorenzo Dow (see Bolton and Hebron), the eccentric and itinerant preacher who drew enormous crowds during the Great Awakening, was born in Coventry.

Wamgumbaug Lake attracted many nationally known vaudeville actors, actresses and radio stars in the late 1920s. They built colorful bungalows near the shores of the lake. For many years there was a sign proclaiming the names of these prominent summer residents.

Inventions, inventors and firsts

Jesse Root, L.L.D. (1736–1822) wrote the first book on common law in Connecticut. A lifelong resident of Coventry, he was a delegate to the Continental Congress and served as Connecticut's Chief Justice.

Notable buildings

Brick School House, Merrow Road, I-84 Exit 67 (860-742-7847). Interesting brick school house.

Nathan Hale Homestead, 2200 South Street, off Routes 44E and 6W (860-742-6917, 860-443-7949). This is the house built by Nathan Hale's father.

Strong-Porter House Museum, 2382 South Street, I-84 Exit 67 (860-742-7847). Eighteenth-century saltbox. The Strongs were early settlers of Coventry. Nathan Hale was descended from them.

Huntington House, South Street, three-fourths of a mile from the green.

Rev. Joseph Huntington kept a boys' school in this house. Among his pupils were Nathan Hale and his brother Enoch, who prepared for college.

Pomeroy Tavern/Loomis-Pomeroy House (c. 1806), 1747 Boston Post Road, Route 44. A popular stopover for stagecoaches, slightly west of what was the center of Coventry.

Brigham's Tavern, 12 Boston Post Road, Route 44. George Washington wrote in his diary for Monday, November 9, "set out about 7 o'clock (from Perkins tavern in Ashford) and breakfasted at one Brigham's in Coventry."

Historic districts

South Coventry Historic District, roughly Main Street and adjacent streets from Armstrong Road to Lake Street, and Lake Street from High Street to Main Street. Though South Coventry was not originally the center of town, but a second center, it is the heart of the town's history: here, over the years, Nathan Hale was memorialized, stagecoaches stopped at the original Bidwell's Tavern, mills hummed, the bells of trolleys clanged, vaudeville stars relaxed, and children of the 1960s sold candles and pottery. Today, there are antique shops, used book stores, and a reinvented tavern, yet the village eschews even a token nod to upscale tourism.

Coventry Glass Factory Historic District, Boston Turnpike, Route 44 and North River Road. Coventry glass production was mostly inkwells and commemorative flasks. In addition to the historic houses, a museum is being developed.

Ellington

Routes 83, 140, 286
Incorporated 1786

Native Americans

Weaxskashuck, meaning "great marsh," was acquired by the Mohegans after King Philip's War. Earlier, Shenipsit (Snipsic) Lake was a favorite hunting and fishing ground of the Podunks.

On Main Street, Route 286, there is a mortar for grinding corn, presumably used by the Podunks. It was moved here from its original site on Somers Road in 1914. The stone has a hollow, approximately eight inches deep and seven inches across.

Historical notes

Ellington was known as Great Marsh in East Windsor and was not settled until 1720. It was also sometimes called Windsor Goshen. When it was incorporated, it was most likely named for the English town.

Life for the settlers was difficult. Fields had to be cleared, houses built, gardens planted and livestock tended. It was not only hard work, but dangerous. Sometimes catastrophe struck. In many Connecticut towns, a stone marker was placed at the site of a tragedy. Most of these stones are lost, washed away in storms, overgrown in forests or removed by development.

Ellington has preserved two such

markers. The first is on Route 83 on the west side of the highway, between 156 and 166 West Road. It reads: "This marker replaces an old stone memorial to the first settler in Ellington. On it was engraved the following: Lieut. John Elsworth was killed here by the fal of a tree Oct. 26th 1720 Aged 49 years and 19 days."

Local historians point out that Elsworth was not actually the first settler in that he was killed while clearing land. Another marker, commemorating an event even more tragic, is on Pinney Street, Route 286, one mile past the synagogue. It reads: "Kild in this place Samuel Field Knight by a cart wheel roling over his head in the 10th year of his age Nov. 8, 1812. But O the shaft of death was flung and cut the tender flower down."

The village of Crystal Lake was a center of early Methodist activity. The first Methodist parsonage in New England was erected here. The Lake (Wabbequassett to the Mohegans and Square Pond to the early settlers), with its clear, cold waters, later attracted summer cottages.

If you look at a map of Ellington, you will see that it has a "finger" in the northeast corner. This seven-mile panhandle, for the most part less than a mile across, was given to the town when settlers complained that their town was smaller than others. It came to be known as the "Equivalent."

In 1925 the Department of Agriculture praised Ellington, saying "Ellington has many features, with the means and possibilities of the ordinary rural community, if only the foresight and the will are present."

Notable buildings

Nellie McNight Museum (c. 1812) 70 Main Street (860-875-1136, 860-875-1597). This is the headquarters of the Ellington Historical Society. In addition to exhibits on town history, the museum contains many heirlooms from the McNight family, including Nellie McNight's weavings and loom.

The Ellington Congregational Church (c. 1916), Main Street, is one of the most photographed churches in Connecticut. It has an impressive Christopher Wren steeple. It replaced the church which was the victim of arson in 1914.

Knesseth Israel Synagogue (c. 1913), Pinney Street, Route 286. This is the oldest synagogue east of the Connecticut River. It was moved here from its original site at the corner of Abbott and Middle Roads in 1953.

Historic district

Ellington Center Historic District, roughly Maple Street, from Berr Avenue to just west of the High School and Main Street from Jobs Hill Road to East Green.

Hebron

Routes 66, 85, 316
Incorporated 1708

Native Americans

Mohegans. North Pond (Amston Lake) was a fishing site for Uncas and the Mohegans. A trail ran past the pond from the Thames River valley to the Connecticut River valley. The land was deeded to John Mason. In the mid-nineteenth century, the pond was dammed by P. W. Turner to power his silk mill. The water level was raised seven and a half feet.

Historical notes

Hebron was part of Joshua's tract (Joshua was Attanhood, son of Uncas). The town was settled in 1704, mostly by families from Windsor. The town was named for the biblical Hebron.

The Reverend Samuel Peters (c. 1753–1826) is Hebron's best known—though infamous—citizen. He was the rector of the church and very wealthy. He kept between eight and thirty slaves. And he was a Tory sympathizer. At the time of the Revolution the local Patriots had no stomach for him, and forced him to read a public confession on the old meeting house green.

Governor Trumbull gave orders to protect him, but Peters thought it best to leave, and sailed to England. Not content to let things rest, he penned a "History of Connecticut," published in 1781. It was less than flattering and was quickly dubbed "The Lying History" when it reached the Charter Oak State. Peter's devoted much of his treatise to a harsh and exaggerated depiction of the "blue laws." His nephew, John S. Peters, who was born in Lebanon and served as governor 1831–1833.

The Connecticut historian Benjamin Trumbull, D.D. (1735–1820) was born in Gilead in Hebron. He wrote *A Complete History of Connecticut, Civil and Ecclesiastical Vol. 1,* published in 1797, and a second edition with two volumes in 1818. He had studied with the Rev. Eleazar Wheelock in Crank and taught at his Indian Charity School (see Lebanon) before going to New Haven. His history of Connecticut is considered a landmark work.

Though primarily agricultural, Hebron had several silk mills, cotton and paper mills, and an iron foundry. Turnerville (Amston) was known for its silk mills in the mid nineteenth century. A mile-long stretch along the Blackledge River boasted three sawmills, a blacksmith shop, textile mill, cider press, and charcoal kilns between 1775 and 1840. The area was called "Factory Hollow." Several taverns flourished.

In the early 1800s brickmaker David Strong operated a kiln in the eastern side of town, on Millstream Road. He made the bricks for St. Peter's Episcopal Church in 1824 (which had Tiffany-designed stained glass windows installed in 1871) and probably for some early homes. Daniel Hodge's up-and-down sawmill, built in 1795 on present-day Route 85, is now part of Old Sturbridge Village.

Gay City, which was in the present towns of Hebron, Bolton and Glastonbury, was for a time a successful village with a huge woolen mill, sawmills, a canal and a Main Street lined with comfortable houses. It was founded just prior to the beginning of the nineteenth century. Inhabitants were required to go to church twice a day, and the men were served hard liquor during the services. The people pretty much kept to themselves, though they welcomed itinerant preachers, and Lorenzo Dow is known to have taught some of the children.

The people of Gay City prospered, suffered financial setbacks during the embargoes, then recovered, but soon fell on hard times again. The older people died, and the younger ones moved away. The houses stood empty. The mill crumbled. Gay City became a ghost town. The last building burned in 1879. Today, the cellar holes, an overgrown canal ditch, and lost mills can be seen when hiking in Gay City State Park (Route 85).

Ghost stories and legends

When the wives of the town's two first settlers, Shipman and Phelps, grew impatient waiting in Windsor for their husbands, who were in the wilderness of Hebron preparing homes for their families, they decided to wait no longer. They set out on foot to join the men. Although they almost reached their new homesteads, darkness enclosed them as night fell. Tired and lost, they climbed up onto a rock and shouted. Some say their husbands heard them and came to their rescue, others say local Mohegans heeded their calls and saved them. In any event, the rock was named Prophet's Rock. It is on private property on the west side on Burrows Hill Road.

Geology

Glacial erratic visible from Route 85 in Amston. This is a sizable gneiss boulder deposited by glacial ice.

Notable buildings

Augustus Post House (c. 1790, Hewitt House), 4 Main Street.

Hebron Town Hall (c. 1838), Route 66. Erected by the Methodist Society, which ended in the mid nineteenth century, and then sold to the town in 1863, the hall is now owned by the Hebron Historical Society.

Burrows Hill Schoolhouse (c. early 1700s), Burrows Hill Road at intersection of School House Road. This is the oldest remaining schoolhouse in Hebron. It served the northwest section of town. Despite the rugged terrain of the Burrows Hill area, several industries thrived here. Canon balls and bullets were made during the Revolutionary War. Later axe heads, shears, clocks and cabinets were made. A road lined with more than a dozen houses connected Paper Mill Road and Burrows Hill. The road and the houses all vanished.

Historic districts

Hebron Center Historic District, Church, Gilead, Main, Wall, and West Streets and Marjorie Circle. Much of Hebron Center burned in 1882, but there are still many fine old houses.

Mansfield

Routes 32, 44, 89, 195
Incorporated 1702

Native Americans

Mohegans

Historical notes

Originally part of Windham, Mansfield became a separate town just twelve years after Windham was incorporated because the residents who lived in the Mansfield Center area (called Pond Place) found it too treacherous to cross the "bad and dangerous" Natchaug River, and could not agree on a place for a meeting house. The land was part of a tract acquired from the Mohegan chief Joshua (Attanhood), son of Uncas.

Mansfield's antislavery society had 300 members in 1837, more than any other town in Connecticut. Curiously, efforts to document local Underground Railroad sites have been unsuccessful, though there are documented sites in several surrounding towns.

Mansfield's Four Corners was a busy crossroads during the turnpike era. The Boston Turnpike, which came through east to west, was pretty much built over the old road from Boston. The Tolland and Mansfield Turnpike led to Somers. The later Windham and Mansfield Turnpike connected Franklin with Stafford, passing through Willimantic and Mansfield. Dan Fuller's Tavern was a well known landmark and a welcome respite for travelers weary from the dusty road and jostling stagecoach. It was torn down in the 1930s.

The Edwin Whitney private school for Civil War orphans was built in 1865. Later, in 1881, the Storrs brothers donated the property to the state for an agricultural school for boys. It became Storrs Agricultural College. The college began to admit women in 1893. Today, the school is the University of Connecticut.

Inventions, inventors and firsts

It was Dr. Aspinwall of Mansfield who first introduced the silkworm craze to New England. In Connecticut, a half ounce of mulberry seed (mulberry trees being the food of choice for silkworms) were supplied to each parish. Mrs. Martin, the wife of the Reverend Martin, went to France to learn how to extract the silk from the cocoon of a silk worm, a skill which she then taught to other townsfolk.

In 1800, Horatio Hanks invented the double wheel head for spinning silk. In 1810, with his brother, Rodney, he erected the first silk mill in the U.S. on Hanks Hill. Rodney invented water-powered machinery to spin the silk. His mill was purchased by Henry Ford and relocated to Dearborn, Michigan, to the Henry Ford Museum. Also invented in Storrs—the buzz saw and the screw auger.

Notable buildings

Mansfield Historical Society Museum. 954 Storrs Road, Route 195 (860-429-6577). This is the original (1843) town hall. Exhibits change annually.

Gurleyville Grist Mill (1835), Stone Mill Road (860-429-9023). The only stone grist mill in Connecticut and one of only a few in New England.

Fitch House (c. 1836), Route 195. Greek Revival mansion.

Historic districts

Gurleyville Historic District, north of Mansfield Center, off Route 195 at junction of Gurleyville and Chaffeeville Roads. A hilltop village.

Mansfield Center Historic District, vicinity of Storrs (Route 195), Dodd, Warrenville (Route 89) and Brown Roads. Because of the heavy traffic, it is difficult to drive slowly enough to appreciate the fine old houses in this area. Early Sunday mornings are best.

Mansfield Hollow Historic District, 86–127 Mansfield Hollow Road. A stone mill and clock tower overlook this picturesque village. The illustrator James Marshall lived here and depicted his house in several of his books.

Mansfield Training School and Hospital District, junction of Routes 32 and 44. Brick buildings with slate roofs from the old training school are being converted to UConn's Depot campus.

Ballard Institute and Museum of Puppetry, 6 Bourn Place, off Route 44 (860-486-4605). The museum has more than 2,000 puppets from all over the world.

Spring Hill Historic District, Storrs Road (Route 195), East Road, and Beebe Lane.

Connecticut Agricultural School, roughly Route 195 at North Eagleville Road. Although only the older, agricultural buildings and properties are officially considered "historic," the rest of the University of Connecticut campus should be included on a visit.

The William Benton Museum of Art (860-486-4520), is located in the old "Beanery." The permanent collection includes work by Mary Cassatt, Alice Neel and Kathe Kollowitz.

The Connecticut Museum of Natural History has native American artifacts and a replica wigwam on exhibit (860-486-4460).

Somers
Routes 83, 186, 190
Incorporated 1749

Native Americans
Agawams
Historical notes
Somers was settled in 1706 as East Enfield in Massachusetts, and incorporated as part of that state in 1734. It was named for Lord John Somers of England. In 1749, Somers was annexed to Connecticut in settlement of a boundary dispute.

Somers was early an agricultural town, with crops of potatoes and tobacco playing an important role. Dairying was also important. Milling of grain and lumber were the first industries. By 1845, Somers was manufacturing straw hats, palm-leaf hats, boots, shoes, harnesses, trunks and wagons. Woolen goods and satinet were produced in the hamlet of Somerville.

Tradition holds that one energetic justice of the peace performed so many marriages in his tavern that the village of Somers became a mecca for couples wishing to elope.

Notable buildings

Somers Free Public Library (c. 1896), Battle Street. Restored and opened as the Somers Historical Society Museum, surrounded by three and a half landscaped acres.

Museum of Natural History and Primitive Technology, 332 Turnpike Road (860-749-4129). Exhibits of native American life, the French and Indian, Revolutionary, and Civil Wars, and natural history.

Historic districts

Somers Historic District, Bugby Lane and Springfield Road.

Somersville Historic District, roughly along Main, Maple, and School Streets, Pinney and Shaker Road.

Stafford

Routes 19, 32, 190, 319
Incorporated 1719, Stafford Springs as a borough in 1873

Native Americans

Nipmucs. The Nipmucs, Podunks and perhaps other tribes prized the waters of the iron and sulphur springs.

Historical notes

The General Assembly voted to sell land in present Stafford to raise money for Yale in 1718. The town was settled the next year.

The springs' curative powers attracted two presidents. John Adams took a drink and a plunge on June 4, 1771, hoping to restore his health. He must have believed the waters were indeed restorative, because he made daily trips until the 7th of the month when he had to leave, but returned on the 11th.

After the Revolution, Stafford Springs became a resort. Visitors came from all over the country to stay in the hotel and benefit from the famous mineral springs. The first hotel was built in 1802 and doubled in size ten years later to accommodate the throngs of tourists. It was torn town in 1896 and replaced with a fancy new hotel.

The Springs flourished until well into the nineteenth century. The hotel burned in 1959. You can find the Springs today on Spring Street (how apropos!), between Grace Episcopal Church and the Stafford Public Library.

Bog iron was mined near Furnace Brook as early as 1734 and continued to be mined through the Revolution, until both the ore and the trees to fuel the furnaces gave out. Gold was unsuccessfully prospected.

As the popularity of the springs and the health spa declined, manufacturing took over, particularly of textiles. Woolen and cotton goods were produced. The Orcutt brothers built oil, saw, and carding mills in what became Orcuttville. Pearl buttons and woolen goods were made in the Staffordville factories.

On March 28, 1877, floodwaters

swept through the town. Freight cars were lifted from their tracks and set down upon factory roofs. The church and many other buildings were destroyed. Fortunately, only two people died, thanks to the early warning of horseman Edwin Pinney, who rode through town urging people to flee for their lives.

The Miner Grant General Store, built in the 1790s on Stafford Street (originally Bank Street, the first street to be laid out), was moved to Old Sturbridge Village and can still be seen there.

Inventions, inventors and firsts

The Stafford Grange #1 was the first grange organized in Connecticut (1874), and served not only as a social locus for farming families, but as a lobby for their interests. The grange movement, which began in the Midwest, reached its heyday in Connecticut during the 1930s when there were 200 chapters and 30,000 members.

In the early years there were secret closed-door meetings and ceremonies, but the main attraction to membership was the opportunity to visit with others engaged in the hard and often solitary agricultural life. Today, membership in Connecticut has dwindled to 8,000, with 100 chapters. The old grange halls, however, remain an interesting architectural feature of many towns.

Notable buildings

N.E. States Civilian Conservation Corps Museum, 166 Chestnut Hill Road, Route 190, I-91 Exit 47E (860-684-3430). This was a working CCC camp. Photographic exhibit.

Holt Fountain (c. 1894), Haymarket Square in the center of Stafford. This imposing granite fountain was erected as a memorial to one of the town's leading citizens. It originally offered refreshment to horse and human alike, with troughs, a faucet and drinking cup. Today, one is most likely to view the magnificent fountain from the window of a car.

Stafford Fair

The annual Stafford Fair was first sponsored by the Stafford Agricultural Society in 1870, and from the start, featured sulky races. Some of the finest horses in the east were highlighted. In 1948 dirt track auto racing began, followed by midget cars and stock cars. In 1968, the Stafford Fair became the Stafford Motor Speedway.

Historic district

Stafford Hollow Historic District, roughly parts of Leonard, Murphy, Old Monson, Orcuttville and Patten Roads. This area includes a few mill owners' homes but otherwise is typical of early rural New England. The Baptist Church (c. 1833), had a bell cast by Paul Revere and his sons.

Tolland

Routes 30, 31, 74, 195
Incorporated 1715

Native Americans

Nipmucs, Mohegans

Historical notes

A committee from Windsor laid out Tolland in 1713 and began settlement in the southern part of town. The first houses were built around Grant Hill and Cedar Swamp. Boundary disputes soon arose with legatees of Joshua (Attanhood), the son of Uncas, who claimed to have title to some of the land. They also claimed the tract was in Coventry, not Tolland. The matter wasn't resolved until 1728 when the General Assembly stepped in. The settlers had to pay for quitclaim deeds which, of course, did not make them happy.

Tolland became the county seat when Tolland County was incorporated from Windham and Hartford Counties in 1785. In the early nineteenth century, the county courthouse was the terminus for five turnpikes, with roads entering from seven directions. This influx of traffic spawned a number of taverns.

Notable buildings

Benton Homestead (c. 1720), Metcalf Road, I-84 Exit 68 (860-870-9599). This is the house with the fabled Tolland ghost. When Elisha Benton wanted to marry the much younger Jemima Barrows, his family was horrified at his choice of a mate. Upset that he was forbidden the hand of his true love, he joined the Continental Army and went off to war. In the hull of a British prison ship, he contracted the dreaded smallpox.

When Elisha was sent home to die, Jemima, who had waited patiently for his return, volunteered to act as his nurse. Despite the family's disapproval of her, they accepted, since the disease was so contagious, and they feared they would contract the sickness themselves. Both Elisha and Jemima died and were buried in the same cemetery, but because they were not married, they rest for eternity separated by a road.

It is Jemima's ghost that most people blame for the mysterious noises and happenings in the house, though some think it is Elisha's. The house was also used to hold Hessian soldiers, so there's the Hessian soldier theory that's also bandied about. Ghost or not, the Benton is a fine, early eighteenth-century house.

Hicks-Stearns Museum, 42 Tolland Green, I-84 Exit 68 (860-875-7552). At first an eighteenth-century inn, with a stone fireplace, iron pots for cooking and a bake oven, this impressive house was added to and remodeled over the centuries. Ratcliffe Hicks, an attorney who grew up in the house, left funds to establish the Ratcliffe Hicks College of Agriculture at the University of Connecticut in 1941.

Old Tolland County Jail Museum and 1893 Warden's Home, Tolland Green, Routes 74 and 195, I-84 Exit 68 (860-875-3544). The jail operated from 1856 until 1968.

John Cady House (c. 1720), 484 Mile Hill Road, Route 31. Also known as the Old Babcock Tavern.

Historic district

Tolland does not have an official historic district, but the green, at the intersection of Routes 74 and 195, could very well be one. Most of the buildings on the green were built a century ago, some longer ago. The sidewalks are made of locally quarried stone.

Union

Routes 171, 190, 197
Incorporated 1734

Native Americans

Nipmucs. Mashapaug, which means "great water," was a summer resort of the Nipmucs.

Historical notes

John Oldham, the adventurer and early explorer of Connecticut, obtained some specimens of black lead or graphite from the Indians in 1633. The authorities in Boston were impressed with the quality of the lead. A mine was opened in Sturbridge some time after Oldham's trip home, and in 1657 near Mashapaug Pond in Union.

The Mashapaug Pond mine had been worked by the Clarke family for over a hundred years by the time Governor Trumbull and the Council of Safety ordered four hundred pounds to be sent to the canon foundry in Salisbury for the Revolutionary War.

Despite the iron mine, Union was the last town to be settled in Connecticut. The rough terrain and poor soil were too foreboding to homesteaders until, in 1720, the General Assembly sold the 12,500 acres that made up Union to twelve proprietors.

Not good farmland, it was excellent timber country. Lumbering and associated activities, such as the manufacture of charcoal, became the main industries. Shoes and axe handles were also produced.

Around 1906, Austin Hawes, the State Forester, hopped a train from Hartford to Willimantic, where he changed trains and boarded the Central Vermont for Stafford Springs. In Stafford Springs he rented a horse and rig and drove to Union, where he bought forest land for three dollars an acre. This was the beginning of the Nipmuc Forest.

Inventions, inventors and firsts

Union was actually the last town to receive electricity. It has the smallest population, and was the last town in Connecticut to be settled. These are all distinctions the townsfolk are proud of, however.

Historic districts

Union Green Historic District, roughly north of the junction of Buckley Highway (Route 190) and Cemetery Road, to the junction of Kinney Hollow and Town Hall Roads.

Vernon

Routes 30, 74, 83
Incorporated 1808

Native Americans

Podunks

Historical notes

Vernon was settled in 1716 by families from East Windsor. It was at first part of East Windsor and Bolton, and later sectioned off. One prescient settler was a Windsor man who traded 500 acres of Bolton farmland for 100 acres plus water privileges in North Bolton (Rockville) in 1726. When North Bolton was incorporated it was named for Mount Vernon, Washington's Virginia estate.

The Hockanum and Tankerhoosan Rivers blessed the town with an abundance of water power. The Hockanum River drops a stunning 254 feet in a mere mile and a half, and boasts spectacular waterfalls.

As early as the late eighteenth century, cotton and woolen mills were humming. It is believed that satinet, a combination of cotton and wool, was first made in one of the Rock Mills.

The original owners of the Rock Mills insisted their workers be Congregationalists and provided a Bible for each worker's bobbin box. Later, thankfully, as the need for employees grew with the growth of the mills, this was impractical.

The U.S. Envelope Company opened a mill in 1856 with machines that counted as well as folded envelopes, which was revolutionary for that time. A silk fishing line mill began operations. More textile mills opened. Rockville became a city.

In the neighboring village of Talcottville, there were also wool and cotton mills. John Brown (see Torrington), was a purchasing agent for one of them. His job was to buy wool in Ohio.

In 1892 Rockville mills took awards at the World's Columbian Exposition, and in 1900 at the Paris Exposition. Presidents William McKinley and Theodore Roosevelt were dressed for their inaugurations in suits made of Rockville cloth.

Except for Rockville and Talcottville, Vernon remained agricultural until after World War II, when farmlands were sold and divided and the town turned residential. By 1952, the last woolen mill had closed.

Ghost stories and legends

The Waffle Tavern, which stood at the corner of Grove and South Streets in 1700, was famous among stagecoach patrons for its waffles. It was said that when a stage was approaching the intersection, the shout "Waffles!" would be given so that, when the stage arrived, the travelers were met with platters of the tasty hot griddle cakes. Across the street from the Waffle Tavern was the King Stage House, later the Town Farm. Lafayette, who maybe didn't like waffles, ate at the King's Stage House in 1724.

Notable buildings

Florence Mill (c. 1864), 121 West Main Street. Built on the site of an earlier mill, this is the earliest known example of a Second Empire Style Mansard roof on an American industrial building.

Minterburn Mill (c. 1906), 215 East

Main Street. The last woolen mill built in Rockville, the Minterburn Mill was consolidated with the American, New England, Springville and Hockanum mills to form the Hockanum Mills Company.

Saxony Mill, 66 West Street. Produced Cassimere, a fine, tightly-woven textile.

Vernon Historical Society Museum, 734 Hartford Turnpike, Route 30 (860-875-4326). Collections include diaries, maps, bound newspapers, textiles and costumes.

Historic districts

Rockville Historic District, roughly bounded by Snipsic Street, Davis Avenue and West and South Streets. In addition to the old mills and spectacular waterfall, Rockville has many splendid old mansions.

Talcottville Historic District, 13–44 Elm Hill Road and 11–132 Main Street.

Willington

Routes 32, 74, 320
Incorporated 1727

Native Americans

Nipmucs, probably primarily hunting grounds.

Historical notes

In 1720, the General Assembly sold the 16,000-acre tract of land which was to become Willington (named for Wellington, England) to men from Windsor, Fairfield, Milford, Stamford and Hartford. The first to live in the new town came from Mansfield and Springfield.

Like most towns in northeastern Connecticut, Willington was agrarian in its nascent century. A few gristmills and sawmills served the needs of the scattered farms. As much as three fourths of the land was cleared. The thin, stony and acidic soils made farming difficult, and sometimes, as in the potato blight of 1844, when two thirds of the potato crop was lost, impossible. Many farmers raised livestock instead crops, and used their lands as pasture.

By the middle of the nineteenth century, the town, though still somewhat reliant on farming, had a glassworks, a scythe factory, four comb factories, pearl button factories, a cotton mill and three silk mills.

The Glass Factory, which opened in 1815, produced whiskey bottles, flasks, inkwells, apothecary bottles, pickle jars and commemorative pieces. Molten glass was blown by skilled workers into clay molds. The factory failed when a shipment of clay for the molds was delayed and then ruined by salt water. The artisans, unable to wait to resume work, left for employment at the Coventry Glass Factory and for upper New York State, forcing the factory to close in 1871.

The New London Railroad was extended to Willington in 1850, opening up markets and possibilities of travel. A decade later, the Gardners built their famous thread mills in South Willington, providing livelihoods for many residents. The mill operated for a century, closing in 1954.

Historic districts

Willington Common Historic District, properties around Willington Common and east on Tolland Turnpike past Old Farms Road. This area was settled as Willington Hill. Though al-

tered over the years, a number of the houses on the green date from the eighteenth century. Ye Old Manse (c. 1728) with a gambrel-roof front and a saltbox lean-to in the rear, sits at one end of the green. The hip-roofed Old Tavern or Glazier Tavern (c. pre 1816) was once the center of village social life.

Windham County

The county is 515 square miles, and has fifteeen towns: Ashford, Brooklyn, Canterbury, Chaplin, Eastford, Hampton, Killingly, Plainfield, Pomfret, Putnam, Scotland, Sterling, Thompson, Windham, Woodstock.

Windham County is Connecticut's best-kept secret. Though once bustling with stagecoach traffic from Boston to Hartford and New York, and later humming with textile and thread mills, today's visitor will find old houses, some still awaiting restoration, now-silent factories, second-growth forests, and, in many towns, a few assertively unpaved roads.

The least densely populated of Connecticut's counties, Windham County is, sadly, also the poorest. Nevertheless, the landscape is breathtaking, and many of the towns unspoiled. There are art galleries, museums, numerous antique shops, and many historical sites worth stopping for.

Interstate 84 clips a tiny corner of Windham County. Otherwise, it is served by Interstate 395. When planning a drive in the area, think first of Route 169, beginning in Woodstock at the Massachusetts line, and continuing south through Pomfret, Brooklyn, Canterbury, and, if you like, on to Jewett City in New London County. This breathtaking stretch of road is the longest scenic highway in the state.

Another pleasant trip is Route 198 from its beginning in Chaplin at the intersection of Route 6, north through the center of Chaplin, with a quick, parallel side trip to see the village, and then on to the center of Eastford, through Woodstock to the Massachusetts line, where if you are so inclined, you can continue to Southbridge and then take Route 131 to Sturbridge.

And you will want to travel Route 44 West from the Rhode Island state line, through Putnam (mill town turned antique mecca), through Pomfret with its private schools, and follow George Washington's route on through Eastford and Ashford.

Ashford

Routes 44, 74, 89
Incorporated 1714

Native Americans

Nipmucs and later Wabaquassets. The Great Path, which led from Boston down to the Podunk villages along the Connecticut River, passed through Ashford.

Historical notes

Originally named New Scituate, Ashford was deeded by Oweneco, sachem of the Mohegans, to Captain John Fitch of Norwich in 1684. In its earliest years, Ashford was subject to contentious land speculation and boundary disputes. Two committees were appointed by the General Assembly to lay out the town, the second in 1710 because the first had failed.

With a hilly terrain and rocky acidic soils, Ashford made farming a challenging undertaking. However, from the first, the town was located on the Boston Post Road, and later the Boston Turnpike, and so benefited from access to the outside world. Industries included grain mills and sawmills, several tanneries, a small cotton mill, blacksmiths and wagon shops.

Thomas Knowlton, an early resident, fought in the French and Indian War. Later, when the alarm came from Lexington, he organized Knowlton's Rangers, which included the young Nathan Hale. He was the highest ranking officer in the battle at Bunker Hill. His descendants donated the stone town hall, named in his honor.

George Washington stayed in Ashford for three days, from Saturday to Monday, November 7–9, 1789. He wrote in his diary, "… lodged at Squire [Isaac] Perkins' in Ashford … Knowing that General Putnam lived in the Township of Pomfret, I had hopes of seeing him, and it was one of my inducements for coming this road; but on enquiry in the town I found that he lived 5 miles out of my road, and that without deranging my plan and delaying my journey, I could not do it."

Isaac Perkins "house of publick entertainment" was after 1804 known as the Clark Hotel.

Already perhaps a little testy because his plans had fallen through, Washington wrote, somewhat grumpily, on Sunday the 8th: "It being contrary to law and disagreeable to the People of this State to travel on the Sabbath day … and my horses, after passing through such intolerable roads, wanting rest, I stayed at Perkins' tavern (which, by the bye, is not a good one) all day—and a meeting house being within a few rods of the door, I attended morning and evening service, and heard very lame discourses from a Mr. Pond."

The Westford Glass Factory was founded in 1857, on Waterfall Road. It was an ambitious undertaking, and at the time the largest commercial venture in town. Thirteen shareholders held a total of twenty shares of stock. The factory produced both free-blown and molded glass. Enormous quantities of wood were required for the furnace to reach the necessary temperature. Near the Westford Glass Factory was a wicker shop which wove wicker and rattan coverings for the glass jugs, bottles and demijohns. The glass factory declared bankruptcy in 1873.

Like so many Connecticut towns, particularly those bypassed by the railroad, Ashford's population declined and many of its farms emptied. Abandoned roads, houses and farms can still be seen deep in some of the woods. But many of the farms were reclaimed in the mid-twentieth century by an influx of mostly Hungarian immigrants. Chicken farms with enormous coops began to crop up. Now these coops have also been passed by the march of time. A drive on the side roads reveals their long silvered walls gradually crumbling into decay.

Inventions, inventors and firsts

Father Dunn, a priest sent in the late 1920s by the Catholic church to administer to the largely immigrant and impoverished farmers of Ashford, organized the first farmers co-operative. Residents could bring their farm products to the co-op and exchange them for other goods.

Dunn bought a truck and drove the surplus to sell in Hartford, thus making the Ashford farmers competitive. In gratitude, the residents brought stones from their fields and, when there were enough, they built him an imposing church. The church, with its copper onion dome, is in the Warrenville (formerly Pompey Hollow) section of town, on the north side of Route 44.

Eliphat Nott, who was born in Ashford, served as president of Union College for more than six decades. He invented the first grate for burning hard coal.

Geology

Ashford is part of the eastern highlands, with altitudes exceeding 900 feet at Westford Hill.

Thomas Hooker leading his congregation through the wilderness in 1636.

Ghost stories and legends

A persistent, though certainly unsubstantiated, legend is that when Thomas Hooker's party traveled along the Great Path, or the Old Connecticut Path, one family was so taken with the beauty of this hilly town that they stayed behind, becoming the first English settlers.

Notable buildings

Ashford Academy (c. 1825), on Fitts Road. This little school, built with a second story so that upper grades could be included, is on Ashford's Green. The green itself may seem somewhat odd to the passerby, as one end of the mowed field disappears into forest. Here is the story:

The first Meeting House was built

Ashford in August of 1835. Once a thriving stop on the Boston Post Road. Except for the Academy, all the buildings in this picture have vanished.

at the west end of the green in 1716. This would have been where Washington heard the boring sermons he complained of in his diary (the Tavern was opposite the intersection with North Road, on present Route 44, and somewhat east). The Meeting House was enlarged and improved in 1795, and destroyed sometime around 1829, probably by lightning.

A second Meeting House, or Congregational Church, was built on the same site in 1830. This was struck by lightning and burned in 1888. A third and last church was built on the same site again, at the end of the green, but it was devastated in the hurricane of 1938. After 221 years, the congregation thought better of rebuilding on this troubled spot, and with dwindling membership, disbanded.

Ashford Center was on the Boston Post Road, later the Boston Turnpike. During the turnpike years, when the road was busy with stagecoach traffic, the center boasted two hotels, a general store, several fine houses and a tannery. The academy and the lovely late eighteenth-century houses on both sides of North Road are all that remain of this village.

Knowlton Memorial Hall, Route 44 (Pompey Road, Boston Turnpike, take your pick). An unusual stone building, donated by the the descendants of Colonel Knowlton.

Mixer Tavern (c. 1710), northeast corner of Routes 89 and 44. John Mixer had the first license to operate a tavern and was the first town clerk. It was known by various other names, including Palmer Tavern and Pompey Hollow Inn.

Brooklyn

Routes 6, 12, 169 (scenic), 205
Incorporated 1786

Native Americans

Nipmucs, Wabaquasset.

Historical notes

Patents were issued to Captain John Blackwell, Jr., of England for 5,000 acres to found a plantation in the Wabaquasset country (southwestern part of Pomfret and the northern part of Brooklyn) in 1686 and 1687. Blackwell's plan was to create a town for Irish and English dissidents and name it Mortlake. It was set up as a feudal manor, outside the jurisdiction of the colony.

The political situation changed in England and the dissidents never came. Mortlake was then divided into two farms, Wiltshire and Kingwood. Israel Putnam, a Puritan and later a Revolutionary War hero, bought part of Wiltshire in 1739. Colonel Godfrey Malbone, of Newport, Rhode Island, bought the rest of Wiltshire and all of Kingswood. Malbone arrived with sixty slaves to work his farm.

When Putnam and the other Puritans decided it was time to build a new meeting house, Malbone asserted that there was no way he would pay taxes for such an undertaking, and to prove his point, he built with the labor of his slaves and his own money the first Episcopal church in the state. Putnam and Malbone continued to quarrel about nearly everything. Ironically, Putnam's son married Malbone's

"The above is the northern view of the central part of the village of Brooklyn. The village consists of about 40 or 50 dwelling houses, 3 houses for public worship, a court house, and 4 or 5 mercantile stores; it is about 20 miles from Norwich, 40 from Hartford, and 30 from Providence." —John Barber, August 1835.

daughter, and, at Malbone's death, inherited his estate.

Mortlake, in parts of Pomfret and Canterbury, finally became Brooklyn (from Brook line, signifying the border with the Quinebaug) and the first town meeting was presided over by Israel Putnam.

Putnam is said to have opened the General Wolfe Tavern at the suggestion of his popular second wife, Deborah Lothrop Avery Gardner, who reasoned that with a public house, they would be able to obtain some reimbursement from their many guests without causing embarrassment.

Putnam was working in the fields outside this tavern when, according to tradition, he got word of the Lexington Alarm and dropped his plow, where it remained throughout the war until his return.

Brooklyn became the county seat in 1820. Prudence Crandall's celebrated trial was held in the County Courthouse here in 1833 (see Canterbury, below).

The state's last public hanging took place a mile and a half east of the green, on Prince Hill. The victim, a man named Watkins, watched from his jail cell as spectators dashed by to get to the execution. Watkins is reputed to have said, "Why is everyone running? Nothing can happen until I get there."

Silverware, tinware, furniture, cotton, optical supplies and furniture were produced in Brooklyn, until the town was eclipsed by the more rapid growth of the textile city, Willimantic.

In 1888, Brooklyn relinquished the position of county seat.

Brooklyn had active male and female abolitionist societies led by the Reverend Samuel May. Beginning in 1834, he took in his first fugitives and sent them on to Worcester or Uxbridge. The town was a hub on the Underground Railroad, which ran through Eastern Connecticut.

Notable buildings

Brooklyn Historical Society Mini Museum, 9 Prince Hill Road (860-774-7728). Features an annual exhibit from the Society's permanent collection.

Daniel Putnam Tyler Law Office, Route 169 (860-774-7728). This was the office of Israel Putnam's great-grandson, who practiced from 1822 to 1875.

Putnam Elms, 191 Church Street (860-774-3059). This house was in the Putnam family for more than 200 years.

Unitarian Meeting House (c. 1771 Second Congregational Church of Pomfret). Southwest corner of Routes 169 and 6. This was Putnam's Congregational Meeting House but became the first Unitarian Society when there was a schism in the membership. The bell is said to be one made by Paul Revere.

Old Trinity Church (c. 1771), on Church Street, is the church built by Godfrey Malbone. It is the oldest Episcopal church in Connecticut.

Chartier Gallery, 481 Pomfret Road,

Route 169 (860-779-1104). Normand Chartier's gallery is in a 100-year-old barn. Close to the road, and planned to be his studio, is a small gambrel-roofed house (c. 1792) which once served as the gatehouse.

Historic districts

Brooklyn Green Historic District, Route 169, Route 205, Wolf Den, Brown, Prince Hill and Hyde Roads. Most of the buildings around the green are Greek Revival. They were built during the town's period of prosperity in the early nineteenth century. The Windham County Courthouse (c. 1820) became the Brooklyn Town Hall when the court was moved.

Bush Hill Historic District, parts of Bush Hill Road, Route 169 and Wolf Den Road.

Quinebaug Mill, Quebec Square Historic District (also in Killingly), roughly bounded by the Quinebaug River, Quebec Square, Elm and South Main Streets. Quebec Square, now in Brooklyn, was once part of Danielson. The rowhouses, restored as low-cost housing, were built in 1881 for mill workers.

Canterbury

Routes 169 (scenic), 14
Incorporated 1703

Native Americans

Quinebaug, later Narragansetts.

Historical notes

James Fitch, of Norwich, settled in Pegscomsuck, in the Quinebaug plantations, in 1697. Although he called his outpost Kent, everyone else called it Pegscomsuck, the Indian name. It served as a trading post with the Indians, and being the only settlement between Norwich and Woodstock, became an important rendezvous for traders, Indians, and civil and military officers. Settlers arrived from Massachusetts, causing a fierce fight over conflicting land title claims of Fitch and Winthrop.

Rope yarns, cloth and hats were made in Canterbury, followed by yokes for Indian water buffaloes and hoops for sailing ship masts. Four foundries operated in the village of Westminster. The town was served by the existing Indian paths, roads, and then turnpikes, but was bypassed by the railroad.

Prudence Crandall.

Prudence Crandall, named Connecticut's Female Hero, is Canterbury's most famous citizen. She opened a school for girls in 1831. Sarah Harris, a young black woman, applied for admission the second year the school was open. Crandall accepted her as a student. This caused an uproar in the town, which prompted Crandall to dismiss her white students and open a school for young women of color.

The heated sentiment against her school led to almost constant harassment and culminated in a riot in front of her house. Angry neighbors threw stones and eggs at her windows, and battered open her doors.

Unable to convince her to close her school, the town put their case to the General Assembly, which passed the Black Laws, forbidding acceptance of black students from out of state except into a public school, and only with town permission.

Fiercely committed to her students and their right to a good education, Crandall refused to back down. She was arrested, but the Reverend May (see Brooklyn) posted bond. She was tried in the Windham County Court (see Brooklyn) and then the case went to the State Supreme Court, where she was convicted. The Superior Court of Errors overturned her conviction on a technicality and released her.

Furious, her opponents then attempted to set fire to her house. Every window was smashed. The Reverend Calvin Philleo, Crandall's new husband, feared for her safety and convinced her to close the school. They moved to Illinois, where she devoted the rest of her life to the education of blacks. Fifty years later, the legislature voted her a stipend.

Legends

On July 3, 1788, nineteen inches of hail fell on Canterbury.

Notable buildings

Prudence Crandall House Museum (c. 1805), Routes 14 and 169 (860-546-9916). Prudence Crandall's school for black women (1833–1834) was conducted in this house. The house is in the Canterbury style. The museum offers changing exhibits that relate to the themes of local and black history. It is located on the green and surrounded by eighteenth and early nineteenth-century houses.

Cleveland Cemetery, Route 169. Moses Cleveland (1754–1806) was born in Canterbury. He became an agent of the Western Reserve Land Company and in 1796, laid out the plans for Cleveland, Ohio, which bears his name. He died in Canterbury, and the Cleveland Chamber of Commerce erected this monument to him on the 100th anniversary of his death.

Captain John Clark House, Routes 169 and 14. This house is considered the best example of the Canterbury style.

Chaplin

Routes 198, 6
Incorporated 1822

Native Americans

Mohegans

Historical notes

Chaplin was incorporated from parts of Windham, Mansfield and Hampton. It was named for Deacon Benjamin Chaplin, a basket-maker and surveyor, who purchased land from out-of-state owners, and who was instrumental in founding the Congregational Church.

The manufacture of silk was an important industry during the mid-nineteenth century. The historian Barber wrote, "The labor of rearing the worms, reeling and spinning the silk and preparing it for market is wholly performed by females."

Other industries were two grist mills, five sawmills, two shingle mills and a hat factory. A paper mill was built on the Natchaug about a half a mile south of the village in 1835. A boot factory, which at its height employed forty hands, manufactured calfskin boots.

Ghost stories and legends

Bedlam Corner was named for a quarrelsome family that was always, well, creating bedlam. They were known for their late nights and raucous, generally lunatic behavior. At least, that is the the explanation people give for the odd name.

Notable buildings

Chaplin Museum, 1 Chaplin Street (860-455-9209). Exhibits of eighteenth and nineteenth-century memorabilia.

Witter House (c. 1828), on Chaplin Street. This brick house, built by Orin Witter, a Chaplin physician, has a monitor roof peculiar to New England.

Chaplin Historic District, on Chaplin Street. This short road, a side trip off Route 198 and back, is a step back in time, lined with many well-preserved older houses.

Eastford
Routes 44, 198, 244, 171
Incorporated 1847

Native Americans

Nipmucs. The Old Connecticut Path crossed Eastford. According to tradition, Crystal Pond was a gathering place for the Nipmucs.

Historical notes

Settled in 1710 as part of Ashford, Eastford was known as the East Parish in 1777, and later as East Ashford. The town was a self-sufficient agricultural community with a few diverse industries. The Phoenixville Manufacturing Company produced cotton batting and twine at its mill on Still River. Wooden handles were made at the Tatem Company.

General Nathaniel Lyon (1818–1861) was the first northern general to be killed in the Civil War. He is credited with saving Missouri. He was born in Eastford (then Ashford). His birthplace, of which only a chimney remains, is in the state forest.

Eastford is the only dry town in Connecticut.

Ghost stories and legends

Supposedly, one of General Lyons' relatives, Ephraim Lyon, founded the Church of Bacchus in Eastford, and attracted followers from surrounding towns. Sometimes Ephraim signed folks up even if they didn't ask to be-come members, and it was said he could tell who was and who was not eligible.

The criteria was hard drinking, and apparently there was plenty of that, especially on long, dark days of winter. There were hogsheads of distilled ci-der ready for drinking stored in the cellar. This was, of course, many years before Eastford decided to become a dry town.

Notable buildings

Benjamin Bosworth House (Squire Benjamin Bosworth's Castle, c. 1800), on John Perry Road. This house looks like a house on top of a house. The frame and sills were laid to align with the north star, the woodwork is heavily carved (it is said that it took one man an entire winter to do the carvings in the upper house), and there are twelve fireplaces. The top of the house was lined with benches and used as a Masonic lodge room.

There is no official historic district, but a side trip from the center of Eastford up Westford Road (Old Colony Road) to John Perry Road is just as good. There are many well-kept, early houses in this area.

Hampton

Routes 6, 97
Incorporated 1786

Native Americans

Nipmucs, Mohegans. The Nipmuc Trail in Hampton follows the Indian Nipmuc trail.

Historical notes

Settled as Canada in 1709, the town of Hampton was formed from the towns of Windham, Pomfret, Canterbury, Mansfield and Brooklyn. There were several mills on the Still River and some industries, such as tin-smithing. The main village was on Hampton Hill, and surrounded a green. During the early twentieth cen-tury, Hampton was a summer colony.

At Clark's Corner (Route 6, imme-diately over the Hampton/Chaplin town line) the two Clark brothers raced to be the first to obtain a license to operate a tavern. Jonathan built an impressive (completed 1844) structure with corner pilasters, a monitor roof, and a Palladian door inside a recessed porch. It took him forty years to fin-ish. His brother, however built a smaller and more modest house—more quickly—and got the license first.

Nevertheless, it is Jonathan Clark who gave his name to the corners (for-merly Goshen), a busy crossroads, with the tavern, a tinsmith's shop, and a cluster of houses. Jonathan Clark kept a diary for much of his life (a copy is kept in the town hall). He built bridges in Windham and as far away as western Pennsylvania. It is said that one Sun-day, when the minister asked a little boy who made the world, the boy answered, "Jonathan Clark, he makes all things."

Jonathan Clark, an ardent member of the Free Soil Society, erected a liberty pole in front of his tavern in

1849. On top of the pole, he placed a signboard with seven hands with seven fingers pointing westward. The sign listed the distances to Hartford, South Manchester, Willimantic, New Boston (North Windham), South Coventry, Coventry, and Chaplin. On top of the sign were the words, "Free Soil Stage Daily." Of course the stage also went east, to Providence, but Clark was apparently an extremist in his support of the western cause. He was a staunch Van Buren supporter. Van Buren's Free Soil Party opposed the extension of slavery in the Territories.

Clark's liberty pole was the last to be erected in Windham County. Over the years it has been replaced and rededicated. The pole stands today, although the topography since Jonathan's Clark's day has been altered by the changed roads. The train replaced the stages and a station was built at the Corner (called on some later maps Chaplin Station). The tavern burned in 1946.

The crack New England Limited (the "White Train") whistled through Hampton on its regular Willimantic-to-Boston run. The conductor, Eugene Potter, was the darling of the Boston social set. He had a reputation for running fast but safe trains, and often wrote articles for newspapers. The night of the blizzard of March 10, 1888, the Limited was snowbound in Hampton, on the steepest grade on the line. It was bitter cold, but Porter kept all 105 of his passengers happy, making sure they were well fed. They slept

"The White Train" offered luxurious travel from Boston to New York.

that night aboard the train. The railroad bed is now a hiking trail and bridle path.

Hampton has enjoyed a unique and rich place in literature. Aspects of Hampton life have been described in detail not only in Jonathan Clark's diary, but in several nationally celebrated books.

The internationally applauded naturalist Edwin Way Teale settled in Hampton, and in addition to his many works of natural history, he wrote *A Naturalist Buys an Old Farm* about his property in Hampton. Hampton residents James Oliver and Janet C. Robertson published *All Our Yesterdays: A Century of Family Life in an American Small Town* about the Taintor family in Hampton. And, more regionally, Susan Griggs wrote *Folklore and Firesides of Pomfret, Hampton and Vicinity.*

Ghost stories and legends

A Mr. Cady told this story before his death in 1939. He lived alone in Hampton in the old Jewett homestead. One day, a man came to his door, and claimed to be a descendent of the buccaneer Edward "Blackbeard" Teach. He had an ancient map which he showed to Cady. The landmarks appeared to point to Cady's property. They agreed to split the find, and together they set about excavating a deep pit. Then one night, the stranger failed to appear at the house as usual, and when Cady went out to the pit, he found his tools and the stranger's boots. The man, however, was gone.

Cady believed that sometime between 1713 and 1718, during Blackbeard's West Indies adventures, he may have come to New London. Then, probably to evade pursuit, he could have hiked the Nipmuc trail to Canada (Hampton), and struck east to the North and South Road, later the King's Highway, and on to the Connecticut Path to Boston, or doubled back to New London. The markers on the map were such things as a stone shaped like a horse's head, another resembling a dog's head, and a third with a fish's eye pointing to the pit. The pit, eight feet deep, was lined with granite walls. The question is, did the stranger find Blackbeard's treasure in Hampton?

Notable buildings

The House the Women Built (one mile north of Hampton village, on Route 97) was constructed during the Revolutionary War. When Sarah Hammond's betrothed, Uriel Mosely, heeded the call to arms, their house had not yet been built. The lumber was sawn into boards at the mill and stood stacked, awaiting construction, on a piece of land Sarah's father had given them.

While Uriel was away, Sarah and her soon-to-be mother-in-law, Mrs. Mosely, set about building the house themselves. They got the help of a carpenter who was missing a leg. When it was time to raise the house, all the women in town turned out to help. Afterwards, as they were celebrating, a post rider from New London sounded his horn, and brought the news that Uriel was injured. Sarah mounted a horse and sped away to fetch her lover. She eventually brought him home, fully recovered, and they were married on September 15, 1788. They raised a family and lived happily together for fifty years in the house Sarah and the women built.

Historic Districts

Hampton Hill Historic District, Main Street, Old Route 6 and Cedar Swamp Road. This district includes sixty-two structures in Colonial, Georgian, Greek Revival, Italianate, Gothic Revival, Queen Anne and twentieth-century styles. A good way to see this pretty village is to drive Route 97 from Route 6 to Route 44 in Abbington (Pomfret). An added treat are two, still thriving, honest to goodness (not touristy) general stores.

Killingly

Routes 6, 12, 21, 101
Incorporated 1708. Danielson incorporated as a borough in 1854.

Native Americans

Nipmucs, Quinebaugs, later Mohegans. There was an Indian fort between the Quinebaug River and present-day Dyer Street.

Early settlers were afraid of the Native American inhabitants. When a group of colonists camped at Mashapaug Pond (Alexander's Lake), to them a frightening wilderness, they were terrified that the resident Indians would attack. One of their members reconnoitered, and discovering a local sachem in a tree, south of Killingly, the colonist shot and killed him. This did nothing to ease local tensions.

Historical notes

The Quinebaug lands came to the Mohegans after King Philip's War. Oweneco, the son of Uncas, deeded what included present-day Killingly to Major Fitch. Settlement began in Aspinock, as it was known, as early as 1696. The town was named for Kellingley Manor, Governor Gurdon Saltonstall's ancestral manor in England. Killingly remained sparsely settled until the nineteenth century when the textile industry grew up along the Quinebaug and its tributaries.

Nicknamed "curtain town," Killingly was the largest producer of cotton goods in Connecticut in the 1830s, and by the 1930s had become the "curtain capital of the world" with five mills operating. Comfort and Ebenezar Tiffany founded one of the earliest cotton yarn mills in Connecticut. Charles Lewis Tiffany, Comfort's son, and his partner, John B. Young, also of Killingly, founded the famous Tiffany & Company jewelers in New York City.

In the earliest years, the pine forests were a resource for the manufacture of turpentine. In 1854 Danielson, located on the Quinebaug River, was chartered as a borough. Killingly also includes the villages of Dayville, South Killingly, East Killingly, Williamsville, Elliotville, and Killingly Center. In 1860, Killingly was one of the sixteen largest cities in the state.

Inventions, inventors and firsts

In 1809, Mary Kies became the first woman in the U. S. to be granted a patent in her own name. Her invention? A "new and useful improvement in weaving straw with silk or thread." Another female first, Emeline Robert Jones, of Danielson and New Haven, took up her husband's profession of dentist upon his death. She traveled throughout eastern Connecticut and Rhode Island, tending to the teeth of many families.

Ghost stories and legends

Loon Island, in the middle of Alexander Lake (formerly Lake Mashapaug), so the story goes, was a mountain where the Nipmucs worshiped. One particularly bountiful year, they reveled on the mountain for four days, forgetting the Great Spirit. The mountain collapsed and sank into the water. One lone woman remained, safe, on the bit of mountain left, Loon Island.

Notable buildings

Elmsville Mill, Route 12, on the Whetstone Brook. The Elmville Manufacturing Company produced sash cords and mill supplies.

Danielson Cotton Mill, Route 12 at Maple and Main. This red brick mill replaced two wooden mills built by the grandson of James Danielson, for whom the borough is named.

Attawaugan Village and Mill, Route 12. This is a good example of worker housing and a mill village.

Historic districts

Danielson Main Street Historic District, Main Street from Water Street to Spring Street. The center of Danielson was north of Davis Park in Westfield Village. Broad Street was the old stage route to Plainfield. When the railroad depot was constructed in 1839, north of Main Street, business shifted and the area became known as Railroad Village. This is now the heart of downtown Danielson. The Killingly Town Hall (c. 1876) was the Music Hall.

Dayville Historic District, Main and Pleasant Streets. Captain John Day manufactured cotton goods here in 1832.

Quinebaug Mill, Quebec Square Historic District (also in Brooklyn), bounded roughly by the Quinebaug River, Quebec Square, Elm and South Main Streets. The Quinebaug Mill, built in 1852, succeeded the mill Comfort Tiffany built in 1827. By 1900 the mill produced 28 miles of cloth a day on 61,340 spindles and 1.656 looms. Production peaked during World War I. Fire destroyed the mill in 1961, but the weave shed (c. 1881) and workers' houses can still be seen.

Plainfield

Routes 12, 14 and 14A
Incorporated 1699

Native Americans

Quinebaugs. Acquiunk Fort was in Wauregan, on the ledge bluff where the Quinebaug and Assawaga Rivers converge.

Historical notes

"Quinebaug Country" was purchased by two sons of John Winthrop, Jr., from Allumps, a Narragansett sachem, in 1653, though Major Fitch asserted some claims. The first settlers arrived in 1689 and probably built their houses on Black Hill.

Plainfield was on the old Greenwich Path connecting Providence and Norwich. The path later became the Providence and Norwich Turnpike, a heavily used stage route. Busy roads to New London and Windham also passed through the little settlement, which greatly enhanced the business prospects of the villagers. Washington came through twice, and Lafayette stayed in the lavish Eaton Tavern.

Plainfield Academy was incorporated in 1784. At that time it was the third incorporated school in the state. The school quickly gained fame. There were sometimes as many as one hundred boarding students. Several of the teachers were the authors of textbooks. In 1850, sixteen youths from the Chicksaw Nation in Texas were students, and later students came from South America. When the school closed, some of the buildings were used by the town.

The first industries were grist and sawmills on the Moosup and Quinebaug Rivers. In the 1800s the textile industry began to appear in Plainfield. The mill villages of Moosup, Central Village, Wauregan, and Plainfield grew up along the rivers. Textile production continued until the 1930s.

Ghost stories and legends

Squaw's Kitchen in Moosup is said to be where the Indians held council and where the last, lone remnant of the Quinebaugs lived in solitude. The cave is twelve feet square with a cleft in the ceiling which forms a natural chimney. Legend has it that, during a cold winter, the chimney fills with ice that doesn't melt until deep into summer.

Historic districts

Central Village Historic District, roughly School, Main and Water Streets, and Putnam Road north to Plainfield High School. The Wyandotte Worsted Mills used the power of the Moosup River.

Lawton Mills Historic District, bounded roughly by Second Street, Railroad Avenue, Norwich Road, and Fifth and Ninth Streets. These were the first mills in the Quinebaug Valley to be powered by steam. The mill buildings were designed and built in the Italianate Industrial style (c. 1905, enlarged 1911). Workers were housed in one hundred twenty five duplexes. There were also fifteen homes for supervisors. The Lawton Inn (now housing for the elderly), was designed as a hotel for single employees. At the height of cotton production, the Lawton Mills had 1,200 hands.

Wauregan Mills and Village, Front, Grove, Lane, North Chestnut, North Walnut, South Chestnut, and parts of Brooklyn, Moosup, Pond, and Putnam Roads. This village has not changed much since the 1850s when eight hundred workers were employed in the fieldstone mill. The cotton mill utilized five turbine water wheels and two steam engines for power. It operated until 1957. Still standing are more than one hundred workers' houses, two boarding houses for single workers, the company store and the home of one of the owners.

Plainfield Street Historic District, roughly Norwich Road from Railroad Avenue to Academy Hill. Sterling Hill Historic District (also in Sterling), Green Lane and Route 14A.

Pomfret

Routes 44, 101, 169 (scenic), 97, 244
Incorporated 1713

Native Americans

Nipmucs, Wabaquasetts

Historical notes

Pomfret was the "Mashamoquet Purchase." Twelve proprietors purchased 15,000 acres in 1686 from James Fitch who had acquired it, along with most of later Windham country, from Oweneco, the son of Uncas. The town was named for Pontefract in England. Captain John Sabin, the first settler, built himself a fort, or fortified house, sometime between 1691 and 1696.

Washington stayed twice in Pomfret. He had hoped to visit the aged General Israel Putnam, but since Putnam lived too far from the main road, Washington went on to Ashford.

In the 1890s, Pomfret was a summer colony for wealthy New Yorkers. It was often referred to as the "other Newport." Pomfret Street (Route 44), where the earliest settlement was located, was lined with extravagant mansions. Most of these houses were later incorporated into two private schools, Pomfret School, founded in 1894, and the Rectory School, 1920.

James A. McNeill Whistler, noted artist, is believed to have spent three years of his childhood here. The poet Louise Chandler Moulton (approx. 1835–1908) was born in Pomfret. She was part of the literary circle that included Oliver Wendell Holmes, James Russell Lowell, and Ralph Waldo Emerson. The English poet Robert Louis Browning was among her fans.

A tornado struck Pomfret a few years back and tore up many of the old trees lining Pomfret Street.

Inventions, inventors and firsts

Miniaturist Anne Hall became the first woman to be associated with the National Academy of Design, in 1835.

Ghost stories and legends

Sometimes, despite official sales and deeds backed by grants and permission from the General Assembly, settlers were surprised to find homesteads on their newly purchased lands. Squatting in the wilderness was probably not all that uncommon.

Such was the case in Pomfret. A portion of Mortlake (see Brooklyn) was deeded to Governor Belcher, who then requested that his holdings become part of the town of Pomfret. Touring his new holdings, he discovered Jabez and Mary Utter already living on his land with their children. They persuaded him to give them a deed to the seventy acres they had already cleared, plus another thirty. However, Jabez was soon (mysteriously) accused of stealing a "black two-year old horse," from Daniel Cady. He was brought to trial in New London and convicted. Poor Jabez could pay neither the heavy fine nor the court costs. He was stripped and given ten stripes with a whip, and then imprisoned. Governor Belcher took back title to the hundred acres. Incarcerated, Jabez was obliged to work for eight pounds a year to pay off his fine.

Meanwhile, Mary and the children remained in the cabin they called home and eked out a meager living. One night a gang of young men from Woodstock came upon them and abused them for the entire night. At the end of it, they threw Mary and her children out of the house and barred the door against her. She managed to make her way ten miles through the forest with her children to the home of Edward Spaulding.

On January 19, 1714, Mary appeared before the magistrate to tell her story, but Woodstock was then a part of Massachusetts and so nothing was to be done. Homeless, Mary likely bound her children out, and perhaps herself, too.

A better known legend of Pomfret is Israel Putnam's slaying of the last wolf, a story much celebrated in years past, but less admired today.

Israel Putnam. General Putnam was a key player in the Revolutionary War.

Notable buildings

Abington Meeting House/Congregational Church (c. 1751) Old Windham Road/Route 97. This is the oldest Connecticut church in continuous use.

Brayton Grist Mill and Marcy Blacksmith, Mashamoquet Brook State Park, Route 44 at the entrance to the park. Exhibits of two Pomfret artisans. The mill dates from the 1800s. The wolf den where Israel Putnam was reputed to have killed the "last wolf" in Connecticut is in the park itself.

Putnam
Routes 12, 21, 44
Incorporated 1855

Native Americans
Nipmucs

Brayton Gristmill, Pomfret.

Historical notes

The commercial center of present-day Putnam was known as Pomfret Factory until 1849, at which point it was called Quinebaug. It was part of Pomfret. In 1855, the city of Putnam was carved from parts of Pomfret, Thompson and Killingly. The Killingly section was known as Aspinock. The town was named for Israel Putnam.

The falls on the Quinebaug afforded water power for mills and influenced the development of the city. The opening of the Railroad in 1840 made Putnam the main freight depot for eastern Connecticut.

The 1955 flood devastated the mill and industrial areas of Putnam and destroyed the railroad bridge. Most of the area was rebuilt but it never regained its industrial prominence. Today, Putnam has reinvented itself as a mecca for antiques.

Notable buildings

Putnam Railroad Depot (c. 1905). This station was built near the site of the Pomfret Factory Depot. The Norwich & Worcester line crossed the Boston-Hartford route at this busy station. Fifty trains a day were common. The comings and goings of the trains at this station inspired Gertrude Chandler Warner to write the popular series, *The Boxcar Children*.

Pomfret Cotton Mills at Cargill Falls. Benjamin Cargill operated several mills at the falls from 1760–1793. Later mills were built on this site by textile-manufacturing families from Rhode Island, including the first cotton mill in Connecticut. Mills have produced textiles on this site continuously since 1807. Nearby, on Route 44, surviving tenements for workers can be seen. The mill owners and professionals built their homes on Church Street.

Municipal Building (1874). Victorian Gothic architecture; was the high school until 1911.

Scotland

Routes 14, 97
Incorporated 1857

Native Americans

Mohegan.

Historical notes

Originally part of Windham. In 1700 Isaac Magoon bought several hundred acres. He kept some and sold the rest. By 1726 he was joined by about eighty families. Though continuing to be part of Windham, Magoon called it "Scotland" after his native land.

In 1706, Josiah Palmer was given a water right to "set up a mill—he, building the same within three years and ditching and damning there as he thinks needful of the Commons, not to damnify particular men's right." He built his mill on Wolf Pit Brook, the first manufactory in Scotland. Merrick Brook supported other mills and small industries.

Agriculture, dairying and poultry raising, however, predominate even today.

Scotland's bid for independence from Windham was not accomplished easily. After a thirty-seven-year effort, Scotland was incorporated, and appropriately, held its first town meeting on the fourth of July.

Notable buildings

Waldo Homestead (c. 1714), Waldo Road, off Route 97 (860-456-0708). This saltbox was owned by the Waldo family for 260 years. Exhibits include antiques, books and farming implements. Some of the work of one family member, the portraitist Samuel Lovett Waldo, hangs in the Metropolitan Museum of Art, as well as in other museums.

Samuel Huntington Birthplace (c. 1700), Route 14, Scotland Center (860-423-6862). The hinges on the outside doors of this old house extend nearly the width of the doors. Huntington signed the Declaration of Independence, and was governor of Connecticut (see Norwich).

Sterling

Routes 14, 49 (scenic), 14A
Incorporated 1794

Native Americans

Narragansetts, later Mohegans

Historical notes

Sterling was part of Voluntown, the long narrow strip of land set aside for volunteers in King Philip's War. When it was sectioned off, Dr. John Sterling offered to build a library in exchange for naming the town after himself. The residents thought they were getting a good deal and agreed. Unfortunately, he reneged on his offer and never built the library, though the name stuck. Donations were solicited and a library was eventually built.

Oneco, the manufacturing center, was named after Oweneco, a son of Uncas, who claimed much of eastern Connecticut. The American Manufacturing Company opened on the Quandock River in 1800, producing cotton. The Sterling Manufacturing Company followed in 1808. Within a decade, the Sterling Co. was running 1,600 spindles.

William Pike, an early industrialist, pioneered using chlorine to bleach fabrics, and later developed dyeing processes. Soon a chemical industry was thriving. Mining began in the 1850's. The stone has been used for curbs, corner pieces and building. The railroad opened in 1854, connecting Sterling with Providence and Hartford. This made the distribution of goods faster and easier.

Historic district

Sterling Hill Historic District (also in Plainfield), Green Lane and Route 14A. The earliest settlement was on Sterling Hill, around the green.

Thompson

Routes 193, 12, 21, 131, 200
Incorporated 1785

Native Americans

Nipmucs. Their village, Quinnatisset, was included in present-day Thompson. They had a stockade on

Fort Hill, near Thompson center. According to local tradition, they frequently camped on the area which became the colonists' green.

Historical notes

Thompson was at first part of Killingly. It was named for the principal landholder, Sir Robert Thompson, who lived in Middlesex, England. Settlement began in 1693.

As early as 1690, Thompson was on the rough road to Plainfield and Boston, with cruder roads to Hartford and elsewhere. The Boston Turnpike was authorized in 1797, followed by other turnpikes. Thompson Hill, where these roads and turnpikes converged, was a popular stagecoach stop, with several active taverns.

Mills took advantage of the Quinebaug and French Rivers, and with the mills came villages. At one time there were as many as eleven manufacturing villages in Thompson. It was typical in Connecticut for the village surrounding a factory or mill to take on the name of the owner. As, during the course of business, the mills changed hands, the villages changed their names, creating confusion for all the local inhabitants.

The village of West Thompson disappeared when it was flooded by the West Thompson Dam to make a flood-control reservoir.

Ghost stories and legends

The Vernon Stiles Inn (c. 1814) on the green was a popular hostelry during the era of stages. It was also a popular place for weddings. Both Massachusetts and Rhode Island required a prolonged announcement of the banns. In Connecticut, however, you could publish your intentions at the morning church service and be married at noon. Stiles, a justice of the peace, was happy to oblige eager couples from adjoining states, and conducted many early afternoon marriage ceremonies.

Notable buildings

Masonville-Grosvenordale Mills, Route 12. The Mason family built a wooden cotton mill here on the French River in 1813, and the village was called Masonville. Later, Dr. William Grosvenordale, who had married into the Mason family, took over and expanded the operation, and the village became Grosvenordale. The five-story brick cotton sheeting mill stands on the site of the Mason mill. Upstream is a three-story, stuccoed fieldstone mill, built in 1826. Across the street are brick and stone double-entry houses for workers. There are also brick houses to the south of the mill.

Historic districts

Thompson Hill Historic District, Chase and Quaddick Roads, Routes 200 and 193. Most of the buildings are of early nineteenth-century vintage. At the corner of Route 193 and Chase road is the Gay-Larned House. Ellen Larned devoted her life to researching and writing the history of Windham County, a project which has not yet been rivaled.

North Grosvenordale Mill, Riverside Drive/Route 12, Buckley Hill Road, Floral Avenue, Market Lane and Marshall, Central, River and Holmes Streets. After Grosvenor had acquired most of the Masonville Company, he bought the Fishville mill and water rights. The village of Fishville became Grosvenordale. Not only is this confusing, the village now had an unpronounceable name.

Grosvenor combined his two companies into one, and built an enormous cotton mill, with a 464-foot-long turbine powered by steam in 1872. At the turn of the century, the mill employed 1,750 hands and was the largest in Windham County. The Grosvenordale mill complex included housing in Three Rows, Swede Village and Greek Village, a company store, a boarding house, and along the railroad tracks, warehouses. The mill closed in 1954.

Windham
Routes 203, 6, 195, 14, 32
Incorporated 1692, city of Willimantic chartered in 1893.

Native Americans
Mohegans

Historical notes
In 1675, the area which became Windham, along with present-day Mansfield, Scotland, Chaplin and parts of Hampton, was bequeathed by Joshua, son of Uncas, to "sixteen gentlemen from Norwich and neighboring towns," including the specula-

tor John Mason. Most of the legatees sold their allotments, but a few sent their sons to make improvements.

The first settler came to Hither Place (Windham Center) in 1691, and within two years, there was a gristmill, a sawmill, and several other settlers. More settlers arrived and built homes at Pond Place (Mansfield Center), and in the valley of the Willimantic River. The town was almost immediately incorporated, and a few years later, in 1702, Mansfield was separated, as the residents complained they could not cross the river in winter to attend worship services.

Because Windham Center was only a mile from the militia training grounds, crowds were drawn to the village on training days and election days. Soon shops, banks and taverns flourished.

During the Revolution, four British prisoners were held in the little jail in Windham. Bored, and also grateful to the Widow Carey, who kept the tavern and provided their food, the prisoners, with only one small knife between them, carved the figure of Bacchus sitting astride a wine cask, holding a basket of fruit. One night, when the jail door was carelessly (one wonders) left unlocked, the prisoners escaped. The Widow Carey boldly displayed the carving the prisoners had left her as a gift, hanging it for all to see in her tavern. It is now in the Windham Free Library on the green.

The Willimantic and Natchaug Rivers converge to form the headwaters of the Shetucket River in Willimantic, a natural resource that was utilized early in the town's history. By 1706, sawmills and gristmills were located at the falls, and shortly after, ironworks. During the Revolutionary War a powder works was built at the falls, followed by paper and cotton mills. Several silk mills began operation in 1838.

In 1854, a group of Hartford capitalists founded The Willimantic Linen Company to produce linen thread. The mill gradually switched to the manufacture of cotton thread and enjoyed an eager market for its goods. Two years before the turn of the century, in 1898, a British conglomerate, The American Thread Company, absorbed the Willimantic Linen Company. For decades Willimantic was a world leader in the manufacture of thread, earning the nickname Thread City.

Willimantic was an important railroad hub in New England, with an average of forty trains a day. You could leave in the morning for a shopping trip in Boston and return home in the evening with your purchases. A night train, with white table cloths on the tables and sleeping cars, took vacationers to Maine in the summer.

Inventions, inventors and firsts

Stafford and Phelps began manufacturing paper in South Windham in 1829. Until then, it was thought that paper could only be made in England, where the air was moist. They were the first to use the Fourdiner machine, which overcame this obstacle. Sometime prior to 1852, Edwin Allen invented a machine for making wooden type in his South Windham shop. Earlier, in 1773, Jedediah Elderkin perfected the first successful silkworm culture. He planted a mulberry orchard and was able to make a coarse silk for vests and handkerchiefs.

Ghost stories and legends

During the French and Indian War, the sleeping residents of Windham were awakened by horrible sounds coming from somewhere in the nearby wooded wilderness. Terrified, they were sure that a party of Indians was preparing to swoop down upon them. They were convinced that the end was near.

Several of the bravest men grabbed their guns and went out to investigate and stave off the dreaded attack. They slipped quietly through the woods, heading toward the blood-curdling shrieks, and discovered, to their relief and chagrin, hundreds, perhaps thousands, of frogs, battling over a diminished pond of water.

This story was immediately reported in the *Connecticut Courant,* and has been repeated many times over the years. Instead of embarrassment, however, the folks of Windham are proud of the tale. Images of the Windham frogs are a familiar and proud sight in this town.

You would expect a place with as many old houses as Windham Center to have a ghost story, and it does. A young unmarried woman was accused of murdering the baby she had secretly borne. She was convicted and hanged. Her shadowy ghost has been seen in the Center ever since, particularly in the old tavern, now apartments, where she lived.

Sometimes only her presence is felt. One modern-day unmarried mother who lived in the old inn reported coming home from work to find a marble placed in the center of her bed. She didn't own any marbles, and had never seen any in her rooms. She took it as a gift from her colonial predecessor, a sign to be strong.

Notable buildings

Jillson House (c. 1825) (860-456-2316). This house was built of stone quarried on the banks of the Willimantic River for one of the mill owners.

The Windham Textile and History Museum.

Windham Textile and History Museum, 157 Union and Main Street (860-456-2178). The museum is dedicated to preserving the history of the textile industry, including the cultures of the workers. It is located within the mill complex.

Historic districts

Main Street, 32, 50 and 54 North Street, 21–65 Church Street, 607–1009 Main Street, 242–280 North Street, 20–22 Walnut Street. In addition to the massive mill buildings, there are many fine Victorian houses, many of them painted in the gay colors of the period.

Windham Center Historic District, Routes 14 and 203. Here you will find carefully restored houses, the fabled Tory carving of Bacchus, and maybe a ghost sighting.

Woodstock

Routes 169 (scenic), 171, 197, 198
Incorporated 1749

Native Americans

Nipmucs, Wabaquasetts. The hillocks of the Wabaquasetts' Woodstock area cornfields were visible well into this century. When the Wabaquasetts learned that the Puritans in Boston were starving, they offered them some of their harvest, which they carried overland on the Old Connecticut Path.

John Eliot, the zealous missionary to the Indians, visited the Wabaquasetts and preached to them from a rock. Those who accepted his teachings formed a community of "Praying Indians." Goodkin, Eliot's associate, when writing about their visit, described the Sagamore's wigwam as "about sixty feet in length, twenty feet in width."

The Wabaquasetts all vanished in King Philip's War.

Historical notes

Originally settled by pioneers from Roxbury as part of Massachusetts in 1686, Wabaquasett (mat-producing country), was first named New Roxbury, and then Woodstock, because the English connotations of its nearness to Oxford, Massachusetts. In 1749, Woodstock became part of Connecticut.

Woodstock remained largely agricultural, though several taverns served travelers. In the nineteenth century, Henry C. Bowen, the editor of the *New York Independent,* entertained numerous presidents in his Woodstock home, bringing the town attention it might not otherwise have received.

Bowen (1813–1896) grew up in Woodstock where his father ran a country store and the post office. When he was twenty-one, he left for New York City and went into the drygoods business. Despite some financial setbacks, he held a controlling interest in the *Independent,* an abolitionist weekly.

At the height of his success, Bowen commissioned a summer house for his family in his home town, and began a personal program of local philanthropy. His credo was, "Make your town … and your home more beautiful every year. Your hearts will be made better and your souls will be richer for so doing." He planted hundreds of trees, fenced the common, set up a fund for Woodstock soldiers in the Union Army, donated a park and revived the Woodstock Academy.

Notable buildings

Roseland Cottage (c. 1846), Route 169 on the Common (860-928-4074). This pink cottage with board-and-batten siding, gables, chimney pots and wooden finials was the fabled summer home of Henry Bowen. The gardens have been carefully restored, and there are several interesting outbuildings.

Quassett School, Route 169. Brick one-room school house, now relocated to the grounds of the elementary school.

Historic districts

Woodstock Hill. This is not an official historic district, but the lovely common is surrounded by orchards as well as houses dating from as early as 1776. Pulpit Rock, where the missionary John Eliot is said to have preached to the receptive Wabaquasetts, is at the north end of the green, on an unpaved segment of Pulpit Rock Road.

South Woodstock. Also not an official historic district, but another pretty green. At the north end of the green is an imposing colonial, the Samuel Mcclellan house (c. 1760). Also of interest is an 1840 two-room school house.

Scenic Roads

Town	Route	Miles	Location
New Hartford	202	5.10	From Canton/New Hartford town line west to Bakersville Methodist Church.
Kent	7	10.50	From New Milford town line north to Cornwall town line.
Redding	53	2.03	From Redding/Weston town line north to southern jct. of Rt. 107.
Greenwich - Stratford	15	37.50	Merritt Parkway from New York State line to Housatonic River Bridge.
Salisbury	44	8.83	From New York State line east to Salisbury/North Canan town line.
	41	8.01	From Sharon/Salisbury town line north to Massachusetts line.
Haddam	154	9.16	From Chester/Haddam town line north to Haddam/Middletown town line.
Barkhampstead	181	1.10	From Rt. 44 north to Rt. 318.
	318	2.60	From Rt. 181 to Rt. 219.
	219	2.60	From Rt. 318 south to end of Lake McDonnough Dam.
N. Stonington	49	10.90	From Rt 184 north to 1/10 mi before Rt. 165.
Voluntown	49	7.90	From Boat Launch area north to Rt. 14A.
Sterling	14A	.70	From Rt. 49 east to Porter Pond Road.
Stonington	234	3.16	From N. Main St. west to Rt. 27.
Branford - Guiford	146	12.20	From Eades St. in Branford to US1 in Guiford.
Sharon	4	3.10	From Rt. 7 west to Dunbar Road.
	4	.80	From Dunbar Road west to Old Sharon Road.
	7	4.29	From Cornwall Bridge north to Rt. 128.
	41	4.00	From Boland Road north to Cole Road.

Town	Route	Miles	Location
Sharon (cont.)	41	2.20	From Cole Road north to Sharon/ Salisbury town line.
	41	2.20	From Boland Road south to New York State Line.
Roxbury	67	.87	From Ranney Hill road south to 3/10 mi south of Rt. 317.
	67	2.90	From Roxbury/Bridgewater town line east to Ranny Hill Road.
	317	.40	From Pointer Hill Road west to Rt. 67.
Glastonbury	160	1.06	From Roaring Brook Bridge west to Connecticut River.
Canton	179	.30	From Burlington/Canton town line to Jct. 565.
	565	.70	From Rt. 179 northeast to Allen Place.
Lisbon - Woodstock	169	32.10	From Rocky Hollow Road in Lisbon north to Massachusetts line.
Guilford	77	11.56	From Rt. 146 north to Durham/Guilford town line.
Preston	164	2.58	From Old Shetucket Turnpike north to Preston/Griswold town line.
Easton	58	3.14	From Fairfield/Easton town line north to Freeborn Road.
Colebrook	183	3.10	From Rt. 182 north to Church Hill Road.
Harwinton	4	1.70	From Cooks Dam west to Cemetery Road.
Norfolk	272	11.00	From Norfolk/Goshen town line north to Massachusetts line.
Washington - Warren	SR 478 45	6.9	From Washington/Kent town line on SR 478 east to Rt. 45 north then Rt. 45 to northern jct. of SR 478 then west on SR 478 to Warren/Kent town line.

Connecticut Facts

State Flower	Mountain Laurel	Indian name	Quinnehtukut (Beside the Long Tidal River).
State Bird	Robin		
State Tree	White Oak	State Hero	Nathan Hale
State Animal	Sperm Whale	Lakes/Ponds	6,000
State Gem	Garnet	Rivers/Streams	8,400 mi
State Insect	European Mantis	State Forests	30
State Song	"Yankee Doodle"	State Parks	91
State Fossil	Eubrontes Giganteus	Shoreline	253 miles
State Boat	U.S.S. Nautilus	Counties	8
Nicknames	The Constitution State. Also Nutmeg State, and Land of Steady Habits.	Towns	169
		Boundary	371 miles
		Indian Reservations	5
Motto	*Qui Transtulit Ustinet* (He Who Transplanted Still Sustains).	Capitol	Hartford

Selected Chronology

1100–570 million years BP, Precambrian Era. Solidification of earth's crust. Avalonia & Proto-North America (ancient continents) are separated by the Iapetos Oceans.

570–225 million years BP, Paleozoic Era. 500 million years ago, the oceans began to close. By 250 million years ago, the continents had collided and melded to form Pangaea. Connecticut was at the heart of the collision and contains the continents of Avalonia, Proto-North America, and the ocean floor of Iapetos. After about 200 million years, Pangaea began to break up and spread apart.

225–65 million years BP, Mesozoic Era. Many cracks formed. One large crack became (eventually), the Connecticut River Valley. The Jurassic and earlier Triassic periods of this era was the age of dinosaurs.

65 million million years BP, Cenozoic Era.

20–25,000 BP, Glaciation. The ice cover was 6,000-7,000 feet thick.

11,000–14,000 BP, First human habitation.

1614, Adrian Block sails up the Connecticut River as far as the Enfield Rapids. This forms the basis for Dutch claims to Connecticut.

1632, Earl of Warwick gives Lord Say and Sele and Lord Brook a grant of land from Narragansett River (Bay) to the "South Sea" (Pacific Ocean.) Edward Winslow, Governor of Plymouth, travels to the Connecticut River Valley to determine the validity of the Indians' claims that the land is fertile. Governor Van Twiller of New Netherlands, purchases land from the Indians at the mouth of the Connecticut River and nails the Dutch coat of arms to a tree.

1633, The Dutch erect the House of Good Hope, at present day Hartford, and set up a trading post. John Oldham, an adventurer, explores the Connecticut River and trades with the Indians. Plymouth Colony sends William Holmes to found a trading post at Windsor.

1634, John Oldham and others settle Wethersfield.

1635, John Steel and 60 others from Newtown settle Hartford. John Winthrop, Jr. and a group of English colonists erect a fort at Saybrook. A group of Dorchester colonists joins those already at Windsor.

1636, Spring. Thomas Hooker and his congregation come overland on the Connecticut Path and settle in Hartford. April 26, first General Court held, in Hartford.

1637, Pequot War: April - Wethersfield colonists killed by Pequots. May 11 - General Court votes to raise 90 men and fight the Pequots. May 26 - Mystic Massacre. Captain John Mason destroys the Pequot fort at Mystic. July 13 - Great Swamp Fight in Fairfield. End of the Pequot War.

1638, Earthquake strikes southern Connecticut. Quinnipiac (New Haven) is settled by 250 men, women and children.

1639, The Fundamental Orders of Connecticut are adopted by reresentatives of Hartford, Windsor and Wethersfield. This is the first written constitution. John Haynes becomes first governor of the colony.

1643, United Colonies of New England is formed.

1646, John Winthrop, Jr., founds New London.

1650, Peter Stuyvesant asserts claims to Connecticut. A compromise is worked out and Connecticut agrees that its western boundary will not exceed more than 20 miles east of the Hudson River. Connecut retains most of Long Island. Code of Laws adopted.

1654, Connecticut seizes Dutch trading post and fort at Hartford.

1657, Shipbuilding begns at Derby.

1660, Uncas is besieged by the Narragansetts. Leffingwell assists.

1662, Governor Jonathan Winthrop, Jr., obtains a liberal charter for Connecticut from Charles II. New Haven Colony loses its separate identity.

1663, Largest earthquake to strike the northeast felt in Connecticut.

1664, New Haven Colony formally becomes part of Connecticut Colony. Duke of York agrees to abandon his claims to western Connecticut in exchange for Long Island. Shipbuilding begins at New London.

1675, Andros, Governor of New York, decides not to attack the fort at Saybrook when he sees the British flag.

1675–1676, King Philip's War.

1682, Earliest recorded tornado in America. Struck New Haven on June 10.

1687, Oct. 31, Sir Edmund Andros, recently appointed Governor-in-Chief of all New England, arrives in Hartford to assume control and demands surender of the charter. Charter is hidden in the Charter Oak.

1689, Connecticut Colony resumes self government under charter.

1701, General Assembly authorizes Collegiate School (Yale).

1702, Collegiate School (Yale) opens at Saybrook.

1708, Saybrook Platform adopted. Established Church (Congregational) now centrally controlled.

1717, Great Snow. Ten to twelve feet deep.

1727, Oct. 27, Great Earthquake.

1740, First tinware in America manufactured in Berlin.

1740's, "Great Awakening" sweeps Connecticut.

1744, King George's War. Connecticut raises quota of 1,000 men to fight French and Indians.

1748, End of King George's War.

1755, Connecticut Gazette begins publication in New Haven.

1763, Settlers from Windham County build the first settlement in Wyoming Valley, Pennsylvania.

1764, Thomas Green, Hartford bookseller and printer, launches the *Connecticut Courant* (now *Hartford Courant*), the oldest continuously operated newspaper in the country.

1765, Widespread opposition to Stamp Act.

1766, William Pitkin defeats Thomas Fitch for governor. Fitch had supported the Stamp Act.

1774, Susquehannah Company area of Pennsylvania officially comes under Connecticut's jurisdiction. Silas Deane, Ellipalet Dyer, and Roger Sherman represent Connecticut at the First Continental Congress.

1775, "Lexington Alarm." Several thousand militia from all over Connecticut rush to Massachusetts. Ultimately, 31,939 men join the Continental forces plus 200 privateers. Seizure of Fort Ticonderoga is planned in Hartford and Wethersfield. April 20, Governor Trumbull

orders Israel Putnam and his militia to join the American forces at Boston. May 10 Ethan allen captures Fort Ticonderoga. June 17, Battle of Bunker Hill. Putnam is the ranking officer. August 30, Stonington raided by British. Benedict Arnold marches his militia through the Maine wilderness and leads a disasterous attack on Quebec.

1776, Samuel Hungtington, Roger Sherman, William Williams, and Oliver Wolcott sign the Declaration of Independence. The Declaration is resoundingly supported by the majority of Connecticut citizens, including Governor Jonathan Trumbull. Sept. 22, Nathan Hale is executed by the British. Wyoming settlement declared a county of Connecticut.

1777, 1General Tryon raids Danbury. Wyoming settlement attacked. General Putnam and his troups spend a harsh winter in Redding, Connecticut's "Valley Forge."

1778, Connecticut is the fifth state admitted to the Union.

1779, General Tryon raids New Haven, Fairfield and Norwalk. He burns Fairfield and Norwalk.

1780, "May 19, The 'Dark Day.' Candles are lighted, fowls go to roost, birds are silent, and colonists consider Day of Judgement at hand."

1781, Benedict Arnold leads the British attack on Groton and New London. Massacre at Fort Griswold. New London burns. Washington meets with Rochambeau at Webb House in Wethersfield.

1784, Slavery abolished in Connecticut. Act provides for emancipation of all Negroes at the age of twenty-five. Tapping Reeve establishes the first American law school in Litchfield. New Haven, New London, Hartford, Middletown, and Norwich are incorporated as cities, the first in Connecticut. Westmoreland area relinquished to Pennsylvania.

1786, Connecticut cedes all western lands to the United States but retains Western Reserve.

1787, Oliver Ellsworth, William Samuel Johnson, and Roger Sherman represent Connecticut at the Philadelphia Constitutional Convention.

1788, Federal Constitution approved by Convention at Hartford, 128-40. First New England woolen mill established in Hartford.

1792, First turnpike company, the New London to Norwich, incorporated. First Connecticut Bank, Union Bank, opens in New London.

1795, Connecticut sells Western Reserve for $1.2 million and uses money to establish the State School Fund. The Mutual Assurance Company of the City of Norwich is the first insurance company incorporated.

1801, Stonington incorporated as a burough, the first in the state.

1802, The brass industry begins in Waterbury.

1807, Noah Webster's dictionary is published.

1808, The Enfield Bridge is built. It is the first to span the Connecticut River.

1812–1814, War of 1812, second war with Great Britain. The War is unpopular in Connecticut.

1815, First steamboat voyage up the Connecticut River.

1816, Year Without A Summer. Summer frosts, hail, and sleet ruin crops. The unusual weather is a result of the eruption of Mount Tambora in Indonesia.

1817, Thomas Gallaudet founds school for the deaf in Hartford.

1818, New state constitution ratified, ending system of Established Church.

1823, Washington College (Trinity) organized.

1825, July 4, work on the Farmington Canal begins.

1826, Longstanding boundary dispute with Massachusetts is settled.

1828, The Farmington Canal opens.

1831, Wesleyan University founded in Middletown.

1832, Boston, Norwich, and Worcester Railroad is incorporated.

1835, Music Vale Seminary is founded in Salem. This is the first American music school.

1837, First railroad to operate in Connecticut runs trains from Stonington to Providence, Rhode Island.

1838, Railroad from Hartford to New Haven is completed.

1840–1850, Height of the whaling industry.

1842, Wadsworth Atheneum is established in Hartford.

1844, New York and New Haven Railroad chartered.

1848, Dec. 29, First railroad cars run from New York to New Haven.

1849, Teachers College of Connecticut is established in New Britain (now Central Connecticut State University).

1860, Largest cities in the state are: Hartford, New Haven, Norwich, New London, Bridgeport, Waterbury, Windham, Killingly, Danbury, Derby, Fairfield, Norwalk, Stamford, Greenwich, Middletown, Meriden, and Stonington.

1861–1865, Civil War. 57,379 men from Connecticut serve, and suffer 20,000 casualties.

1871, Samuel Clemens moves to Hartford.

1872, The Hartford and New Haven Railroad and the New York and New Haven Railroad are consolidated to form the New York, New Haven and Hartford Railroad.

1875, Hartford made the sole capital city.

1878, The world's first commerical telephone exchange is established in New Haven. Tornado strikes in Wallingford on August 9, killing 34.

1881, Storrs Agricultural College (University of Connecticut) is founded.

1888, March 12–14. The Great Blizzard dumps up to twelve feet of snow on the state.

1897, Pope Manufacturing Company begins pruduction of automobiles in Hartford.

1901, First law regulating speed limits.

1917–1918, World War I.

1922, WDRC begins to broadcast. This is Connecticut's first radio station.

1936, March 18–25, disasterous floods.

1938, September 21, Hurricane followed by floods and heavy loss of life and property, including 600 deaths. 180 mile per hour winds along the shore. First section of the Merritt Parkway is opened.

1941–1945, World War II.

1955, August 18, Huricane Diane followed by floods, and heavy loss of life and property, including 184 dead, 4,700 injured and $182 million in damage.

1959, County government abolished.

1974, Ella Grasso is elected governor. She is the first woman to be elected governor of a state who has not succeeded her husband.

1973, December 17 ice storm. Northeast Connecticut declared a disaster area.

1978, February 6 an 7, Blizzard of 78.

1979, October 3, tornado struck Windsor Locks, killing 3.

1981, Gypsy moths defoliate 1,482,216 acres.

1985, September 27 Hurricane Gloria. Power outages for more than a week in some parts of the state.

Resources for Further Information

Connecticut State Historical Society
59 South Prospect Street
Hartford, CT 06106
(860-566-3995)

Connecticut Historical Commission
59 South Prospect Street
Hartford, CT 06106
(860-566-3005)

Bureau of Outdoor Recreation
State Parks Division
CT DEP
79 Elm Street
Hartford, CT 06106-5127
(860-424-3200)

Connecticut Office of Tourism
865 Brook Street
Rocky Hill, CT 06067-3405
(860-258-4355).

Connecticut Trust for Historic Preservation
940 Whitney Avenue
Hamden, CT 06517-4002
(203-562-6312)

UConn Co-op
(books on Connecticut history and town histories)
81 Fairfield Road
Storrs, CT 06269
1-800-U-READ-IT

Selected Bibliography

Alexopoulos, John, *The Nineteenth Century Parks of Hartford: A Legacy to the Nation,* Hartford, Hartford Architecture Conservancy, 1983.

Andrews, William L., *Journeys in New Worlds: Early American Women's Narratives,* Madison, WI, University of Wisconsin Press, 1990.

Allis, Marguerite, *Historic Connecticut,* New York, Grosset & Dunlap, 1934.

Ashford Connecticut 1914–1964, and supplement, Town of Ashford Two Hundred Fiftieth Anniversary Committee, 1964.

Ayres, Harrall, *The Great Trail of New England: The Old Connecticut Path,* Boston, Meador Publishing Co., 1940.

Bailyn, Bernard, *Voyagers to the West: A Passage in the Peopling of America on the Eve of the Revolution,* New York, Alfred Knopf, 1987.

Barber, John Warner, *Connecticut Historical Collections,* New Haven, Durrie and Peck, 1838.

Beardsley, Thomas R., *Willimantic Industry and Community: The Rise and Decline of a Connecticut Textile City,* Willimantic, Windham Textile & History Museum, 1993.

Bell, Michael, *The Face of Connecticut,* Hartford, State Geological and Natural History Survey of Connecticut, Department of Environmental Protection, 1985.

Bickford, Christopher P., and J. Bard McNulty, *John Warner Barber's Views of Connecticut Towns 1834–36,* Hartford, Acorn Club, The Connecticut Historical Society, 1990.

Bourne, Russell, *The Red King's Rebellion: Racial Politics in New England 1675–1678,* New York, Atheneum, Macmillan Publishing, 1990.

Bragdon, Kathleen J., *Native People of Southern New England, 1500–1650,* Norman, OK., University of Oklahoma Press, 1996.

Buckley, Dr. William E., *A New England Pattern: The History of Manchester Connecticut,* Chester, Globe-Pequot Press, 1973.

Burpee, Charles W., *Burpee's the Story of Connecticut,* 4 vols., New York, the American Historical Company, Inc., 1939.

Bushman, Richard L., *From Puritan to Yankee: Character and the Social*

Order in Connecticut, 1690–1765, Cambridge, MA, Harvard University Press, 1967.

Calloway, Collin G., ed., *After King Philip's War: Presence and Persistence in Indian New England,* Hanover, NH, University Press of New England, 1997.

Calloway, Collin G., *New Worlds for All: Indians, Europeans, and the Remaking of Early America,* Baltimore, MD, Johns Hopkins Press, 1997.

Caplovich, Judd, *Blizzard! The Great Storm of '88,* Vernon, VeRo Publishing Company, 1987.

Carpenter, Delores Bird, *Early Encounters: Native Americans and Europeans in New England,* East Lansing, MI, Michigan State University Press, 1994.

Committee For a New England Bibliography, John Borden Armstrong, chairman and series editor, Roger Parks, ed., *Connecticut: A Bibliography of Its History,* Volume 6 of Bibliographies of New England History, Hanover, NH, University Press of New England, 1986.

Connecticut: A Guide to its Roads, Lore, and People, American Guide Series, Works of the Federal Writers' Project of the Works Progress Administration of the State of Connecticut, Boston, MA, Houghton Mifflin Company, 1938.

Connecticut Forest & Park Association, *Connecticut Walk Book,* 14th ed., East Hartford, Connecticut Forest and Park Association, 1984.

Crofut, Florence S. Marcy, *Guide to the History and the Historic Sites of Connecticut,* Volume I & II, New Haven, Yale Univeristy Press, 1937.

Cronon, William, *Changes in the Land: Indians, Colonists, and the Ecology of New England,* New York, Hill and Wang, a division of Farrar, Straus & Giroux, 1985.

Cummings, Hildegard, Helen K. Fusscas and Susan G. Larkin, *J. Alden Weir: A Place of His Own,* William Benton Museum of Art, the University of Connecticut, 1991.

Daniels, Bruce D., *The Connecticut Town: Growth and Development 1635–1790,* Middletown, Wesleyan University Press, 1979.

DeForest, John W., *The History of the Connecticut Indians,* St. Clair Shores, MI, 1970 from 1852 edition.

Demers, Ronald, *A History of Willington Connecticut: Modernization in a New England Town,* Willington, Willington Historical Society, 1983.

Dolan, J. R., *The Yankee Peddlars of Early America: an Affectionate History of Life and Commerce in the Devloping Colonies and the Young Republic,* New York, Bramhall House, 1964.

Faude, Wilson H., and Joan W. Riedland, *Connecticut Firsts,* Old Saybrook, Peregrine Press, 1985.

Feder, Kenneth L., *A Village of Outcasts: Historical Archaeology and Documentary Research at the Lighthouse Site,* Mountain View, CA, Mayfield Publishing, 1994.

Highways & Byways of Connecticut, Hartford, G. Fox & Co., 1947.

Grant, Ellsworth S., *Yankee Dreamers and Doers: The Story of Connecticut Manufacturing,* Hartford, The Connecticut Historical Society and Fenwick Productions, 1996.

_____ , *The Miracle of Connecticut,* Hartford, The Connecticut Historical Society and Fenwick Productions, 1992.

Griggs, Susan, *Folklore and Firesides of Pomfret, Hampton, and Vicinity,* Hampton, Griggs, 1949.

Grumet, Robert S., ed., *Northeastern Indian Lives 1632–1816,* Amherst, MA, University of Massachusetts Press, 1996.

Hardy, Gerry, and Sue Hardy, *Fifty Hikes in Connecticut: A Guide to Short Walks and Day Hikes in the Nutmeg State,* 2nd ed., Woodstock, VT, Backcountry Publications, 1984.

Hauptman, Laurence M., and James D. Wherry, *The Pequots in Southern New England: the Rise and Fall of an American Indian Nation,* Norman, OK. University of Oklahoma Press, 1990.

Heermance, Edgar L., *The Connecticut Guide: What to See and Where to See It,* Hartford, Emergency Relief Commission, 1935.

Holbrook, Stewart H., *The Old Post Road: The Story of the Boston Post Road,* New York, McGraw Hill, 1962.

Holcomb, Robert, N., *The Story of Connecticut,* Vol. II, Hartford, The Hartford Times, 1936.

Hollister, G. B., *The History of Connecticut: From the Settlement of the Colony to the Adoption of the Present Constitution,* 2 vols., New Haven, Durrie and Peck, 1855.

Hoopes, Penrose R., *Connecticut Clockmakers of the Eighteenth Century,* 2nd ed., New York, Dover Publications, 1974.

Johnson, Gil, and Bennett W. Dorman, *Savin Rock Memories,* West Haven, Committee for the Preservation of Local History, 1993.

Johnson, Malcolm, *Yesterday's Connecticut,* Miami, FL, E. A. Seemann Publishing, Inc., 1976.

Johnson, Steven F., *Ninnuock (The People): The Algonkian People of New England,* Marlborough, MA, Bliss Publishing, 1995.

Karr, Ronald Dale, *Lost Railroads of New England,* Pepperell, MA, Branch Line Press, 1989.

Karr, Ronald Dale, *The Rail Lines of Southern New England: A Handbook of Railroad History,* Pepperell, MA, Branch Line Press, 1995.

Kelly, J. Frederick, *Early Domestic Architecture of Connecticut,* New York, Dover Publications, 1963.

Knapp, Alfred P., *Connecticut's Yesteryears, So Saith the Wind,* Old Saybrook, Alfred P. Knapp, 1985.

Little, Richard D., *Dinosaurs, Dunes, and Drifting Continents: The Geohistory of the Connecticut Valley,* Greenfield, MA, Richard D. Little, 1984

Main, Jackson Turner, *Society and Economy in Colonial Connecticut,*

Princeton, NJ, Princeton University Press, 1985.

Mavor, James W., Jr., and Byron E. Dix, *Manitou: The Sacred Landscape of New England's Native Civilization*, Rochester, VT, Inner Traditions, 1989.

Metsack, Barbara A., researcher, *Ashford 1714–1989: Moments from History*, Ashford, CT, Ashford 275th Anniversary Comittee, 1990.

Miller, James W., *As We Were on the Valley Shore*, Guilford, CT, Shore Line Times, 1976.

Milne, George McLean, *Connecticut Woodlands: A Century's Story of the Connecticut Forest and Park Association*, East Hartford, CT, Connecticut Forest and Park Association, 1995.

Morgan, Ted, *Wilderness at Dawn: The Settling of the North American Continent*, New York, Simon and Schuster, 1993.

Moynihan, Ruth Barnes, *The Connecticut Historical Society Bulletin*, vol. 53, Hartford, Connecticut Historical Society, 1988.

Nutting, Wallace, *Connecticut Beautiful*, Garden City, NY, Garden City Publishing, 1935.

Philips, David, *Legendary Connecticut*, Hartford, Spoonwood Press, 1984.

Phillips, Christopher, *Damned Yankee: The Life of General Nathaniel Lyon*, Baton Rouge, Louisiana State University Press, 1996.

Price, Edward T., *Dividing the Land: Early American Beginnings of Our Private Property Mosaic*, Chicago, Il, University of Chicago Press, 1995.

Radde, Bruce, *The Merritt Parkway*, New Haven, Yale University Press, 1993.

Raymo, Chet, and Maureen E. Raymo, *Written in Stone: A Geological History of the Northeastern United States*, Chester, The Globe-Pequot Press, 1989.

Robertson, James Oliver, and Janet C. Robertson, *All Our Yesterdays: A Century of Life in an American Small Town*, New York, HarperCollins Publishers, 1993.

Robinson, William F., *Abandoned New England: Its Hidden Ruins and Where to Find Them*, Boston, New York Graphic Society, 1976.

Ronson, Bruce G., *Bolton's Heritage*, Essex, Pequot Press, 1970.

Roth, David M., *Connecticut: A History*, New York, W. W. Norton & Company, 1979.

Russell, Howard S., *Indian New England Before the Mayflower*, Hanover, NH, University Press of New England, 1980.

Ryerson, Kathleen H., *Rock Hound's Guide to Connecticut*, Revised Edition, Chester, CT, The Pequot Press, 1972.

Salisbury, Neal, *Manitou and Providence: Indians, Europeans, and the Making of New England, 1500–1643*, New York, Oxford Univesity Press, 1982.

Sanford, Elias B., *A History of Connecticut*, Hartford, S. S. Scranton and Company, 1888.

Selesky, Harold E., *War & Society in Colonial Connecticut,* New Haven, Yale University Press, 1990.

Sherer, Thomas E., Jr., *The Connecticut Atlas,* 2nd ed., Old Lyme, CT, Kilderatlas Publishing Co., 1992.

Slater, James A., *The Colonial Burying Grounds of Eastern Connecticut and the Men Who Made Them,* Hamden, CT, The Connecticut Academy of Arts and Sciences, 1987.

Speiss, Mathias, and Percy W. Bidwell, *History of Manchester, Connecticut,* Manchester, Centennial Committee of the Town of Manchester, 1924.

, *Connecticut Circa 1625, Its Indian Trails, Villages and Sachemdoms,* The Connecticut Society of the Colonial Dames of America, Inc., 1934.

Stave, Bruce, and Palmer, Michele, Palmer, Mills and Meadows: A Pictorial History of Northeast Connecticut, Virginia Beach, The Downing Publishing Company, 1991.

Sterry, Iveagh Hunt, and William H. Garrigus, *They Found a Way: Connecticut's Restless People,* Brattleboro, VT, Stephen Daye Press, 1938.

Stewart, George, Jr., *A History of Religious Education in Connecticut to the Middle of the Nineteenth Century,* New Haven, Yale University Press, 1924.

Stilgoe, John R., *Common Landscape of America, 1580–1845,* New Haven, Yale University Press, 1982.

Stommel, Henry, and Elizabeth Stommel, *Volcano Weather: The Story of the Year Without a Summer 1816,* Newport, RI, Seven Seas Press, 1983.

Stone, Frank Andrews, *African-American Connecticut: African Origins, New England Roots,* Storrs, The Isaac N. Thut World Education Center, 1991.

Strother, Horatio T., *The Underground Railroad in Connecticut,* Middletown, Wesleyan University Press, 1962.

Taylor, John M., The Witchcraft Delusion: the Story of the Witchcraft Persecutions in Seventeenth-Century New England, Including Original Trial Transcripts, New York, Random Value Publishing, 1995.

Taylor, Robert J., *Colonial Connecticut: A History,* Millwood, NY, KTO Press, 1979.

Travel Historic Connecticut: A Guide to Connecticut's Town Historical Markers, Madison, WI, Guide Press Co., 1987.

Trigger, Bruce G., ed., *Handbook of North American Indians,* Vol. 15, Northeast, Washington, DC, Smithsonian Institution, 1978

Turner, Gregg, and Melancthown Jacobus, *Connecticut Railroads: One Hundred Fifty Years of Railroad History,* Hartford, The Connecticut Historical Society, 1986.

Tuttle, Sam, *Sam Tuttle's Picture Book of Old Connecticut,* Scotia, NY, Americana Review, 1979.

Van Dusen, Albert E., *Connecticut,* New York, Random House, 1961.

Vaughan, Alden T., & Edward W. Clark, eds., *Puritans Among the Indians: Accounts of Captivity and Redemption 1676–1724,* Cambridge, MA, and London, England, Harvard University Press, 1981.

_____ , *New England Frontier: Puritans and Indians 1620–1675,* Boston, Little Brown, 1965.

Weatherford, Jack, *Native Roots: How the Indians Enriched America,* New York, Crown Publishers, 1991.

Weishampel, David B., and Luther Young, *Dinosaurs of the East Coast,* Baltimore and London, Johns Hopkins University Press, 1996.

Wetherell, Diana V., *Natural History Outings on Connecticut's Traprock Ridges,* Storrs, Diana Wetherell, 1992.

Whipple, Chandler, *The Indian and The White Man in New Enland,* Stockbridge, MA, The Berkshire Traveller Press, 1972.

White, Glenn E., *Folk Tales of Connecticut,* Volume I & II, Meriden, Glen White, 1981.

Whitehead, Russell, and Frank Chouteau Brown, eds., *Architectural Treasures of America: Early Homes of New England,* New York, Arno Press, 1977.

Wilbur, C. Keith, *The New England Indians,* Chester, The Globe Pequot Press, 1978.

Willauer, George J., Jr., ed., *A Lyme Micellany 1776–1976,* Middletown, Wesleyan University Press, 1976.

Wood, Frederic J., *The Turnpikes of New England: A New Edition of the 1919 Classic,* abridged with an introduction by Ronald Dale Karr, Pepperell, MA., Branch Line Press, 1997.

Wood, Joseph S., *The New England Village,* Baltimore, Johns Hopkins University Press, 1997.

Acknowledgements

Thanks to John W. Shannahan, Director, State Historic Preservation Office; Tom Daly, Department of Transportation; Patricia Koch-Lewin, Connecticut Office of Tourism; Andover Historical Society, especially Marti Hardisty; Association of Northeastern Connecticut Historical Societies, especially Marge Hoskin; Avon Historical Society, especially Terri Atkinson; Bridgewater Historical Society; Brookfield Historical Society, especially Marilyn Whittlesey; Falls Village-Canaan Historical Society, especially Marion Hock; Canton Historical Society Museum, especially Kathleen Woolam; Connecticut Firemen's Historical Society, Inc., especially Richard N. Symonds; Cromwell Historical Society, especially Joanne Sansone; Historical Society of the Town of Greenwich, especially Susan Richardson; Darien Historical Society, especially Louise McCue; Hartland Historical Society, especially Joan Stoltze; East Granby Historical Society, especially Betty Guinan; Ellington Historical Society, especially Mildrod Dimock; Fairfield Historical Society; Stanley-Whitman House Museum; Historical Society of Glastonbury; Griswold Historical Society, especially Mary Deveau; Hebron Historic Properties Commission, especially Grace R. Grubert; Mystic River Historical Society, especially Helen Keith; Haddam Historical Society, especially Jan Sweet; Hamden Historical Society, especially Martha Becker; Mark Twain House Museum; Lebanon Historical Society, especially Alicia Wayland; Meriden's Heritage and Cultural Commission, especially Bernice Shelberg; Meriden Historical Society, especially Allen Weathers; Middlesex County Historical Society; Monroe Historical Society, especially Marge Tranzillo; Naugatuck Historical Society, especially Verna Blackwell; Newington Historical Society; Suffield Historical Society; Marlborough Historical Society, especially Sandra J. Soucy; New Canaan Historical Society, especially Janet Lindstrom; New Hartford Historical Society; New Haven Colony Historical Society; Christopher Leffingwell House Museum; Sherman Historical Society, especially Gloria Thorne; Totoket Historical Society; Lockwood-Mathews

Mansion Museum, especially Joanna Torow; Florence Grisowld Museum, especially Laurie Bradt; Indian & Colonial Research Center; Old Saybrook Historical Society, especially Donald Swan; Orange Historical Society, especially Harry Jones; Plainville Historical Society, Inc., especially Ruth Hummel; Prospect Historical Society, especially John R. Guevin; Keeler Tavern Museum, especially Pat; Salisbury Association, Inc.; Seymour Historical Society; Sharon Historical Society; Massacoh Plantation; Somers Historical Society, Inc., especially Mary Harrington; Fort Stamford Period Garden, especially Sarah Tyrell; Stamford Historical Society, especially Grace K. Bounty; Stafford Historical Society, especially Esther Da Ros; Stratford Historical Society, especially Hiram Tindall; Tolland Historical Society, especially Mary Lafontaine; Torrington Historical Society, especially Mark M. Eachem; Trumbull Historical Society, especially Wayne Sakal; Vernon Historical Society, especially Jean Hopkins; Webb-Deane-Stevens Museum, especially Pat Warner; Wethersfield Historical Society; Willington Historical Society, especially Isabel Weigold; Windsor Historical Society; Mattatuck Museum, especially Rachel Guest; Windsor Locks Historical Society, especially Mickey Danyluck; Winchester Historical Society, especially Milly Hudak; Woodbridge Historical Society; Woodbury Historical Society, especially Mary Tyrrell; Prudence Sloane of Hampton.

And very special thanks to Lary Bloom, champion of writers, champion of Connecticut, and champion extraodinaire of things interesting, and Ann Charters, who, at always just the right moment, offered enthusiasm and encouragement, and Wally Lamb, who sets the example, and Gina Barreca, and to independent booksellers all, especially Sally Lerman (always), Kathy Anderson, Fran Keilty, Peter Sevenair (!), Carole Horne, Roxanne Coady, Jan Owens, Henry Berliner, and of course the crew at the Co-op, Clare, Alec, Michael, Julie, Marc, Jim, Anne, and Olu.

Index